America's Battalion

Also by Otto J. Lehrack

No Shining Armor: The Marines at War in Vietnam
The First Battle: Operation Starlite and the Beginning of the Blood Debt in Vietnam

America's Battalion

Marines in the First Gulf War

OTTO J. LEHRACK

THE UNIVERSITY OF ALABAMA PRESS

Tuscaloosa

Typeface: Goudy and Goudy Sans

∞

The paper on which this book is printed meets the minimum requirements of American
National Standard for Information Science—Permanence of Paper for Printed Library
Materials, ANSI Z39.48–1984.

Library of Congress Cataloging-in-Publication Data

Lehrack, Otto J.
  America's battalion : Marines in the first Gulf war / Otto J. Lehrack.
     p. cm.
  Includes index.
  ISBN 0-8173-1452-0 (cloth : alk. paper)
  1. Khafji, Battle of, Ra's al-Khafjāi, Saudi Arabia, 1991. 2. Persian Gulf War, 1991—
Campaigns. 3. United States Marine Corps. Division, 3rd. Battalion, 3rd—History—
20th century. I. Title.
  DS79.735.R37L44 2005
  956.7044'242—dc22
                                                              2004016593

To the memory of my father, Otto J. Lehrack Jr., and to my grandsons, Brett Matthew Martin and Nathan Edward Martin

Contents

viii   Contents

List of Illustrations

Preface

Those familiar with my first book, *No Shining Armor: The Marines at War in Vietnam,* will know that book attempts to portray the American infantry experience in Vietnam through the efforts of a single unit—the 3rd Battalion, 3rd Marines. It was not a book about politics, generals, grand strategy, or other lofty topics except as these subjects affected the day-to-day lives of our fighting men in Vietnam. It was essentially a book about men at war. This book is an attempt to once more deal with the human side of warfare, but in a different setting, against a different enemy, and with a fundamentally different public perception about the worth of the efforts of the American warrior.

By chance rather than design, the unit I chose to represent in the first American effort against Saddam Hussein was the same unit portrayed in my book about Vietnam. At the time of Desert Shield and Desert Storm I was living in Hawaii. As luck would have it, the 3rd Battalion, 3rd Marines was stationed at Marine Corps Base Hawaii and was one of the first units deployed to Saudi Arabia in response to the Iraqi invasion of Kuwait. As Desert Storm ended and the unit returned to Hawaii, I contacted the unit and asked for permission to interview members of the battalion about their recent experiences in the Persian Gulf. Colonel John Garrett, the commanding officer, and his staff demonstrated the fullest cooperation in allowing me access to members of the command. The fact that I had served with the unit in Vietnam and had written a book about it helped to establish my credibility with individual members of the unit, and, I would like to think, created an atmosphere of trust an outsider may not have had access to.

I was by no means sure what my efforts would produce. The 3rd Battalion, 3rd Marines was, after all, just one of the twenty-nine Marine infantry battalions deployed during the conflict. The entire operation consumed only seven months and, of those, only four days of ground combat. As such things go, it was relatively bloodless. Twenty-four Marines died in Desert Storm, more than half of those from "friendly fire." To the families of these Marines, Desert Storm was as great a tragedy as Vietnam, but to put this in perspective, one can read in my earlier book of a single platoon from this battalion that lost even more men in a single morning during a heart-wrenching ambush in the demilitarized region of Vietnam in early 1968.

I had doubts about whether the experiences of a single battalion, in a very brief war, would provide enough material to justify trying to put it in book form. After just a few interviews, however, my fears about a lack of material were put to rest. As happy coincidence would have it, the 3rd Battalion, 3rd Marines participated in more events that made the headlines back in the United States than any other battalion in the war. They were the only unit that had just returned from one deployment and were required to immediately redeploy. They were part of only the second Marine regiment to arrive in Saudi Arabia after making a historic movement in conjunction with the Maritime Prepositioning Force, a concept long in being that had never before been executed. They had the experience, almost unique in Desert Storm, of training closely with our allies in the Arab Coalition. They participated in the first allied ground operation of the war, which involved artillery raids launched in response to Saddam Hussein's use of missiles against allied forces. They also had a key role in the battle for the city of Khafji, and a small group of these Marines attempted, unsuccessfully, to rescue Melissa Rathbun-Nealy, the only woman soldier to be captured by the Iraqis during Desert Shield/Desert Storm. Finally, this unit was the first through the Iraqi wire and minefield barrier, infiltrating two days prior to the official beginning of the ground war, with the mission of providing flank security for the main attack.

Those readers who are interested in the bloodier aspects of warfare may be disappointed with this account. I trust that those concerned with the actions and reactions of young American men engaged in the stressful and uncertain activities of combat will not be. Almost to a man, and almost apologetically, the Marines whom I interviewed made mention of the fact that they had incurred very few casualties. To each of them I replied that they need not take off their hats to anyone. They performed as magnificently as any fighting men in our history, and to the end of their days they, and we, should be profoundly grateful for their relatively small loss.

The nature of this conflict, however, brought about a major change in my collection and organization of material. Vietnam was rightfully described as a "squad leaders' war." Dominated by small unit actions, necessitated by the requirements of fighting an elusive enemy in jungle terrain, that conflict often seemed to be a series of such actions. In those fights an unprecedented burden of responsibility rested on the shoulders of junior enlisted men. For that reason, the majority of my interviewees were the enlisted men who carried that load. In the Persian Gulf, on the other hand, the terrain and enemy dictated a more conventional type of warfare. Fire team and squad tactics, while certainly an essential foundation for the success of larger operations, did not in their own right play a major role in the conflict. In the words of Major General John H. Admire, who served as a lieutenant in Vietnam and commanded the 3rd Marines in the Gulf as a colonel: "The tropical jungle and guerrilla warfare characteristics of the Vietnam conflict contributed to the small unit nature of the war. But the vast desert expanses and the conventional characteristics of the Gulf War contributed to division level operations. In Vietnam, a majority of the daily or routine activities focused on squad or platoon level patrols and ambushes. But on the Arabian Peninsula the focus was on battalion and regimental assaults, coordinated at the division level."

For these reasons, the majority of the interviewees in this work are the officers and senior noncommissioned officers whose actions had a measurable impact on the battalion's operations as a whole. This is certainly not meant to detract from the performance of the junior enlisted men, whose performance, as always, was outstanding.

Acknowledgments

Several people deserve special thanks for helping me with this project. Major General Mike Myatt was kind enough to spend some time discussing his insights as the commanding general, 1st Marine Division, for Operations Desert Shield and Desert Storm. As usual, the Marines and employees of the Marine Corps Historical Center were more than cooperative. Many thanks to my old friend Colonel John Ripley, the director. Charles Grow's help was especially valuable. He not only did much of the USMC artwork during the operation but was also kind enough to copy much of it for my use. Charlie's efforts on behalf of the Marine Corps will enrich our understanding of this campaign for generations. Also helpful was Lieutenant Colonel Charles Cureton, USMCR, who did the official monograph on the 1st Marine Division in the war and was able to point me in the right direction for some material I might have missed. Finally, and especially, there is Pierrette, *mon amour.*

America's Battalion

Introduction

The Interwar Years

At the time the 3rd Battalion, 3rd Marines were withdrawn from Vietnam, in the autumn of 1969, America was winding down its participation in its longest and most unsuccessful war. Within eighteen months the participation of our ground troops in that unhappy adventure would come to a halt. Lyndon Johnson was driven from the presidency by the war, and his successor, Richard Nixon, clearly recognized the political liability of continuing the conflict. Our inability to formulate and carry convincing objectives had divided a nation and led to the new administration's "Vietnamization" of the war. Turning the allied effort over to the South Vietnamese promised slow but certain victory for their northern brethren—a promise that was fulfilled with the fall of Saigon in 1975.

In America, the counterculture movement was at its peak, and antiestablishment, antimilitary sentiment carried the day. Under pressure from these groups, the draft was ended in 1973, and the following year President Nixon was forced to resign because of the Watergate scandals.

The United States Marine Corps, heir to a long and proud history of service to the country, was beset with unprecedented challenges. Desertion, drug abuse, racial and disciplinary problems, all of which were largely rooted in the Vietnam War, were rending the fabric of the Corps. In 1973 fewer than half of enlisted Marines were high school graduates. A full 20 percent were in Mental Group IV, the lowest acceptable level for entrance into the armed forces. Eighty-eight percent of first-term enlistees opted to not reenlist. Officers and senior noncoms spent an inordinate amount of their time, for the first half of the 1970s, dealing with the disciplinary issues wrought by the Vietnam era. As the decade drew to an end, positive change began.

The rebuilding process was slow, but under the guidance and determination of a succession of commandants, it was nevertheless certain. The Corps rid itself of a large number of misfits by simply discharging them, preferring to take on its national defense missions with fewer, but better, Marines. By 1982, 85 percent of new enlistees were high school graduates. Three years later the figure was 97 percent, and an identical number of new Marines scored in the top three mental categories. Reenlistments were at an all-time high, and disciplinary problems had receded to the point that the Corps' leaders could once again concentrate on forging their units into efficient fighting forces.[1]

Under President Ronald Reagan, the Marines and their sister services benefited from the administration's goal of having an armed force second to none. Weapons systems were upgraded or superceded, and ammunition stocks were increased, from a nineteen-day supply in 1980 to a fifty-eight-day supply in 1986. Funds were made available for training in every conceivable climate and condition. Marines were deployed to Norway for winter combat training, to the Philippines for jungle warfare exercises, and conducted desert maneuvers at the huge training facility at Twenty-nine Palms, California. Infantry training for all Marines, regardless of military occupational specialty, was once more adopted as standard policy.

Strategic priorities were revised. The oil crisis of 1973 focused American attention on the Persian Gulf and was to have a far-reaching effect on strategic planners. Although the Soviet Union continued to dominate thinking for some years to come, the Middle East situation prompted the United States to form the Rapid Deployment Force in the early 1980s and the U.S. Central Command (known as CentCom), the headquarters that would eventually run Desert Storm, in January 1983.

With the collapse of the USSR, the shift of thinking away from intense land warfare on the plains of Europe, and the reduction of a nuclear threat, operational analysts rediscovered the Marine Corps. Emphasis now came to bear on the rapid deployment of military forces to Third World hot spots. Assigned new missions, the Corps' antiarmor capabilities were improved, and one unit, the 7th Marine Expeditionary Brigade, was designated as the rapid deployment force in case of need in Southwest Asia. They were moved from Camp Pendleton, California, their peacetime home on the coast for decades, to the desert station at Twenty-nine Palms.

Concurrently, forward thinkers like General Paul X. Kelley began to wonder how they would deploy and sustain Marines if they *did* have to fight in a remote country like Saudi Arabia. A result of this concern was the Maritime Prepositioning Force (MPF), a concept devised during the Kennedy administration but shelved because of the exigencies of the Soviet challenge, and later, the Vietnam War.

The idea of MPF is to preposition supplies and equipment for a rapid deployment force aboard squadrons of ships stationed in several strategic locations around the world. This would permit the immediate dispatch of U.S. Marines by air to imperiled regions, where they could meet up with the resources they needed to commence combat operations. Since the Maritime Prepositioning Ships (MPS) are not combatants but belong to the Military Sealift Command, operated largely by civilians, it is necessary, under this concept, for the forces and material to join together in a benign port near the conflict area. One study, examining the possibility of supplying, for example, a 12,500-man Marine expeditionary force by air alone, estimated that the first thirty days of combat would require 4,500 flights by transport aircraft, a level of operation that would severely tax our air-supply resources. An MPS squadron could supply the same thirty-day level of supply by itself, buying time for the U.S. forces to augment their ability to sustain themselves.

Thus, by the time of the Iraqi invasion of Kuwait, three MPS squadrons had, for some time, been deployed in the eastern Atlantic. Although training exercises had rigorously tested the MPS concept, neither the concept nor the ships had been through the real thing.

America's Battalion

On 2 August 1990 Saddam Hussein's army swarmed across the Iraqi-Kuwaiti border to seize and occupy the tiny oil-rich Kuwaiti nation, setting off alarms around the world. In less than seven months' time, and after less than seven weeks of air warfare and four days of ground fighting, this same army, the world's fourth largest, was routed and forced back into its own territory, with great loss of life and material. This victory, the product of almost unprecedented cooperation within the United Nations and among regional powers in the Middle East, was remarkable for numerous reasons. Diplomatic and military cooperation aside, the war was a test for new methods of war fighting and new technology. It was also a test of American willpower, a quality considered questionable since Vietnam. All of these are important objects for study and analysis, and a flood of books has already examined them in detail. This book does not consider any of these topics except peripherally, but returns to an older topic—the personal and professional experiences of the American fighting man at war. It is an attempt to portray how the American grunt, whose timeless mission is to "locate, close with, and destroy the enemy," performed in the shadow of more spectacular events. It is mostly about the experiences of a single unit—the 3rd Battalion, 3rd Marines—in the war against Iraq.

Like all of our military units, the 3rd Battalion, 3rd Marines was made up of a wide representation of America's sons and, like many, has a long record of dedicated service to our country. She fought against the Japanese in the Bougainville, Guam, and Iwo Jima campaigns. In Vietnam she landed across the beaches of Chu Lai in 1965 to counter the Viet Cong forces that were endangering the country. Her struggle in that land took four and a half years, in which she ranged the length and breadth of I Corps, South Vietnam's northernmost provinces, and she engaged in bitter combat with one of the world's best infantry forces, the North Vietnamese army. In that war the battalion established a remarkable reputation for courage and élan that was matched by few other units.

Since Vietnam the battalion has been stationed at the Marine Corps Base, Kaneohe Bay, Hawaii, with her parent regiment, the 3rd Marines. From this home base the battalion has traveled the world to train in "every clime and place" in which a force-in-readiness might be expected to fight.

Somewhere along the way the battalion acquired the sobriquet "America's Battalion." Although the officers and men represented here belong to one Marine unit, they are truly representative of America—not only sharing and reflecting our values but also demonstrating the willingness to risk the ultimate sacrifice so that other men and women might also have the opportunity to partake of those values. This, then, is the story of how your battalion—your sons, brothers, fathers, and husbands—performed in the First Gulf War. It is told, for the most part, in their own words.

Note: A number representing the battalion, followed by a slash and a number representing the regiment, generally represents Marine infantry and artillery battalions in writing. The 3rd Battalion, 3rd Marines, then, is generally written as "3/3" and pronounced as "three three." The companies in a third battalion are Headquarters and Service (H&S), Weapons Company, and three rifle companies called by their phonetic designators—India, Kilo, and Lima.

I / The Alert

Infantry Marines can expect to make periodic deployments to various parts of the world, where they train in different conditions and act as a ready reaction force for that part of the globe. Lasting up to six months, these deployments are unaccompanied. This means that these men say good-bye to their families and go off to serve wherever needed. On 2 August 1990, the day Saddam Hussein invaded Kuwait, 3/3 was just finishing a six-month deployment in East Asia.

The other units of her parent regiment, the 3rd Marines, were scattered. As 3/3 returned home, 2/3 had deployed to Okinawa to relieve her. In the last week of July the remainder of the regiment, along with its artillery battalion (1/12), reconnaissance, and engineer and amphibious support, had moved to the Big Island of Hawaii to conduct a thirty-day training exercise. The regiment was one of the units immediately alerted for deployment in Southwest Asia.

Major General, then Colonel, John H. Admire, Commanding Officer (CO), 3rd Marines

This was an extremely challenging time period. We were deployed in a demanding training schedule with the regiment plus deploying and redeploying two of our battalions. After the alert we continued a rigorous training schedule while simultaneously preparing for an emergency redeployment from Hawaii to Oahu and then on to the Persian Gulf. We continued to conduct tactics, live fire, and chemical warfare training almost until the day of our eventual departure. The initial unit to deploy from Oahu to Saudi Arabia was 3/3.

Colonel, then Lieutenant Colonel, John Garrett, Battalion Commander, 3/3

There is something special about 3/3. They do special things and they do things extremely well. I wouldn't be able to explain it to you . . . I had the premonition that we would do something uncommon about deploying. I kept thinking that something's going to happen. I thought, *Well, what could that be?* They might call us down to the Philippines for a problem down there while we were in Okinawa or something. Something special.

We did really well on our tour on Okinawa, but 27 to 28 percent of the battalion is married and it was time for them to come home. It is very difficult enough to be away six months and then have to go back out again. Had we not been in a pretty high state of motivation, I think it would have been a very difficult thing to put on people. But it worked out just fine.

Major Craig Huddleston, Battalion Executive Officer (XO)

The second and third of August 1990—that's when we came back. The day the first increment of the battalion left Okinawa was the first day of the invasion of Kuwait. We were getting a bit of news about that, but not much, because we were mainly tied up with getting out of Okinawa and getting home.

My outcall with Colonel Strickland, who is the CO of the 9th Marines on Okinawa, was on the third of August. That afternoon I went up to the regimental headquarters to say good-bye to him about 1600, just prior to getting on the bus to go to Kadena Air Base. As I was coming into the regimental headquarters, Colonel Strickland grabbed me, pulled me into his office, and showed me a message that said things were degenerating in Kuwait and it looked like the 7th [MEB—Marine Expeditionary Brigade] was going to deploy.

The 7th MEB was the first Marine unit to deploy. Based at the Marine Air-Ground Combat Center, Twenty-nine Palms, California, in California's Mojave Desert, the brigade was commanded by Major General

John Hopkins. His brigade specialized in combined arms operations in a desert environment. Over the next forty days, the Marines were to deploy the majority of the Marine Corps to Saudi Arabia with the mission of protecting the oil and port facilities at Al Jubail, Juaymah, and Ras Tannurah.[1]

The first U.S. troops on the scene in Saudi Arabia were elements of the Army's 82nd Airborne Division. One of America's elite units, the 82nd Airborne was nonetheless lightly armed for desert warfare and incapable of sustaining itself against Iraqi armored divisions. Their chief function at this point was to provide an American presence of some sort in hopes that it would give Saddam Hussein pause if he intended to carry his invasion across the borders of Saudi Arabia.

The MPF concept paid off for the Marines and for America. The 7th Marine Expeditionary Brigade (7th MEB) was airlifted and was met in Saudi Arabia by the Diego Garcia–based squadron. It was a close thing. Two of this squadron's ships were out of position at the time of the invasion. One was undergoing routine maintenance in the U.S. and another was on its way back from a similar task. Both were rapidly redeployed and carried out their mission of supplying the 7th MEB. Just seven days after the order to deploy was issued, the ships were in Saudi Arabia offloading their cargoes. On 14 August, members of the 7th MEB began filing off the aircraft that had lifted them into Saudi Arabia. The Saudis were so unprepared for the rapidity with which the Marines arrived that they didn't know what to do with them. There were many Saudis who were worried about the presence of non-Muslims on Saudi soil. Because of this, the Saudi authorities would not permit the Marines to tactically deploy away from the port area but housed them in huge warehouses in heat that reached 120 degrees. General Norman Schwarzkopf, commanding general of the U.S. Central Command and responsible for all U.S. forces in the Gulf, took a number of steps to reassure our Saudi allies. First, he issued an order that imposed a total prohibition on alcohol for U.S. forces. Second, the flying of U.S. flags was not officially permitted at any U.S. installation. Third, Christian religious services could not be held where local civilians could observe them, and chaplains were referred to as "morale officers."[2] With these and several other measures in place, the

Marines were finally permitted to tactically deploy northwest of the port of Al Jubail.

The arrival of the 7th MEB and its equipment constituted the first credible antiarmor capability for U.S. forces in the Gulf. The 1st MEB, of which 3/3 was a part, was right behind them.

Major Craig Huddleston, Battalion XO

I was kind of in shock because we thought it would be the standard drill—stern diplomatic protests and sending the carrier battle group over there until the other side backed down. We really did not have any indication that it would be bigger than that. In addition, the message that Colonel Strickland showed me contained words to the effect that Maritime Prepositioning Squadron One should be prepared to execute a positioning operation. MPS One supported the 1st MEB in Hawaii. So we knew we were leaving the 3rd Marine Division to come back to the 1st MEB and were going from the frying pan into the fire.

The invasion was big news. There was a lot of talk, speculation, scuttlebutt going around with the officers and the staff NCOs [noncomissioned officers].

I was the battalion's senior Marine who was still on Okinawa, so I took most of the questions. In the back of my mind, I said, *This could be big.* But I didn't want to tell the Marines that, so I said, "I don't know what we're going to do. I think it's probably going to be pretty light. Don't worry about it."

We got on the 747, with the staff and officers on the top part. Once we were airborne, I grabbed the S4 [logistics officer] who was flying with me, the S3 Alpha [assistant operations officer], the headquarters commandant, and some of the other key players. I said, "Look, I don't want you to get too apprehensive, but we need to be thinking about, as soon as we hit the deck, deploying again."

So they started thinking about it. We got home on the third and had a ninety-six-hour pass over the weekend. The plan was, we were going to get together Monday morning, the morning of August 6th, to talk about what was going on.

Sunday evening, the evening of August 5th, Lieutenant Colonel Garrett called me at home and said, "I'm not going to be at the meeting tomorrow morning. I have to go to the Pohakaloa Training Area on the Big Island of

Hawaii to meet with the regimental commander." I asked, "Why do you have to go there tomorrow morning?" He replied, "I can't tell you."

The regimental headquarters was over there and 1/12 and 1/3. Well, when he told me he couldn't discuss it, I knew immediately what he was talking about. So we reported in. Everybody came back, and at 0730 on the sixth of August we commenced staff planning for deployment to Saudi Arabia.

Captain Michael J. McCusker, Commanding Officer, India Company

We were briefed by the XO and the CO about how Kuwait had been invaded and how we had established contingencies for that. The colonel came up to me on Wednesday and said, "You are now the commanding officer of India Company, 3/3. Take your company and pack them up tonight. I want you to be prepared to leave as of tomorrow. You will be leaving independently in advance of the battalion." It was August eighth. We actually left on the fifteenth, so I had seven days to prepare the company to mount out. The colonel said, "Mike, go forth and multiply." So we did our thing.

I immediately went over to the company and said, "Hey, I'm your new CO. Start packing. We're leaving." It was a big change, because I hadn't seen my wife and child for a long time. We had been separated for six months for the Okinawa deployment. That was the tough part. But the colonel told me, "You know, I really agonized over giving you this job, but you're the best person to do it for me." I'd been the company commander of Kilo Company. "I want someone who can go off and operate by themselves. You're the person I want to take the company." The boys in the company were real good. They had done operations by themselves in Thailand and were very competent at operating by themselves.

Captain Leon M. Pappa, Commanding Officer, Kilo Company

There was excitement mixed with apprehension and some disappointment that we were no sooner back than we were going right back out again. I was surprised that there was almost no complaining about that. What there was went away very quickly because there was so very little time to think about it. We were no sooner back a few days and already we were drawing gear, securing weapons, and training on the weekends. Over the days and weeks as we got ready to leave, I started gearing them up. "Remember who you are.

You are Marines. Yes, they're Iraqis, and they have the third or fourth largest army in the world. But don't forget what stock you come from." I felt I really had their attention in the weeks before we left. You could see it in their faces. They were afraid but excited at the same time, and I thought that was good. I would be suspicious of anyone who wasn't afraid.

1st Sergeant Wylie R. McIntosh, First Sergeant, Weapons Company

You could see it. The first reaction was total silence. The men were shocked. I'd been telling them ever since I had been with the battalion that one day we were going into a conflict. It would happen. I don't think anyone really believed it.

Major Craig Huddleston, Battalion XO

It was a very difficult time for us. We were trying to get equipment and supplies that we needed to deploy to a potential combat zone. We came back from Okinawa with our sea bags and that was all. We had to issue weapons. We had to draw equipment and supplies, do some training. We had to battle-sight-zero our weapons, test our communications equipment, and all the while we never had a firm date for deploying.

Captain Mark A. Davis, Battalion Logistics Officer (S4)

When we got back from Okinawa we had to do all the things that a battalion does—pull out all the Marines' personal effects from storage, pick up their cars from storage, issue linens and gear, and dozens of other things. Now we had to reverse the process, turn all that stuff in again. An infantry battalion is like a newborn baby. It has very little in the way of an organic support mechanism. Like a baby, it requires a lot of people to take care of it. It can breathe and see and touch and hear, but it cannot feed itself, water itself, clothe itself, take care of its own medical needs, or go to the bathroom by itself. That was my job.

Major Craig Huddleston, Battalion XO

My first impression of the Marines' reaction was one of excitement. They were excited about being part of something that could be very big. That placed an obligation on the senior leadership—NCO and officer—to try to tone that down a little bit and say, "Look, be careful what you ask for. You just may get it. You want to go to war? You've never seen a war. You might find out what it is like and not think it is such a great idea." At the same time, we had to ensure that the men were ready. After the initial excitement wore off, the hard work that was ahead of us became a reality. I would say that the emotion changed to one of resolve. "Let's get on with it, let's go get the job done." I sensed that from the most junior PFC [private first class] to the battalion commander. "We don't know how long we're going to be deployed, we don't know what the situation is going to be over there. We know we're facing a potentially serious foe. Let's do it. Let's just go get it done." That emotion tended to feed on itself to the point that we began to feel pretty confident.

Corporal David Bush, Driver for the Battalion (S3)

When it first started I thought it was unreal. It would be like Afghanistan, something we'd hear about and talk about but not actually do anything about.

Sergeant Major James W. "Bo" Pippin, Battalion Sergeant Major

There were 252 married Marines in the battalion, so roughly 25 percent of the battalion was married. Most of them had children. Getting back from deployment from Okinawa and then in a matter of three or four days know-ing you had to depart again was quite emotional for those married Marines. I don't mean to take anything away from the unmarried Marines. It was emotional for them too. They had leave planned, they had bought tickets to go home—the whole bit. A few Marines had already departed on leave and had to be called back. The families didn't all understand the situation at the time. How do you prepare a family for something like this?

Lieutenant Ivan Wray, Artillery Forward Observer (FO), with India Company

I didn't think we would go. I had this joke about the 1st MEB being the 1st Mothball Brigade. After all, the invasion of Panama took place just a year earlier and didn't affect us at all in Hawaii. If war came, I thought we would go in sometime after the Girl Scouts.

Captain Kevin Scott, Commanding Officer, Lima Company

I had a wife and two children. The children were very small. They had a rough time when I was in Okinawa, understanding where I was. Lisa did a good job of explaining it, but when I got home and Saddam did his thing, and knowing that I was leaving again and the children asking where I was going . . . at that point it took the wind out of my sails. But then I remembered that the nation had been called on, and I had been called on to do my job.

Captain Osamah "Sam" A. Jammal, Company Commander, Headquarters and Service (H&S) Company

I'm Jordanian by birth. I came to the States in 1970. Around 1979 I qualified and was entered in the Platoon Leaders Class program and was commissioned in '82.[3] I've been in the Marine Corps for approximately nine and a half years. I reported to 3/3 in August 1990. Approximately three weeks after I reported in, the battalion was packing up to go to Southwest Asia. I was scared and anxious, but I wanted to do it. I put all that aside and started concentrating on what it is I'm going to do in 3/3. I was given H&S. It is made up of the headquarters and service elements—e.g., logistics, intelligence, communications, et cetera—that do not properly belong with one of the operational companies.

I didn't really have time to think about anything else except getting the unit ready to deploy. I didn't have any fear or anxiety once I got busy. The first question from everyone was, "You're an Arab, what do you think?" I'd say, "What do I think? I think we ought to go over there and kick some ass." I was no different than anyone else.

I remember Major Huddleston saying, "Be careful what you wish for. You just might get it." He was right. We shouldn't wish for something we might not really want to get. I didn't have the slightest hesitation about going over there. It needed to be done. Where I come from Saddam was well liked, but not by everyone. I don't think what he did was proper in the Arab sense. The Arab coalition forces proved that.

I never thought I would speak Arabic for the United States Marine Corps. I learned English in elementary school in Jordan from the British and I did not know what to expect in Saudi Arabia. Jordan is a different climate, a Mediterranean climate. It is more like Southern California. So I didn't know what to expect. All I knew about Saudi Arabia was that it was going to be hot.

The other thing I didn't know and I thought was very important was getting to know about 230 names and faces and all that. My biggest fear was, assuming that we did go to war, was that I would not have time to know my people. Our basic leadership training tells us that we need to know everyone's names and faces. So it was important to get to know the people. At the same time, I was wrestling to get the company going. H&S is different from a line company. You can't just say, "Fall in," and have everyone do that, because if you did, everything else would come to a halt in the battalion.

We were given a few classes on Arab culture before we left Hawaii, and I didn't think they were very well presented, so I spoke up and was allowed to tell the Marines what I knew about it. We were a little too sensitive about uses of the left hand and right hand and saying this but not saying that. I told them that the Arabs were a certain way but once you broke the ice with them it was not necessary to be so formal.

Captain Joseph Molofsky, Liaison to the Saudi Brigade

On graduation from Amphibious Warfare School in the spring of 1989, I was sent immediately to the United Nations Troops Supervision Organization in Palestine. I served in patrol duty in the Sinai and on the Gaza Strip. I left there in June 1990, reported to the 3rd Marines on 2 August, and prepared to deploy to Saudi Arabia on the fifteenth.

I left the Middle East planning on *never* going back. I wasn't here in Hawaii for two days before I found out that the whole regiment was going there. I was immediately put on a program of developing classes in area orientation, Arabic culture, and also desert survival techniques, based on my experience in Sinai and Gaza. I spent the two weeks we were in Hawaii traveling around and giving lectures, some to as many as a thousand people at a time, on Arabic culture and so on.

Lieutenant Daniel S. Henderson, 3rd Platoon Commander, Kilo Company

I had plans to go away with my wife. Everything like that got cancelled. A lot of my Marines who were on leave got recalled. Being the NBC [nuclear, biological, and chemical] warfare defense officer was one of my extra duties assigned by my company commander. I went to NBC School here at Kaneohe Bay, so I was up on that and took over the NBC duties. My priorities included getting gas masks, new filters for the masks, and going over the different NBC kits. There was a lot of maintenance that we had not done before and we had to do immediately, because by the time we reached Saudi Arabia there would be a chemical threat to every single man in the battalion. We changed all the filters to make sure they were up to date. We issued decontamination kits for the skin. We had atropine [anti–nerve gas] injectors all set to issue once we got there. We had just three weeks to do all this plus the reissue of weapons and the normal training of my platoon. We missed a lot of weekends.

Tempers were beginning to flare after the first few weeks, because it was "Let's go, let's go," and then we would wait. This happened several times. Then, all of a sudden, they said, "We're leaving now." It was the real thing.

Sergeant William D. liams, Reconnaissance Team Leader, Company A, 3rd Reconnaissance Battalion

None of the younger Marines knew who Saddam Hussein was or where Kuwait was. Fortunately, I had been stationed in Lebanon for a couple of years and had done some research on the area. And when I was in Okinawa, I was involved in antiterrorism training. So I knew a little about what was going on.

I thought from the first day that if they are spending this much money and making this much effort, there is going to be a war. I didn't think we were going to sit in the desert as long as we did. It is too bad we had to wait for the Army, but we always do.

It was real interesting, the whole buildup. It's amazing how with the problems we had sometime with color, creed, race, and all, when the flag goes up, all that gets put aside. Everyone does their job and everything turns out the way it should. Of course, we have a great bunch of guys in company. We're kind of a unique bunch of men. There are no personnel problems. Some of the younger guys ran off and got married just before we left, because they thought they were going to die and they wanted to make sure their girlfriends were set up.

Major Craig Huddleston, Battalion XO

After all the things we'd been doing back in Hawaii, it was a relief when we deployed our first increment to Southwest Asia. "All right, now we're going to start doing something. We're under way. We're involved and we're going to do it."

As the end of August approached, it became very confusing here. "When were we going to go? When were we going to do it?" In the families we had a common experience with our wives after a while who were saying, "Why don't you just get out of here?" I'd go home and tell my wife we were leaving in two days. We'd make our plans and say our good-byes, and then a couple of hours before we boarded the aircraft, we'd come back home again. This was more stressful than just about anything.

This went on and on, and finally we deployed about half the battalion. The battalion commander led the first increment over, and I stayed back with about three hundred Marines waiting to go. We went through the process again and again for another four or five days.

2 / India Company Leads the Way

The battalion was not to deploy together but incrementally. Captain McCusker's India Company was the first to leave. They were to be flown to the Far East to provide security for the Maritime Prepositioning Force ships that would travel from Guam to Saudi Arabia.

Captain Mike McCusker, CO, India Company

We had gotten some very, very basic briefs as to what Saddam Hussein had been doing. Our initial impression was that there is nothing over there to stop him from continuing what he is doing, to continue down south and invade Saudi Arabia too. The 7th Marines were there, but there wasn't much else to slow them down. The biggest deterrent was just the fact that the United States was there.

I initially thought that no one was going to start throwing rounds down range because of the last twenty years. The United States did not want to get involved in a war, because we'd been such a paper tiger for a long time. So I was really amazed when we actually deployed that night. A small side note: My new first sergeant had just stepped on deck that same day. He was a friend of mine from our days in the 3rd Battalion, 6th Marines—Gunnery Sergeant Carrington. I hadn't seen him in a long time. We had gone to Beirut together. I was a platoon commander then and he was my platoon sergeant. So at times in the Marine Corps, you come back and see each other again. It was nice to have someone I knew, who I could trust to go right in, get them prepared, get the boys ready to go and take off.

Colonel Counselman was my boss in his role as the task force commander of the security detachment of the Maritime Positioning Force. Under that task force was us, the security personnel, which was being run by a major from the Brigade Service Support Group. During the seven days of getting ready to leave, we had gone twice to the airfield, ready to go, and then at the last minute they would cancel. We had packed everything and put it on pallets in just an amazing few days. That was because Gunnery Sergeant Carrington really turned to and got people going.

Then we got on planes and flew to a different country, which we had to sneak through because of the classification of the whole thing. In the middle of the night they put us in covered vehicles and transported us to the docks. We snuck aboard the ships. It was really late. Two of the ships were under way before the sun came up.

The ammunition came in. The last ship came in so that it could pick it up and shove off by a certain time. We still had to transfer all of this ammo before we could get out of there. The ships were prepared for the equipment on board and other things, but because this was an actual wartime scenario they were not prepared for the security forces, us, who were on board to take care of terrorist activities.

I had a platoon with Lieutenant Mike Doggin aboard one ship and Lieutenant Tim Mundy, the commandant's son, on another. Colonel Counselman and I put together a whole set of security orders to guard these ships. We had to build gun mounts. We welded them to the ships, mounts for the .50-caliber and the M-60 machine guns. Then we set up full machine gun drill aboard ship against possible air, submarine, and small boat attacks at sea. We were expecting the worst. The ship, the Navy, and all the civilians— Merchant Marines—really helped out.

During the whole crossing we prepared. Our understanding was that we would land somewhere near the objective area, but we didn't know where. It turned out to be Al Jubail, Saudi Arabia. We were not sure what was there or what security measures were in place. We had to prepare for every type of defensive countermeasure there, from guerrilla-type operations to counterterrorist operations. On the way, the Marines had classes on all the possibilities, and they had physical training, you name it. They did a hell of a bang-up job.

Lieutenant Ivan Wray, Artillery FO, with India Company

I spent some time on the bow and some time on the stern just looking out at the sea. It was peaceful going through the Straits of Malacca and then heading past Sri Lanka. We weren't too far off shore and could see the topography. The time we spent on that ship was spent preparing myself and preparing these kids. They were so young. They're just good kids, good young men. If someone asked me to choose any place on earth I could be, it would be with those men.

Captain Mike McCusker, CO, India Company

We finally got the word we were going to Al Jubail. During the time of our crossing, three incidents happened. One is that something came up on the radar screen one night—something that was following the ships. It could have been a submarine, we didn't know. It was in the middle of the night and we had a full reaction drill. Everyone was out in a Condition One Alert. The ship's captain was grateful we were there. After a while, whatever it was faded from the radar screen.

In the second incident we had unmarked helicopters flying through. They turned out to be "gray Navy" flying for some other ships. We had to send a message to Command Task Force telling them that if they didn't want to get shot out of the air, they should stay away from our ships, because there were Marines on board who were fully armed and prepared to knock down anything that wasn't authorized to be there.

The last one was when we had this civilian cigarette boat come hauling at us. This was just about the time we entered the Persian Gulf. We had no idea who they were, but we went into full reaction again and had everything trained on this boat. We saw the Arabian people on board and had no idea who they were. We thought, *Oh, shit, terrorists attacking the ships!* They drove the boat between two of the ships and started waving.

Lieutenant Ivan Wray, Artillery FO, with India Company

We were not even sure they were combatants. They were coming toward us and they couldn't see what was on board, and everybody's heart is pumping pretty bad. I was up on the bridge and they were coming toward our right side. We had a .50-caliber machine gun mounted right there. The gun was half loaded, and when they came in closer the gunner loaded up all the way. They got close enough to recognize the gun, and one of the guys saw it and his eyes popped. The boat turned to the left, and they went speeding down our column and left.

Captain Mike McCusker, CO, India Company

Just after that we got into the port of Al Jubail and took over port security from Echo Company, 7th Marines. There was a lot to be done. We had nothing to work with. I mean I had my organic weapons—M-60 machine guns and mortars—but we had no assets to move me around and get where I needed to get. As soon as we got in, there was a go-around to see who was in charge of what. We were attached to a Brigade Service Support Group. A lieutenant colonel was in charge of overall security, but there was not much being done. So I called my gunnery sergeant in and said, "What do we have in vehicles?" "Basically nothing," he replied. "We have to do everything on our own." I said, "Go forth and get me what I need." And, like a good gunny does, he came back with a truck, two Humvees, and everything from sandbags to camouflage hats to whatever I needed. He was a major, major go-getter and solved a helluva lot of problems for me, especially during that time.

We then proceeded to make defensive positions all through the pier area, looked at what was done for security, and beefed it up 110 percent from what had been done. Marines had constant security patrols going around the whole thing and just did a bang-up job of getting the whole thing ready.

At that time we were living in a big warehouse. The gunny got me everything from cots to a freezer you could put water in to make it cold. You name it, he got it while we were there. He was amazing.

Lieutenant Ivan Wray, Artillery FO, with India Company

We had one guy who I guess you could call our Radar O'Reilly. His name was Spinks and he was a clerk in the CP [command post]. He was a Georgia boy and a helluva character. He could get anything. He could get an icepick. He could get steaks off the ships. He also had friends among some cooks who were with us in Thailand. After our original evening meal, which we didn't have enough of anyway, he'd pull up outside the warehouse, and the Marines would file out and get rice, steaks, pork chops, whatever he could get off the ship. India Company was doing well.

With the arrival of India Company and the MPF ships, the antiarmor capability of the U.S. forces nearly doubled and was growing. The first 140 tanks to arrive in Saudi Arabia were Marine tanks. Three hundred assault amphibian vehicles, designed to operate over a defended beachhead, served as armored personnel carriers and greatly enhanced the land mobility of the Marines. Thanks to the MPF, these vehicles arrived with at least thirty days of supply. Still more Marines were on the way. The 4th MEB had been diverted from a NATO exercise in Norway and it, too, was en route.[1] In the meantime, the main body of the battalion was getting under way from Kaneohe Bay, Hawaii.

Major Craig Huddleston, Battalion XO

Finally, on the first of September, the entire battalion was deployed. Our flight over—I don't think any of us experienced anything like it before— thirty hours on an airplane. We flew from Hawaii, landed in Seattle. From there to Bangor, Maine, and then to Brussels, Belgium, and then straight into Dhahran, Saudi Arabia.

The apprehension built about what we were getting into. The sensation was exactly the same as when I got on the bus to go to boot camp. I was excited. I was looking forward to it and at the same time wondered what was going to happen to me when I got there.

I was in a little different situation than the rest of the battalion. About ten days prior to our deployment, with all this apprehension and nervousness, I was riding my bicycle at Pearl Harbor on the bike path and I hit a chicken. The chicken got in the front spokes of my bike. I went over the top and broke my collarbone in three places. I was worried that I might not be deployable. By that time I had been in the Marine Corps for twenty-one years, and I thought that this was going to be the biggest thing that has happened to the Marine Corps during my career and I couldn't miss it. So I had to deal with this broken collarbone—and I did. I went to Saudi Arabia with my shoulder in a brace. I had a little physical pain, but it wasn't anything like the mental apprehension, which was far worse than the pain from my broken collarbone.

Captain Joachim "Joe" W. Fack, Forward Air Controller (FAC)[2]

I'm Captain Joe Fack, as in forward air controller with a "K" on the end. I was in Marine Aircraft Group 24 in Hawaii when a FAC position opened up. I volunteered for it and for what I thought would be an on-island tour. I was at Tactical Control Party School in Coronado, California, when Iraq invaded Kuwait. I didn't think much of it and *Sure, no problem.* The course was supposed to be twenty-nine days long. It ended up being nine days, with a weekend included. I checked into 3/3 when I returned to Hawaii and nine days later was on an airplane to Saudi Arabia. I didn't know what to think right then. I was assigned to Kilo Company.

Major Craig Huddleston, Battalion XO

So anyway, we were flying to Saudi Arabia on United Airlines. Our last stop was in Brussels. All the way over, the aircrews, the flight attendants, they treated us like kings. All the flight crew, from the pilots down to the last flight attendant, were volunteers, and many of the flight attendants were middle-aged men and women who had flown the freedom flights out of Vietnam. They said that's why they wanted to do it. They volunteered to fly us over there, perhaps to relive their youth a little bit, but also because I think they knew how to handle people going into battle or coming back from battle. I've never been treated better by anybody. They fed us, they showed continuous movies, they gave us everything they could. They asked me, as senior man on the flight, as we approached Brussels, if there was anything they could do at their last stop to help us prepare. The only thing I could think of was water. I told them we are going to need water, and we need to start hydrating because it is going to be hot there. We needed a lot of water. So they radioed ahead, and when we landed they put about forty cases of bottled water on the airplane for us and handed them out. Each Marine got a couple of bottles of water, and we started drinking it and it was real good.

1st Sergeant Wylie McIntosh, Weapons Company

Our airline was TWA. We couldn't have been treated better. The only way we were treated better was when we came back. All of the flight attendants were a little older. Two of the five were vets who had flown Marines to Vietnam. The reason they were there was because they were the old warhorses. The younger ones had all pooped out on them because they couldn't carry the load of flying as much as they did. They gave us pencils, paper, and envelopes and encouraged us to write letters. They collected the letters and mailed them, paying the postage out of their own pockets. We turned them in in San Francisco, and again in New York. I was very impressed.

Major Craig Huddleston, Battalion XO

It was dark when we left Brussels, something like 0200. We flew down the Red Sea, and they told us that was to avoid Iraqi antiair missiles. That was a kind of reveille for everybody.

We flew down the west coast of Saudi Arabia and then turned due east, heading for Dhahran. At about that time the sun came up. The pilot told us to look out the windows. As the sun came up we looked out at absolutely nothing, just an empty desert, an empty wilderness. It was there for four hours of the flight, and we didn't see any lights or anything until we approached Dhahran. At that point we were all greatly sobered. We knew it could be very bad.

Corporal David Bush, S3 Driver

I had a window seat. I looked out and it was light and dark all the way across Saudi Arabia. All you could see was the different textures. For miles and miles and miles. I remember thinking that I hoped we didn't have to stay there too long. I didn't think I'd be able to deal with not seeing anything.

Major Craig Huddleston, Battalion XO

We had no idea what was going on. We had received an intelligence update at Hickam Air Force Base in Hawaii just before we departed and were told that the Iraqis were continuing to move forces south, that they were consolidating their positions in Kuwait, and that they were bringing in larger forces and moving to the border of Saudi Arabia. We knew at that time that our mission was going to be to deter the invasion of Saudi Arabia and, if necessary, defend Saudi Arabia and, finally, be prepared to counterattack. We also knew that we were flying over there with just our personal weapons, so if we were flying into a war we were going in pretty light. We were a little concerned about that.

The airline pilot was a former Marine pilot from Korea. He put on a garrison cover, his old khaki piss-cutter, and he came out and talked to all of us. He walked around and tried to reassure the Marines. He told them all that he was proud of them and knew they would do the best job they could. He was very good and so was the rest of the flight crew. I think they sensed that we were nervous. All of them volunteered, down to the last guy. We went through something like three flight crews in this thirty-hour period. On a 747 that's a total of about seventy or seventy-five people. For some of them this was their third trip to Saudi Arabia already. As we approached Dhahran we could see this huge airport. None of us had ever seen that many tactical aircraft in one place at one time. When we looked we noticed that all the aircraft were loaded with live ordnance. We knew we had arrived.

The pilot got on the intercom and said that they had a lot of expendable supplies on the aircraft. He told us that if it wasn't nailed down we could take it with us. We walked off with pillows and blankets, bottles of water, cases of soda pop, and sandwiches. The flight crew was not allowed off the aircraft, but they stood on the ladder and waved good-bye. They all had their hankies out and were waving. It was a poignant moment, and it shook us a bit because we knew we were severing our ties with the United States.

Major General J. M. "Mike" Myatt, Commanding General, 1st Marine Division

We arrived in August 1990, the middle of August. The 7th Marines landed with the 7th Brigade, and then the rest of the division came on in, and we were all there by the end of August. We weren't quite sure if Iraq wasn't going to come further into Arabia. The only thing standing between the Iraqi military and the oil fields early on, from August, September, and October, was the 1st Marine Division. And then in September in came a couple of brigades of the Army. The 82nd Airborne, which was so foot-mobile and of little use, to be honest, and the Saudi Arabian National Guard, the SANG. The 2nd SANG, commanded by Colonel Turki [Efirmi].

We started preparing for defense, and our whole focus was how to defeat an Iraqi invasion further into Saudi Arabia. We worked pretty closely with the Saudi 2nd SANG. They were really not a balanced force. They didn't have enough artillery, and they didn't have any air support or experience with it.

Upon their arrival, the 3rd Marines were attached to the 1st Marine Division while in Saudi Arabia. Since their home base was Hawaii, they were called Task Force Taro after the nutritious tropical plant that provides the makings for poi and other foods.

3 / Saudi Arabia
The Warehouses

Major Craig Huddleston, Battalion XO

When we got to Saudi Arabia it was about 110–115 degrees that day. We marched off to big tents that were set up for us to await transportation to wherever we were supposed to go, and we didn't even know where that was. About fifteen minutes after we got to the tents, the press descended upon us. Reporters from Italy, Germany, the UK, Reuters, AP, the *New York Times* all jumped us. Here we'd been on an airplane for thirty hours, arrived in a country where we'd never been and didn't know anything about the situation, and they asked us what we thought. That was our initial experience with the media. They knew more than we did, and we asked them more questions than they asked us.

Where we were and where we were going were foremost in our minds. We finally got on buses and took off for the port of Al Jubail on the eastern coast of Saudi Arabia. It was there that the ships offloaded. We pulled into the port and got off the buses and moved into very large warehouses, each of which housed about a thousand Marines. I wondered if we had learned anything from Beirut. Here we were, a couple of thousand Marines living elbow to elbow in a situation that is just as dangerous, if not more dangerous, than Beirut. That served as an impetus for us to speed the offload process, acquire our gear, and get out of there as quickly as we could. We stayed in that port for about nine days.

1st Sergeant Wylie McIntosh, Weapons Company

There must have been five thousand Marines in these warehouses, all packed in together. We sat there for approximately nine days. The longer we sat there, the more we got to thinking, *The man is going to run tanks through here at any minute*, or, *We are going to get a gas attack right here*. Here they had all these people piled up. One rocket could take out an entire battalion. If Saddam had used his head and fired on us while we were still in those warehouses, the war might have had a whole different outcome. We were about 110 miles from the Kuwaiti border and he could have reached us with a Scud. I don't know why he didn't, but I'm glad he didn't.

Captain Joseph Molofsky, Liaison to the Saudi Brigade

We went straight from the airfield to the port of Al Jubail and were billeted; unfortunately, the whole damned regiment was put into a series of warehouses right across the pier from a Russian cargo ship that spent two weeks loading, then unloading . . . then loading again.

Contingency plans were made for a quick defense of the port. Had Saddam Hussein chosen that moment to attack, he would have killed thousands of Marines. As the ammunition came off the ship it was still in conex boxes. It wasn't distributed. It was piled up in an ammunition supply point that, if it had been detonated at one time, would have made a crater out of the entire port facility.

There were eight thousand Marines down there, many of them without ammunition, and there was nothing between them and Kuwait City except one Saudi brigade that would have gotten walked over. Saddam could have roared down to the port, killed five thousand Marines and I think that American will, which is our real center of gravity, would have disappeared and we would have pulled out. He could have defeated the Americans had he not blinked and hesitated at that moment. There was nothing to stop him. The air support that was there wasn't real coordinated.

Captain Mike McCusker, CO, India Company

Two or three days after I got there, the battalion commander showed up with about one-third of the battalion. Again, no mail, no contact with home as to what was going on, and everything was classified, so you couldn't tell your family where you were or what was going on, just that you were gone.

Corporal David Bush, S3 Driver

We had India Company that went before us. They were on guard detail and they hadn't seen anything. They were ready for anything that came in. We had a sandbag perimeter, machine guns in the corners, patrols all the time. The MPs [military police] had the gates.

Colonel John Garrett, Battalion Commander

Captain McCusker got there first. He was really smart; he put his platoons really spread out. We're talking about a four- to five-square-mile area.

His trip was historical, providing security for the first time for a real deployment of MPS ships to a port that we hoped would be benign when we got there.

I'd walk around those warehouses and look at those guys sleeping in there on the cots and things. You know, we'd already been together for a significant amount of time in one deployment. We learned to adapt. We didn't have the tan paint that we needed for our vehicles, so we traded with the MPS people and used that. There was an extra piece of cloth in the back of the desert cammies [camouflaged uniforms] that's useless. It always gets caught when you put it on. They cut that out and they put it on their rifles. They invented a way to keep water cool. They'd take these water bottles we got, and they would fit precisely into a green issue sock. So they'd make the sock wet and just hang it at night or carry it around wet and it keeps your water cool. The biggest problem about water is it's always hot, and it's barely palatable when it's like that, but you must drink. You've got to drink all the time.

Major Craig Huddleston, Battalion XO

It was a mental shock, a culture shock. We came to a place that was like a brown ocean. We could see forever and ever. Our initial impression was "there's no vegetation in this place, there's nothing but roads and sand." It wasn't the desert of California or Yuma, Arizona. It appeared flat, initially. It appeared very hostile—no water, no vegetation, no anything. It was very hot. We were pretty depressed by the sight.

What was going through my mind—as well as, I know, the commander's—

was how, as an infantry battalion, how were we going to defend against a mechanized force in this terrain.

Sergeant William D. Iiams, Recon Team Leader

When we flew into Saudi Arabia, it was just unbelievable. First of all, I don't understand why people would fight over that country. Once we got off the plane on the tarmac, it was hot. The wind was blowing. There were Arabs standing in their tribals [native clothing].

Corporal Patrick A. Sterling, Reconnaissance Team Member, Company A, 3rd Reconnaissance Battalion

When we got on the plane when we were leaving for Saudi Arabia, I thought they were going to issue ammunition on the plane and when we got off, we were going to be shooting.

Captain Mike McCusker, CO, India Company

We started doing extensive recons out of the port area with all of the company commanders, the colonel, the staff personnel—extensive mobile reconnaissance of the desert, spending full days up there, driving around, checking areas out. We actually drove all the way up to the triangle below Khafji just doing mobile reconnaissance, seeing where we wanted to go, where the battalion wants to be, making contingency plans. Colonel Garrett had all the platoon commanders out there going over the ground as much as we possibly could, which was the best thing to do. I've always said the time you spend on the reconnaissance process is never ill-spent.

We did a lot of it. At the same time, our company gunny was out there scrounging every bit of material I'm going to need in the desert, from sand bags to camouflage nets to wood. I mean you just can't build a hole in the ground. It has to be reinforced.

1st Sergeant Wylie McIntosh, Weapons Company

The Army set up there, and they already had a lot of supplies, so they "loaned" us a lot.

Lieutenant Dan Henderson, Platoon Commander, Kilo Company

As far as you could see, there were just little dips in the sand as a terrain feature. It was real hostile because of the heat, and I knew that if something would happen and we were stranded out there, you could pretty much forget about making it back. We had gotten basic classes on survival in the desert, but out there, there were few watersheds or water holes. They were marked on the map, but it was hard to get oriented.

It was kind of exciting. We'd stop along the road that had Kuwait signs and took pictures in front of them and all that fun stuff. But it was miserable. I would ride on the back of a Humvee for five or six hours, and I'd get back and I would just collapse; I was so tired, physically tired, and I wasn't even walking. So I was thinking, *Gee, what's going to happen when we start putting on a pack?*

Captain Joe Fack, FAC

We were in the warehouses for about two or three weeks, thinking, *This is boring, it's going to be over soon.*

Captain Mike McCusker, CO, India Company

We were briefed on Saddam and his forces—that they were capable, that they were very good on engineering, and we knew their chemical capability. We were briefed a little bit about their nuclear capability—that it may be there, and that was a major problem. Of course with all of that was their reasoning since they'd just fought the Iran-Iraq war. We got some pamphlets concerning customs and courtesies, very minimal on language—flags, pictures, that type of thing. But I don't think we were ever really prepared for how vast the desert is.

Sergeant William D. liams, Recon Team Leader

I guess just because of guerrilla warfare and the lessons learned in Vietnam, we were briefed on the common people. We were really concerned about that sort of situation.

I was real surprised the way they lived, the common Saudi people out where we were at. Out where we were at were a lot of goat herders. There were a lot of peasant people. They seemed very humble, but they also seemed very frightened. I would say that they are religious fanatics. They were very hesitant about us. It was fortunate, or unfortunate, with us being in recon, we were pretty much away from this society. We were out in the bush a lot.

The Bedouins were real interesting people. They had what was probably the toughest and loneliest life. You're out by yourself in the sand dunes for days and days. It's just you and the sheep and your family members.

Captain Joseph Molofsky, Liaison to the Saudi Brigade

With some limited background in Arabic culture and the ability to speak just a little bit of Arabic, and serving with a group of Arab officers who were for the most part American-trained and who spoke English, I spent hours and hours discussing Saddam Hussein.

They believed sincerely that Saddam Hussein was mad and a danger to the sovereignty of the kingdom of Saudi Arabia. But they believed that the Iraqi army must not be destroyed. The Iraqi army needs to be used in the future to fight the real enemy, and of course that's the Zionists. Almost to a man, they believed that all those tanks, all those APCs [armored personnel carriers], all those Scuds, sooner or later, they were going to be allies with the Iraqi soldiers to relieve Jerusalem. Unbelievable! Unbelievable, but a sincere perception, I believe, on most of the officers' parts.

They looked at the whole thing from an Arabic perspective. It was all a matter of bluff, of bluster, and show of force and blinking and manliness. They believed that Saddam was going to push as far as he could push and then find a way to save face and back down, still achieving most of his strategic objectives. Saddam Hussein may be mad, but he's certainly one of the most shrewd politicians around.

Corporal Patrick Sterling, Recon Team Member

At times I felt pretty helpless, because being in the open desert like that, I felt if we were to come into contact with anybody, it would have been over because we had no cover. We'd just have to lay behind our rucksack or something. Sometimes it was a helpless feeling.

Corporal Scott Alan Uskoski, Recon Team Member

It wasn't hard to navigate around things; it was hard to find things to shoot resections off of out there. You had to follow the stars. You had to really pay attention to the stars, because there was nothing to guide off. You'd end up doing circles. When you'd look at the stars, you'd see that it wasn't left, it must have been right, and you'd go the wrong way.

Colonel John Garrett, Battalion Commander

When we were in these warehouses, we'd go up into the offices where the warehouse manager had been, and we'd put our maps up on the wall. We tried to game through this. It was like a war game I'd learned at Fort Leavenworth [where the U.S. Army Command and General Staff College are located]. We could expect more than ten thousand rounds of artillery in a half hour. What does that mean for us? Overhead cover! But there was no lumber there yet. The lumber had not gotten into the country. There was tons of lumber that had been used as dunnage on the ships. So when we did move out, about ten days later, from the warehouses, we took with us seven or eight P7s [LVTP-7 amphibian tractors] full of lumber. Subsequent to that we had three or four trailer loads of pallets brought out.

Colonel John H. Admire, CO, Task Force Taro

We deployed to areas previously occupied only by nomadic Bedouin tribesmen. The isolated remoteness of the desert sands slowly became less alien and more of an ally—a temporary home. We adjusted to its harshness by constructing defensive positions and conducting training primarily at night. In the summer heat we became nocturnal. We reduced day activities to rest and to nonphysical functions. Our desert night awareness and confidence continually improved.

4 / Cement Ridge

Captain Joe Fack, FAC

Then we moved out to the field, which was a place we called Cement Ridge, and we started doing a lot of exercises with F18s, Harriers, running SIMCAS [simulated close air support] shoots. We got real proficient.

SIMCAS was a new type of close air support because we couldn't drop bombs in Saudi Arabia. The Saudis wouldn't let us. They even wouldn't let us try artillery until we set up a range and showed them what we could do on the range. Then we finally got to shoot artillery. I think what they were concerned with was Bedouins and camels and all that stuff. We were at Cement Ridge for about four months.

For air operations I used the Joint Operations Graphic Air Map, but I also used the 1:50,000 [infantry tactical map] to get even closer. We were using a lot of lats and longs,[1] because the map error was so great. We used the GPS [global positioning system] for our location. And we'd use a target azimuth and a range with the 1:50,000. If you can get the aircraft within a mile of the target, all you have to do is talk to them on the radio, describe what it is.

Sergeant William D. Iiams, Recon Team Leader

GPS is spectacular. It's something that we need, in reconnaissance especially. Lightweight. I'm surprised the military got it since it's lightweight. It should have weighed fifty pounds. I swear by it.

Captain Mike McCusker, CO, India Company

So we're confiscating, for lack of a better word, as much wood as we possibly can. Someone would take something out of the box, they throw the wood away, so we're getting all that to make shoring for our bunkers. That's all we had. The Marine Corps didn't have notice to prepare for that big of an operation, which required shoring up bunkers and fighting in the desert.

For sandbags and camouflage nets, all we had were green things. The tan ones were found coming in, but we only had three per company. Every bunker needed them, so you actually needed about fifty tan camouflage nets to get things right.

Colonel John Garrett, Battalion Commander

We built the best defensive positions that you could ever hope to work on or train on. If we'd have gone home the next week, the Marines would have gotten experience in defensive operations that you'd never get anyplace else. This was against the expected ultimate ten thousand rounds of artillery in thirty minutes.

EMDCOA

Captain Mike McCusker, CO, India Company

We set this whole defense position in. This was probably the first time some of these Marines have ever dealt with a very intensive defensive perimeter. You name it, the wire to the bunkers, sandbags, you just can't do that in Hawaii. They weren't used to that. They went to town and, as always, the Marines turned in good work.

It was one of the best defensive training tactics I've ever done in my whole Marine Corps career. We laid everything—supplementary wire, defensive protective wire—we did it all. We were constantly patrolling every night. We were patrolling three times a day. This was live, it wasn't Memorex. You still got frustrated with it, because you still couldn't register your weapons for FPF [final protective fires], which still to this day I think was wrong. We had rounds in weapons. We had constant observation out there, checking networks, monitoring long-range patrols. People were learning how to do it right—everything from the basic patrol to fast foot formation up to the brigade level.

Colonel John H. Admire, CO, Task Force Taro

Once established in the new TAOR [tactical area of responsibility], we created a three-grid-square-by-six-grid-square training TAOR south of Khafji.[2] The concept was to create a company-level, and below, training area. Companies, platoons, and squads could then conduct relatively independent patrols and ambushes without immediate supervision from battalion or regimental commanders or staff. Small unit confidence and capabilities improved significantly. This team-oriented approach to and investment in training accrued multiple dividends in the subsequent war. Good squads ensured good platoons; good platoons ensured good companies. These techniques resulted in tactically proficient battalions and a well-trained regiment capable of multiple missions.

Lieutenant Ivan Wray, Artillery FO, with India Company

These Marines had never really been pressed that much, as much as we'd like to think we have training challenges in the Marines. These Marines were smart guys. Here in the desert, these Marines were just taking charge. The combination of fear and excitement made these young Marines think they were invincible. They thought they were like the Knights of Templar. I'm getting kind of romantic, but they saw themselves as doing something important. They were not thinking, *Oh, well, I don't have to impress the lieutenant today on this little field exercise out here,* like they sometimes did in Hawaii or on Okinawa. Here they were thinking that this was important and it had to be done right.

1st Sergeant Wylie McIntosh, Weapons Company

We finally moved down to this rock quarry, which had real good defensive capabilities, so we started digging in there. They assigned us the mission of defending the highway that ran through there. We were off a few hundred yards, and we had to defend and stop anything coming down that road.

The Dragon [vehicle-mounted antitank weapon] platoon had three sections, so we had one section out with each infantry company. We set the Dragons up there with on-call artillery, and the AT4s [shoulder-fired antitank weapons], and everything that goes with them in an infantry company.

Staff Sergeant Don Gallagher, Platoon Sergeant, Weapons Company

When I reported to Southwest Asia I was sent to the regiment as a replacement, and they were attaching replacements to the battalions. For some strange reason I got 3/3 in my head. They asked me where I was supposed to go. I told them I would go where I was needed but I wanted to go to 3/3.

When I reported in to 3/3 at Al Jubail, Sergeant Major Pippin told me he had two openings for a staff sergeant. One was in the armory, and the other in the motor pool. I thought to myself that I didn't want any of that, so I piped up and told him that I was good with heavy guns. He looked at me and told me that that was a lot of responsibility, but that was what I wanted and he sent me. I wanted to get into something with heavy firepower, something I knew about with vehicles and mobility. I'd never worked with them, but I'd been with TOWs [vehicle-mounted antitank weapons] and they used many of the same concepts, so I felt pretty familiar with it.

Captain Sam Jammal, CO, H&S Company

We dug in. And we learned a little bit about the desert. It did rain, for example. I had the dilemma of putting in the Combat Operations Center [COC], and the colonel didn't want it to look like a COC. He wanted it to blend in with the front line. The area where the communicators had put up their relay sites and their antenna was set up so it would look like a COC, which was behind the lines and kind of centered. We also learned that camouflage netting in the desert only shows you that there is somebody there. The most you can get out of it, if you do a decent job, is you can't tell *what* is under it. They might be able to tell if it's a tank or a truck, but they can't tell if it's the platoon CP or the company CP or the battalion CP. They're not going to be able to decipher the difference unless you telegraph it with antennas.

Aside from that, they are going to know you are there. We flew an RPV [remotely piloted vehicle] over the battalion earlier, and you could tell where the CP was. That's where we learned that when you set up the CP, you set it up along the battalion defensive line and blend in with all the bivouacs of the company so you couldn't really guess a lot about it. That was an important lesson. And the environment did change. It got colder, a lot colder. We had our stocking caps on. We slept in our sleeping bags and didn't really want to take a shower.

Colonel John Garrett, Battalion Commander

We'd get out from our positions and go on these long recons. We'd send out TOW and heavy machine gun patrols—twelve, fifteen, twenty miles out. It was really a test for the communications. It was a test for the logistics. It was a test for the tires on the vehicles.

There were all kinds of probers around. Two or three nights in a row we would have groups of two or three Arabs pretending to be workers with a stalled car. There were just too many people like that for it to be a coincidence.

We stayed in that defense until about October or November, until it looked like Saddam was not going to attack. Even for seasoned combat veterans it was scary. We also knew by this time that we were not going home in November or December—going home was not right around the corner.

Sergeant Major Bo Pippin, Battalion Sergeant Major

The Marines worked on their own individual living areas. The companies had three general-purpose tents set up. We tried to make it as comfortable as we possibly could. We didn't have a mess hall and we didn't have a PX. There were a lot of discomforts, but Marines know how to make the best of what they have got.

About every ten days or so we would move a group of Marines back to the rear area for a little rest and relaxation for a few days. In the rear we had a regular mess hall, and we had a PX and tents with cots. It wasn't the greatest thing in the world, but it was a lot better than what they had in the battalion defense position.

Captain Mike McCusker, CO, India Company

When we rotated back to the rear, we would get cleaned up, get our uniforms cleaned as much as we possibly could in a three-day stint. There would be no patrolling, and we would have a chance to clean our weapons real good. But it wasn't all relaxation, because they started reaction drills in the rear too. We never had an air-conditioned place like people saw on TV in the States. We were not authorized to go to town. That pissed a lot of us off, because people in the States thought we were seeing civilians. We were stuck in the desert, nowhere near a town. We didn't even have electricity. It was all flashlights and candles and chem lights.

Lieutenant Dan Henderson, Platoon Commander, Kilo Company

About the end of October or the beginning of November there were some short-wave radios for sale for twenty bucks. That helped a lot. Just about every officer and staff NCO bought one, and we could listen to the BBC and Voice of America, stuff like that.

Corporal David Bush, S3 Driver

I heard a lot of things about Saddam. He is a ruthless guy. He'd been in power a long time and had done awful things. A book came out during the war by two reporters from *Time*. It was the story of Saddam Hussein and his life in power. There was a lot in there about the things he'd done, the tortures and all. I believed every single one of them. For seven months Saddam didn't back down, but his people didn't want to fight for him. If they had really fought back it would have gone on a lot longer.

Lieutenant Dan Henderson, Platoon Commander, Kilo Company

The thing we missed the most was books, so people would ship us over big boxes of books so we would have something to do in our spare time.

The work schedule would be—from five-thirty or six o'clock in the morning—up for chow. You'd work until about ten hundred and then stop until after dark because of the heat. If you did work during this time you might last a half hour, because the heat was so intense.

Captain Sam Jammal, CO, H&S Company

We couldn't have books with any sex in them over there, so the best-read book in Saudi Arabia was the Victoria's Secret lingerie catalog. I'll always support them.

Captain Mike McCusker, CO, India Company

People complained about being bored. I never had time to read one book over there. That's how unbored I was. My Marines were constantly going all the time. Constant patrols, constant classes. When we finally got mail it was a saving grace. Mail is a precious commodity. Even when other things were screwed up, receiving mail helped make up for it.

Colonel John H. Admire, CO, Task Force Taro

The uncertainty of how long we would be in Saudi Arabia and how long before we would return home to friends and loved ones were continual concerns and topics for conversation. In late October plans for a rotation system were considered. At the senior Unified Command and Service levels a variety of options were considered for rotating units from Saudi Arabia and for providing replacement units. This planning was somewhat preempted, however, when those of us in the field were notified on 10 November that the president had established a timetable for hostilities. The effect of the president's decision and announcement was to reduce all uncertainty regarding tour length. Now we knew exactly how long we would be in Saudi Arabia—for the duration. We would be in the Gulf until we had won and were done.

Major General Mike Myatt, Commanding General, 1st Marine Division

Then, in the middle of November they made the announcement that instead of being just on the defensive, that we were actually going on the offense. We were the only connection that the Saudis had with the rest of the alliance.

They were going to be on our right flank, and on the Marines' left flank were the other Arab forces—the Egyptians and the Syrians. So we had the 2nd SANG on the right flank with the Qataris and the Moroccans, and as we were getting prepared to go north, we maintained our ANGLICO firepower control teams with 2nd SANG.[3]

Major Craig Huddleston, Battalion XO

I think the biggest complaint that the Marines had—and it was somewhat justified—was the uncertainty of the situation. We didn't know when we were coming home. And to my knowledge, never in any previous engagement had that been the case. Because even in World War II, where our men were gone so long, they had something to aim for. They were at war and they'd go home when the war was over. At Korea, you had a point system. When you'd hit so many points, you'd rotate home. Of course Vietnam was a thirteen-month tour.

Here we weren't at war. We didn't know if we were going to go home. And I think what probably grated on everybody's nerves more than anything was the open-endedness of the situation. The longer we stayed there, the more we came to say, "Right, wrong, or indifferent, let's just kick it off. Let's go into Kuwait, start the war, and then whatever happens, happens. At least we'll know we got something to aim at."

I think the biggest blow to morale came prior to Thanksgiving, when we started hearing we weren't going to be alone in this, that 2nd Division and all its assets were not coming in to relieve us, they were coming in to reinforce us. That was a pretty clear indicator to the dumbest private in the organization that something was going to happen.

When the word came down that 5th MEB, 2nd Marine Division and just about anything that was an amphibious ship was coming over, and almost all of our tactical aircraft were coming over, there wasn't any doubt in our minds that there was going to be a serious confrontation.

Actually it served to help us, because now we had something to focus on. We knew we were going to war. Nobody told us, but we sensed it within the battalion. Our training became more realistic. I think people trained harder. Our staff exercises became more serious. It was a backhanded blessing when we realized we were going to war.

Morale improved. After the initial shock, morale got better, because now the Marines knew when they went out on a training exercise, it wasn't just to be occupied, and it had a meaning. We also started getting clear indications of what our mission might be. Several objective areas were identified so we could start focusing on that type of terrain, that type of enemy force, and prepare to attack.

Colonel John H. Admire, CO, Task Force Taro

At that point we began to aggressively train for the offensive. This transition from defensive tactics enhanced the morale of our Marines, and we knew with certainty that we were on our way home.

Captain Leon Pappa, CO, Kilo Company

I thought the Marines were good in Okinawa, but in Saudi Arabia, when they finally accepted that we're not going home right away and there's no sense whining about it, they were great. It was refreshing. It was motivating. It was exciting to see corporals and sergeants really taking care of their people. Maybe because I was with them, and everybody was in a fishbowl there, I saw things. I'd see corporals talking to lance corporals. I'd see sergeants with their arm around a lance corporal. Even up on my level, you knew the guys that weren't getting mail.

Colonel John Garrett, Battalion Commander

The commandant [General A. M. Gray Jr.] came over and said, "There will be morale." Our Marines had some adjustments to make. They were human beings that didn't know what was happening to them; you'd have to not be human to not have some understanding about what's going through their minds.

Major Craig Huddleston, Battalion XO

There was a lot of press and a lot of media concern with our morale. "Oh, morale's terrible. Soldiers and Marines are complaining. There's problems here, problems there, blah, blah, blah."

General Gray said, "Well, they're going to have good morale, because I say so." A lot of us were there when he said that. Of course, we all know the commandant. He was making a joke out of the thing. We all laughed. We thought it was pretty funny. The press didn't know General Gray, and they took it literally when he was just being one of the boys. It was like, "No liberty call until morale improves." It was a big joke. What I saw was the fact that the morale of the Marines was fine. Again, I was one of the more experienced fellows in the battalion, and it wasn't any different than anything I'd seen before. A group of Marines would complain about the chow, which they've done since Caesar's day, but there was a reporter there listening to them and he'd say, "Oh, the Marines are complaining about the chow. The food must be no good." It was the same food we've always had. It's just that it was now receiving national exposure.

Lieutenant Dan Henderson, Platoon Commander, Kilo Company

I was surprised by the chow. I don't remember a day, unless we were on an extended operation, that we didn't get hot meals. I was happy, surprised, shocked, to tell the truth, to get hot chow once a day.

Captain Sam Jammal, CO, H&S Company

Eating out in the open every night became a social gathering. No matter what you did all day, as you go on trying to do your work, there would be a little bit of horseplay and talking and shooting the breeze about anything. But when it came to dinner, that's when you really did it. It was our time to just line up. Everybody'd line up. You were always getting ticked off at the Marine who was late. They'd get in line and eat, and you'd get in line, and you'd grab your food and make some comments about it.

Between Colonel Garrett and myself, I was the headquarters commandant, so I hated hearing that word, because it meant something was wrong. "Headquarters commandant." "Yes, sir?" "What are we having for dinner?" I wouldn't know until it appeared, because we didn't have a menu. And he knew that, but he used to like pulling my leg, and I would say, "Chili mac." A couple of times I was wrong.

Major Craig Huddleston, Battalion XO

Five months after we arrived, I had an entirely different impression of the desert, but initially it had looked like an impossible situation. When we first moved to Cement Ridge, we didn't know what we were going to do. We had very light antitank assets. We were between 90 and 120 kilometers from the Kuwait border. We knew that if the enemy attacked, it could be there in short order, within a few hours anyway. So we did a lot of reconnaissance, a lot of driving around in our sector, which was quite large. Initially our frontage was about 22 kilometers and about 18 kilometers in depth, and that was for about 1,100 men, a foot-mobile battalion. We didn't know what we were going to do. The desert appeared hostile. We were suffering the effects of the heat, which was quite bad for us.

But as we became acclimatized, as we became used to the desert, our impressions changed greatly. We found that maybe the high ground wasn't the best place in the desert, maybe the low ground was. And in fact that's what we did—we took the low ground, because it was the only place you could conceal yourself. And we found that the limited cover that was available was in the low ground. Then we put the outposts on the high ground so you had good observation.

We decided we would form a battalion position defense that would be as difficult as possible to penetrate. It was on the north-south road that connected Kuwait and Saudi Arabia. Our scheme was to hold on to that road and make it so dear and, also, anticipating fighting isolated, that the enemy would be obliged to bypass us and try to mop us up later, thereby giving us the opportunity to fight trucks, supply, refuelers, replacements, not tanks or mechanized vehicles. In other words, we hoped to present the enemy with such a formidable defense that in order to save time he would bypass us, hoping to clean us up later. We were betting that we could hold on long enough to ruin his logistics.

It turns out that the position we were in was about one refuel from Kuwait and also about one refuel from Dhahran, which would be a primary objective, so we thought that this was going to be a place that the enemy would need if he invaded, in order to connect his combat service support. So we very carefully decided that we would not try to defeat his armor. We would try to make his armor bypass us, and we would fight his combat service support. And so for the next four to five months we continued to work on that type of defense.

As we stayed there, we became very familiar with the desert. We learned how to use things. We learned that the desert was neutral, not an enemy. If we could find a way to use it to our advantage, then it's our friend. If we don't use it to our advantage, it may be the enemy's friend.

One of the things we found was that from our particular position we could observe mechanized vehicles up to forty kilometers away, day and night. That was an advantage to us, because that put them about an hour away from us and we could really bring some heavy fire support in on them in that intervening time.

Sergeant William Iiams, Recon Team Leader

Twenty-nine Palms has hills. This had none. It was completely flat. It was all new to us. You're looking at a different type of reconnaissance. You're looking at mobile reconnaissance in a Humvee, or you're looking at engaging your enemy miles and miles away. Looking at your E&E [evasion and escape] routes. That was very, very important to us, getting the hell out of Dodge fast. With a mechanized force going up against us, I think it was better sometimes that we had plans to just let them roll over us.

Another problem we had was foot patrols, especially in September and October because of the heat. We were carrying nine or ten quarts of water each with us, and that was practically not lasting at all, plus our radios and our ammunition. We were moving at night. We had a real bad problem in the desert with our radios, because our radio waves were being sucked up by the sand, so we had a problem with VHF radios. We had to use a lot of HF radios instead.

The desert wasn't survivable. There were no animals to eat. There was no place to hide. At least in the mountains or in a jungle environment, you can live off the land. You couldn't live off the land there. There was no fresh water. It was real chaotic.

Major Craig Huddleston, Battalion XO

We found that we were able to patrol quite well there, mounted and dis-mounted, and that we were able to control the terrain by very aggressive and active patrolling. Probably one-third of the force was on patrol at night, every night we were there . . . long patrols.

We worked it several ways. Dismounted patrols might only go four or five kilometers on a leg, so they might have a total patrol route of maybe ten or twelve thousand meters a night. They would depart right after dark and be home at first light.

Mechanized or mounted patrols could go out much further, sometimes they went twenty to forty kilometers on a leg, and they could cover that ter-rain at night without great difficulty. What we also did with the motorized patrols is use them to drop off foot patrols. In other words, send them out maybe fifteen, twenty kilometers in front of our position and, during what we hoped would appear as a security halt, an eight- or ten-man patrol would quickly dismount from the vehicles, the vehicles would drive away, and that patrol would stay out there the next day and they would be picked up the next night.

The longest one of our patrols stayed out was two nights and three days, and that was a patrol for snipers. They constructed a high position about ten kilometers in front of our position, were dropped off by a motorized patrol and remained in position for two nights and three days, and were picked up on that third night and brought home.

44   Cement Ridge

Captain Sam Jammal, CO, H&S Company

I accompanied a couple of reconnaissance patrols, and I remember not being able to stand in one spot for too long because my boots would burn from the heat.

Major Craig Huddleston, Battalion XO

 The limiting factor on the length of the patrols was clearly water. We couldn't carry enough water. In the jungle, or rather, more temperate terrain, you could expect a patrol to live off the land a little bit. It just wasn't possible here. For a dismounted patrol, each man carried a minimum of four quarts of water, and they spent the day resting and hydrating, drinking as much water as they could. The four quarts of water would last about one evening, and it would be a close thing if they didn't get home right away. We had to have a back-up plan, so if a patrol was required to remain longer, we had to resupply them with water.

In addition, on some of the motorized patrols, part of their mission might be to cache water. At night they would take out four or five water cans, bury them at a point in the desert, and then one of the longer-range patrols would have to navigate to that water, find it, and resupply themselves in order to keep going. If they couldn't find the water, we had to abort the patrol right away.

During the first couple of months we were there, we were very aggressive in our patrolling. The reason for that was we were convinced we were under surveillance. We were convinced for several reasons. We observed people with binoculars, we observed people with cameras, and on a couple of occasions we observed vehicles whose actions led us to believe they had night-vision devices. When a patrol would approach to within maybe one thousand or two thousand meters of one of these vehicles, whoever was there would quickly mount and drive at right angles, four or five thousand meters, and set up again. It was difficult to trap them or to hold them off.

One night we had three groups of four Arab individuals hit our lines at roughly the same time. Two of them ran away, and we captured one group. They had proper identification as Saudi nationals. They didn't have cameras or binoculars or anything on them. All of them said they were lost. We found that a little squirrelly.

Our sister battalion captured a Saudi officer in front of their lines who had a car, and in his car were binoculars and several cameras and lots of film, so we don't know who was watching us. It may have been Saudis. It may have been Palestinians. It may have been Iraqis. Clearly we were being observed. So therefore there was a need for aggressive patrolling to keep them away from us as much as possible.

Also during the first months of Desert Shield, we spent a lot of time training. We didn't have a real offensive mission, so we worked on our defense. By the middle of October it became apparent to us—although we didn't have any official documentation, we sort of had this gut feeling—that we were going to have to go into Kuwait. So our training started to become more and more offensive and less and less defensive. It took the form of infiltration tactics. When we didn't have any transportation assets, we practiced infiltration on foot. When we could get mechanized assets, we did mechanized work. When we could get helicopters, we did helicopter work. I think we concentrated more on helicopters than just about anything.

Along about mid-November, we started to get a sense from things we heard from higher headquarters and others that we might be expected to conduct heliborne offensive operations, so we started really concentrating on helicopters. In fact that's what our assigned mission was about mid-December, when we were told we would be a helicopter-borne force and probably the division reserve. So we really concentrated on helicopters. Of course we had to be careful for operational and security reasons not to tell our people at home what was going on, and we did a good job of that.

Captain Sam Jammal, CO, H&S Company

I can't tell you that I had a particular day when I just hated living out there. I missed my wife greatly. I missed my family. I was afraid for myself, afraid for my people. But the day-to-day getting up in the morning and going to sleep at night, I didn't have time to sob about it or think that I didn't want to be here.

5 / The Chemical Threat

Lieutenant Dan Henderson, Platoon Commander, Kilo Company

For once the Marines took NBC warfare as a serious threat. Chemical warfare hung over our heads. We didn't know if the Scuds would have chemical warheads on them or not. We'd tell our Marines that they had better learn to use the gear. Their lives could depend on it. MOPP4 [mission-oriented protective posture, level 4] is full chemical gear. You have on your gas mask, hood, gloves, rubber booties, and full chemical protection suit. MOPP level 1 is just with the suit on—no booties, no gloves. MOPP level 2 is with the boots on too. MOPP3 is with the boots, suit, and hood, but without gloves and mask. We trained all the time. We worked in the chemical suits. We did a lot of alerts and sent out monitor teams and set up decontamination sites.

Captain Kevin Scott, CO, Lima Company

We knew Saddam had chemical and biological capability because of what he had done to his own Kurd population. We had to remember what the symptoms are for a particular agent, when to use atropine, and all this other stuff. There wasn't really an antidote for his biological weapons.

We practiced a lot with the NBC gear. The corpsmen did many classes on NBC defense, the treating of NBC casualties, donning the gas mask. We inspected the gear constantly. When we went forward to Al Mishab, we got more intensive with it, because we knew we were in the center of the bull's eye.

The first time I came across the border into Khafji we had to go to MOPP4. It took about three or four minutes of straining to get into this gear. Then it took about five minutes to report back that everyone's got it. It could take longer if you haven't packed your pack to make it easily accessible.

First you stop breathing until you get the mask on. Then you put on the trousers and then the blouse. The blouse zips up and then snaps with a flap. There are three snaps in the back that snap on the trousers. It has an elastic waist with a drawstring. You tighten that.

Then you have rubber gloves you pull on. The sleeves of the blouse come over the gloves. There is a Velcro thing that you can use to tighten up on the cuffs.

Then there are these big rubber boots, just like cow-manure boots—big enough to slip our regular boot into. You tie them up with shoestrings, lace them up your leg. The legs of the trousers are split and have a zipper to zip down over the boot. There is a tie to tie it off.

The hood goes on when you put on your gas mask, and it protects the head and neck. So if you get a mist or spray of some type of chemical that hits you, you want it to be able to roll down off your head, down off your body and back off your gloves or boots onto the ground. We'd check each other once we were done.

Captain Mark A. Davis, Battalion Logistics Officer

Water for decontamination of chemical agents was a problem. The simple thing was the battalion did not possess any tanker support, none of the 5,000-gallon refuelers or 1,500-gallon water tankers. If we needed water we would have to call and have it sent out in 900-gallon tanks. I could get an initial load, a drop, but then the nature of the beast is that if the colonel wants to go somewhere, he is going to have to make a hard call—abandon that water and go without, or hold tight to where the source is? That doesn't mean we couldn't have gone on and done things like hasty decontamination and use 5-gallon water buckets and just wash guys off like that. We could have done that, and we were prepared to do so.

We had chemical decontamination teams back at the battalion aid station. We had the corpsmen ready to perform the many steps where you start on one side of the facility and you're fully contaminated, and you walk through the decontamination process and start losing bits and pieces of clothing as you come through until you come out the other side clean. We did that.

We got some old NBC garments and practiced how to treat casualties in a chemical environment. We learned not to take chemical casualties on board a helicopter unless they had been decontaminated, because if you put a dirty person on that helicopter, then the whole helicopter is now dirty.

So we worked real hard to figure out how we could get more water up there quicker. One way of doing that was to have dedicated truck assets to take care of it. That doesn't mean that I would hold them at my level. Maybe the regiment would hold it at their level, and when a unit got hit, then they'd just take all the truck assets and run them over.

I was scared. The thing that got me was when the NBC officer told us that they could hit us with a blood agent and then come back with a nerve agent. The blood agent would wipe out the filters in the masks, and then the nerve agent would just go right through it because there was nothing to stop it. So we really, really concentrated. Before this, NBC was kind of like, "Oh, shit, do we have to do this again?" Now we were looking at this thing eyeball to eyeball. Some guys who used to fall asleep in NBC classes were asking a lot of important questions.

We used to look at the Pam II Chloride anti–nerve gas agent that comes with its own syringe for self-injection and wonder if we could stick ourselves with a needle. Now we just walked up to that door, opened it, and went through. We would have been able to do the self-injections.

Our commanders kept telling us that we had the best equipment we could possibly have and that if we followed procedures we could live and fight in a chemical environment. But if we shortcutted them we would be in trouble. That's why guys stayed awake and paid attention in NBC classes.

When suddenly you're looking directly at this thing, life becomes different. Things get more precious. You'd stop, look, and listen. You start looking at the sun rising, notice how the sun sets in a different way. The air smelled clearer. Food never tasted better. Friendship, camaraderie—you prized it. A letter from home made people seem closer. The bond was there. The only way we could get through this was to remind ourselves that this was our job, and by trusting in our fellow Marines to do their jobs to the best of their abilities, we would get through this thing together.

6 / Holidays

Captain Leon Pappa, CO, Kilo Company

I was very attached to my Marines, but not to the point where it would obscure my judgment if I had to make hard decisions. Many a night I lay awake wondering if I had covered everything, but I never had. At one point in Saudi Arabia, I wrote to every one of my Marine's families—about 150 letters. I sent them out in November and December just to say that they were okay and we were taking care of them. I didn't make it too heavy and I didn't make it patronizing. I was inundated with responses and I saved them all. So I was getting very attached to these Marines even though they pissed me off at times. I just didn't want to write the other type of letters, the casualty letters.

Major Craig Huddleston, Battalion XO

Of course, while this was going on we celebrated the Marine Corps' Birthday.[1]

Lieutenant Dan Henderson, Platoon Commander, Kilo Company

We had the Marine Corps' Birthday with a picnic with a barbecue and chili. Our company had a cake, and we did a 215-mile run for the 215th Marine Corps' Birthday. We did the first mile as a company and the last mile as a company and the rest individually. Each Marine ran three miles.

Captain Mike McCusker, CO, India Company

November 10th we had a really good birthday. I'll remember it for the rest of my life. We got a cake and put that on a nice cot. I was with the company command group, and we had a company formation but with the platoons dispersed so if a rocket did come in, only one tent would be taken out.

We took all the staff NCOs and officers and picked up the cot with the cake and took it down. The Marines loved it. We had a table set up with a big dinner—ham and turkey.

After we marched the cake down, we read the commandant's traditional message. If I had my choice to be anywhere, I would rather have been with those Marines than anywhere else in the world. We had near-beer to go with the cake, so we all had our toast to the Corps. We went through the ceremony with the whole company and they all enjoyed it. Thanksgiving, Christmas, and the Marine Corps' Birthday were great. They couldn't have been better.

By tradition, the oldest and youngest Marines present are served the cake first. Our oldest Marine was Gunnery Sergeant Carrington and the youngest was Lance Corporal Washington.

Major Craig Huddleston, Battalion XO

Thanksgiving and Christmas were rather melancholy. By mid-November every man in the battalion knew we were going to fight. We just didn't know when. So we were wondering if this would be our last Thanksgiving or our last Christmas. Would we see our families again? It was kind of tough.

Lieutenant Dan Henderson, Platoon Commander, Kilo Company

Thanksgiving I won't forget, because one of my Marines got in trouble and threatened to commit suicide, so I spent Thanksgiving with him down at the psychiatrist's. He was having family problems, and he got drunk on some moonshine he got from a civilian driver. He was drunk on duty and that is how he got caught.

Sergeant William Iiams, Recon Team Leader

One thing I do think was really good about the desert was the policy of no alcohol. I think our casualty rate would have been higher if we'd had it. There would have been a lot more dehydration. With no alcohol everyone had a clear head and body.

Captain Mike McCusker, CO, India Company

My father sent me a bottle of Jim Beam bourbon in a loaf of hollowed-out bread. I called it the "gateau la guerre," the war cake, and saved it until the eve of going into battle. We had a little toast, the officers and staff NCOs, just before the war started. It was a somber moment for all of us.

Corporal David Bush, S3 Driver

The holidays were rough. We couldn't sit there and dwell on it, because we'd get more down. There were a couple of other corporals with me who were married too, so we hung out. I spent my first wedding anniversary over there, and it was a down point for me and for the other two guys who had gotten married about the same time I did. I'd talk to them and tell them how I felt about it, and we talked it through.

Sergeant William liams, Recon Team Leader

The holidays didn't bother me. No matter where Marines are at, no matter what the holidays, they always make a blast out of it. We're a family and we have a good time no matter what. There were jokes. The American public was unbelievable with all the packages they sent, all the candy. Our families were real supportive. Of course we wanted to go home, but I don't think there was a holiday over there where everyone just sat around and said, "Well, this sucks."

Captain Mike McCusker, CO, India Company

Thanksgiving came and went and we had another big dinner. All this time we were training. My Marines were continuously asking if we were going to war. I told them that I didn't think so. I thought we would move up and the Iraqis would give up when they realized what could happen to them. At first there was a lot of talk about going home in December. Finally I told them it would be around February, if anything, and we weren't going home for Christmas.

Once they were told that, they wanted to know when we were leaving. No one could tell them. I even asked the general when he came around, and he couldn't tell us either. If we could have told them they would be here for six months or a year it would have been better. To leave it open like it was, was the hard part. It made it hard every day.

Christmas was a real good time. My wife had been sending me packages, and the other Marines were getting packages. I had a lance corporal that had to go back to the States because his mother had a heart attack. He sent us packages because he knew the situation. The civilians really helped a lot with letters and packages. That was great. That kept morale very high. We got Red Cross packages, which were great, getting people what we weren't getting and augmenting what we had.

I saved a lot of stuff from the packages my wife sent, and cooked my CP group a full-course breakfast—scrambled eggs, sausage, the whole nine yards. She sent eggnog. She must have spent about eight hundred dollars sending all this stuff to me. She sent a table cover, little Christmas cups, a little Christmas tree. It was real nice.

By that time we were practicing mechanized operations. Just before Christmas we did a practice attack on a hill out there. Afterwards, we got axes and chopped down this big, huge bush. I had to haul it with one of the tracks. The troops asked what was going on, and I told them their CO was doing a Christmas tree raid. We put it in the track and off we went to the bivouac area. We were still at Cement Ridge. Then we got the thing ready to set up. It was something to keep their minds off of being so far away and to make some sort of Christmas there in the desert, and it worked. The Marines used to give me shit about it: "Gee, sir, this Christmas tree is so ugly that we are going to burn it." But it gave them something to look at, and I think it did what I wanted it to do. We decorated it with engineering tape and tinsel and little Christmas ornaments that school kids made and sent to us. I took chem lights and hung them on the tree on Christmas Eve and made a big cross on top. It was round like a big bush. It was five or six feet tall, and the camels used to come and chew on it and we had to shoo them away. It served its purpose. A reporter came by and said it was the best Christmas tree he had ever seen out there.

The camels were weird. I'd always laugh when I saw the damned camels running across the road. They didn't care where they were but would come out of nowhere hauling ass. You couldn't hit them with a vehicle or they'd kill you.

1st Sergeant Wylie McIntosh, Weapons Company

Santa Claus arrived in his Humvee. We enjoyed it, but it is the time of year you need your family around. Even though you had your big family around, you missed your small family.

Captain Leon Pappa, CO, Kilo Company

We had a CBS crew stay with us on Christmas Eve. They were interviewing my Marines, and after hearing them the interviewer asked me if I'd like to comment. I couldn't talk. I was getting choked up listening to them, and I don't think they were doing it for the camera. The same knucklehead the day before . . . They were saying things like, "Of course we'd like to be home with our family. Who wouldn't? But this is my family. This is where we get our strength. Sure, we won't be home, but the quickest way to get home is to do our jobs." That will always stay in my mind.

Lieutenant Dan Henderson, Platoon Commander, Kilo Company

The Hyatt Regency Hotel on the Big Island of Hawaii sent us boxes, so each Marine got a wrapped Christmas present. I answered an "any Marine" letter from New Hampshire. It was a schoolteacher. She had a fourth grade class and my Marines adopted them. We got little things from them, Christmas decorations. My platoon received at least ten letters a day. I'm going up to New Hampshire and meet with those kids. Little things like that help us Marines a lot, because they get to see what we are like.

We were in an unsecured area, so pretty much the whole time we were out there we had to have security patrols. I drew the security patrol Christmas Eve, which lasted until about four A.M. Christmas morning. Usually I had one of my squad leaders go out, but I volunteered to take the patrol. It was me, about six other Marines, and four NCOs.

Corporal David Bush, S3 Driver

By the time the war started, we knew we had the support of the American people. At first we didn't know and that was the last thing on our minds. I just wanted to get through it and come out alive and come back. As time went by, we heard from people, and by the time we were really into it, we knew that the American people were behind us.

Lieutenant Dan Henderson, Platoon Commander, Kilo Company

After the Christmas Eve patrol I went on, an Italian reporter asked if he could go on patrol with us. I told him yes as long as he didn't smoke or anything while we were out there.

At times there would be people out there and we'd tell them to move on. We were worried about terrorists, unoccupied vehicles, and things like that.

Colonel John Garrett, Battalion Commander

Around January the momentum seemed to be picking up a little bit. We moved from Cement Ridge up to Al Mishab, with a brigade of Qataris.

1st Sergeant Wylie McIntosh, Weapons Company

Most of the men had come to Saudi Arabia with a pack and a sea bag each. Most of them needed another sea bag just to haul the goodies people had mailed to them. We probably buried three hundred pounds of goodies, candy, and stuff like that we couldn't take. We had no one to give it to.

7 / Al Mishab

Working with the Arabs

Major General Mike Myatt, Commanding General, 1st Marine Division

When John Admire came in with the 3rd Marines in early September, one of the missions I gave him, as part of the defensive posture, was to work closely with the Saudi Arabian National Guard. That then became a larger force as they brought in other elements of the various forces around the Gulf—the Qataris, the Moroccans, and several others like that—but they were really battalion-size units. The biggest unit of that was the 2nd SANG, and Colonel Turki was sort of the de facto leader of all of them. Colonel Admire got in there and did some combined training with this and gave them some confidence that we knew what we were doing and that if they ever got in trouble, we would provide them with firepower control teams—the FCTs, the ANGLICO—and that we could provide them with the capability to use our supporting arms, and then they could be successful.

We did quite a bit of training with ANGLICO integrated into, primarily, the 2nd SANG. What was really interesting was we got a lot of push-back, because at that point in time there was a bit of interservice rivalry and the Special Forces folks were looking for a mission, and they said, "It's our mission to be training indigenous forces." They would resist us training the 2nd SANG and I just simply ignored it, and I told General Boomer that, "We have got to give them the confidence that we can do it." Because what the Special Forces role is, is to train them to use their own gear, not to interface with our gear and our capabilities. It caused a little bit of heartburn and wasn't the only thing that caused heartburn in the alliance, but I did it.

Admire did a great job. He spent a lot of time drinking tea with Colonel Turki, just talking in their tents about how they could work together in wrapping up this training. This was like September, October, early November 1990.

Colonel John Admire, CO, Task Force Taro

The inhospitality of the Arabian desert is in stark contrast to the gracious hospitality of the Arab people. Although contact was limited because most Marines were forward deployed, far from the Saudi population areas, friendships prospered. Saudi military representatives, Bedouin tribesmen, and highway travelers invariably offered greetings in both traditional and modern styles. We were invited by Saudi military personnel into Arab tents, with their classic rugs and cushioned pillows, to partake of family-style meals. We shared fruit and drink with Bedouin tribesmen and shepherds on isolated desert plains. We exchanged waves, smiles, and victory signs with businessmen, truckers, farmers, and children in passing vehicles. We received smiles and waves of thanks from Kuwaiti refugees fleeing from the horrors of their homeland. We were recognized rather than ignored. Our actions demonstrated respect for the Saudis. The Saudis responded with approval for, and support of, our presence.

Major Craig Huddleston, Battalion XO

Al Mishab, which was about twenty-five kilometers south of the Kuwait border, was a Saudi port and also a Saudi naval base, and fledgling Saudi marines were also stationed there. They had a very large airstrip and a pretty large port. My opinion is the real reason we went to Al Mishab was to bolster Saudi forces in the area. The Saudis had a very large portion of their national guard and their army to the north of us along the Kuwaiti border.

Captain Joseph Molofsky, Liaison to the Saudi Brigade

On October 1st a request came from the Saudis for a Marine liaison officer because of the proximity of the 3rd Marines to the Saudi unit. Because of my recent experience in the Middle East, I was sent up there. I reported to Colonel Turki Efirmi, the brigade commander of King Abdul Aziz Brigade. Turki is his first name, but he was known as "Colonel Turki." His brigade had a brigade of Qatars attached to it. They were mechanized infantry equipped with American-made Cadillac-Gage V-150 armored personnel carriers. He also had an artillery battalion. The Qatars were French trained and had a company of French Mark F3 tanks and mostly French equipment. They had a retired Egyptian brigadier serving as their advisor and wearing captain's rank, and one man who had been severely wounded in the Sinai in 1969. The correct pronunciation of Qatar in Arabic is "guttar." The Qatars were very capable, very professional, but totally inexperienced, never having been deployed from Qatar before.

The Saudi brigade was not a national guard in the American sense but the protectors of the king, mostly from Bedouin backgrounds, who joined the brigade to show loyalty to King Faisal.

The brigade was quartered where the Sunni population of Saudi Arabia lives, to make sure the Sunnis don't rise up against the government. They had some fighting experience. They were the people who go to Mecca every summer to police the annual pilgrimage. They attacked the Grand Mosque after it was captured by Iranian dissidents and killed some 279 of them. After being told they couldn't use their normal weapons, they attacked the place with pistols and knives. They had also deployed to the Yemeni border a couple of years earlier, but as far as mechanized warfare in the open desert, there was nobody that had any idea what the hell was going on.

Colonel John Admire, CO, Task Force Taro

Major General Myatt, Commanding General, 1st Marine Division, encouraged and directed the 3rd Marines to become the division's focal point of training with the Saudi Arabian King Abdul Aziz Brigade. The Saudi brigade was located on the Saudi-Kuwaiti border, and training with them provided American Marines with opportunities to train and operate in terrain in which they would later conduct combat operations. We were very careful to present the cross-training as a reciprocal program. We acknowledged the Saudi expertise in desert tactics and asked them to teach us desert survival, desert navigation, and desert tracking. In the process, a vital relationship began developing. Arab and American friendships emerged, founded on the common bond of brotherhood of arms.

A unique camaraderie developed as a natural result of the challenges of desert life. American Marines were invited into Saudi tents for meals and began to experience Arab culture and hospitality. The friendships transitioned into a special trust and confidence between Arabs and Americans and became the foundation for future battlefield actions.

Major Craig Huddleston, Battalion XO

President Bush said to the Iraqis that they had until January 15 to get out of Kuwait, or we end the diplomatic process and war begins. As we came closer to that, a couple of weeks away from that time, it was decided that U.S. forces probably ought to be up there to backstop the Saudi forces. I think that was a poor estimate of the Saudis' resolve. My reaction and interaction with their forces was very positive. They were poorly trained, and I don't know that they had the leadership they needed. But at the individual level, I think that the Saudi, Qatari, and Kuwaiti were as good as anyone. He just wasn't trained very well.

And there were some serious cultural differences between them and us. We had daily interaction with these folks. From 31 December on, we were training with the Saudi marines and the Qatari brigade. You would never find a more hospitable people, a braver people, a better-educated people. They were all very well educated. Some of our folks were bilingual, but most of theirs were. They were very astute politically, whereas most Americans are naive politically. Good people—clean, hard-working, very religious. I was pleased with them. I thought they were good people. On the military side they were poor. They just had no training. Their equipment wasn't well maintained. I think their officers took the British model to the extreme, because they didn't do anything with their men. They didn't lead them from the front, that was for sure. But aside from that—and I think that was cultural and not part of their basic human value—they were good people.

Colonel John Admire, CO, Task Force Taro

Personal contact and friendships in Arab society are traditionally deliberate and cautious, with an element of formality and reservation. In contrast, the American style is more often quick, carefree, informal, and open. Despite the incongruities, Arabs and Americans gravitated toward an accommodation. We became more patient; they became more understanding of our aggressiveness. We became an influence on each other. An illustration of this may be made by describing a four-day live-firing exercise with the Saudi marines. Officer leadership in the Saudi military is often characterized by a focus on society or class distinction. Officers devote the majority of their time to schools, professional training, or administrative issues. Enlisted personnel train primarily with staff NCOs. The opportunity for officer-enlisted interaction in a training environment is often minimal.

In our Saudi and U.S. Marine firing exercises, however, the Saudi officer assumed a new role. His English language proficiency was required to translate the class to the Saudi enlisted marines. Initially the Saudi officers and enlisted men remained separate as they observed the weapons demonstrations. But once classes began, the cultural, class, and societal barriers between them and their men began to dissolve.

The Saudi officers developed a sense of pride in assisting the American Marine instructors and were adept at weapons nomenclature, assembly/disassembly, and firing procedures. The Saudi officers recognized their contribution and appreciated the closer involvement in the training. The Saudi enlisted men formed a new respect for their officers based on shared experiences and contact.

At the conclusion of the exercise it was apparent that what was truly learned or taught was neither weapons systems nor antiarmor tactics. Instead it was leadership. U.S. Marines, by personal example, demonstrated the importance and contributions of every Marine in the chain of command. The value of command, professional, and personal relationships was recognized and adopted by the Saudi marines. The U.S. Marines learned that their professionalism and their example could make a difference.

Captain Sam Jammal, CO, H&S Company

Initially it was the "ragheads this" and the "ragheads that." The Marines put all the Arabs together in their thinking about them. I can tell you without a shadow of doubt that by the time we left there, those perceptions were thrown away. They got to know the people, and they worked with the Qataris and thought they were good fighters. They knew how to identify them by their country and not by their race or religion. I thought it was a damned good experience for our people.

The Marines got a couple of surprises over there as we moved around the desert in different missions. They found that some of these Arab units were tactically proficient and could carry out the mission and were capable and willing to do it.

None of us really comprehended what it takes for an Arab to fight an Arab, especially if you're a Muslim, although it was always on the news. I couldn't tell you how it feels for one Muslim to fight against another, but I know that it is not acceptable by Muslim rules. We got a feel for the fact that these guys were willing to fight anyway.

We found that the Saudis and Qataris were as curious about us as we were about them. They had their own preconceived notions about us. Some of them were real pompous and arrogant and we were approached that way. But they found out that each one of us is different. What really threw them a curve was the fact that we have so many mixed cultures—black, Hispanics, Arabs—you name it, we had it. I think they found that interesting.

One time some Arabs came by because my name is sort of a Muslim name, although in Arabic it isn't when it is spelled out. They thought I was Muslim and came looking for me. When they found out I was an officer, they apologized and walked away. Then they sent an officer group to welcome me as a brother Muslim. When I explained to them that I was a Christian, they said, "Oh, well, we like you anyway, but think about Islam." They did try to indoctrinate our Marines, the Saudis more than the Qataris. A lot of Marines got pamphlets and read about it and made their own choice.

It was a real cultural experience for the American public because of what little we know about the Arabs. We hear about other countries all the time, but we relate to most of them more than we can to the Arab world. To a certain extent, the Arabs have dealt themselves the deal that they've gotten from the Western world—by their isolation and by their lack of concern about what people thought of them. On the other hand, the U.S. has never gone as far as we have with other countries to try and understand them. We have tried to understand the Japanese, I think. We haven't done it with the Arabs because of the relationship between the Israelis and us and the Arabs.

I think the Arabs realize the need, too, for them to publicize themselves. They can't go back into isolation now because of human rights issues and all things culturally acceptable to them and not to us. We can't force our hand on them. If we do, they'll shut the door. I think that has happened in Kuwait since the end of the Gulf War. Kuwait went right back to the old way of doing things after the war. Maybe that's not the right answer for us, but it's the right answer for them. We need to try and look at things from their perspective. You can't judge them by our rules. It isn't that human life is worth less over there. It's just looked at in a different way. Principle is more important than logic or who is right or wrong. From their perspective it doesn't matter.

Major Craig Huddleston, Battalion XO

Regarding pejoratives. I started out in August before we left by gathering the officers and saying that I wouldn't tolerate that in the battalion. If I heard anybody doing it, they'd answer to me. The two pejoratives that I heard most were "ragheads" and "sand nigger." When I heard that, I jumped on people. When you use a pejorative to describe your enemy, you are underestimating him. The Marines, if they had been let loose—and I saw it in other units— might tend to group all Muslim people as these "ragheads." Well, there was only one Muslim nation that was opposed to us and that was Iraq. Almost all other forces were our allies, and we couldn't afford that type of thinking. In fact, Arab forces surrounded our battalion. We were in a perimeter that belonged to a Qatari brigade.

We tried to open up as many personal contacts with the locals as possible. We went to dinner with them. We invited them to dinner. We had tea and coffee with them. We went and talked with them. We exchanged information. We opened up landline communications between their headquarters and our headquarters. We did everything we could to firm up this relationship. I recall, from talking to people who were advisors in Vietnam, how important it was to nurture that relationship. The Marines would talk about these people: "What they do, they eat a goat." "Their hair is all singed off." "They eat a big pile of rice." I'd say that it was true, but that is the way they were. I had a conversation with a Saudi major one time, and he opened up to me a little bit and asked me if it was true that we had cemeteries for dogs. I admitted that we did. And he asked if it was true that murderers could be paroled from prison for good behavior. *How was that possible?* he wanted to know. The point I'm making is that we were just as strange to them.

Another one that caused some problems until we talked to them was our view of how they treated their women, that they totally subjugated them. The women appeared to be slaves to the men. An Arab man has a different perspective. He will tell you that they worship their women, that is the reason they spend so much time and effort protecting them. Their point of view was that they were putting their women on a pedestal. Perspective is very important.

We tried very, very hard to avoid underestimating our enemy. At times I think we overestimated them. They were real human beings to us. I think that's good. We tried as hard as we could to open up lines of communication between our Arab allies. We were always in their area, and at Colonel Garrett's insistence anything that we had of intelligence interest we shared with them. We may not have told them the source, but we told them what we knew, and after a while they told us what they knew. It was very helpful, and as we got into combat it paid dividends. They had brothers, cousins, aunts, and uncles. Also, there were the Bedouin people who traveled freely between the borders, who were not afraid to discuss things with the locals. So we got pretty fair information. If we didn't get good information, we got explanations of why this or why that. For example, Friday evenings were initially pretty scary for us because there was so much traffic on the road—civilian traffic and bonfires in the desert and groupings of people, just out in the middle of the desert. The first couple of Fridays we couldn't figure it out. Then we talked to some Saudis, and they told us that it was the night that families gathered and it was a regular occurrence. We just didn't know what it meant. Things like that helped greatly.

We learned that the best time to be on the road in convoy was about the time of mid-afternoon prayers, because all the traffic left the road and pulled off to the side. They'd get out and cleanse themselves and pray, and we'd have a straight shot of about fifteen or twenty kilometers without anybody on the road but U.S. forces. We tried to be respectful of their religion. We told them that we may not subscribe to your religion, but if we are doing something wrong, tell us and we'll stop. We need to work together on this.

There was quite a bit of press about whether the Arabs were committed to this and what they would do if Israel were attacked. Blah, blah, blah. We knew because we worked with these folks, and knew that they were good and they were going to fight. They'd hear things on the BBC or see it in our *Stars and Stripes* newspaper, or they'd see the international edition of the *London Times* and they'd ask why we didn't trust them. I'd say that personally I trusted them, but I couldn't account for the people back in the States. It is hard for them to understand, because they do not really live in a democracy.

They'd read our editorials and ask if we liked them. I'd tell them that we liked them and were with them 100 percent.

Captain Sam Jammal, CO, H&S Company

The company commander of Weapons Company was informed that one of his corporals left a weapon on top of a vehicle and he forgot it was there and drove off. If flew off and a Qatari captain found it. He was a platoon commander, and he knew that someone was going to have to formally answer for it if he sent it up to his brigade commander, across to our regiment, and back down to the battalion. Instead, he notified us directly. I think that gave us a sense that the same things that we complain about as company commanders and letting people get into our business, the chain of command, was the same in both Arab and American forces.

We thanked him a lot and asked him to stay for tea. He stayed and, lo and behold, he brought out a TV set that ran on batteries, and there are the Baker-Aziz talks. That's where they both came out and gave their speeches that they had tried and failed and the negotiations were over. That was that. That was the last-ditch attempt. I remember thinking how the media could reach out and get to us. Then it sank in a little more—there was still some hope that the war wasn't going to go. This was in January, just before the air war started.

8 / The Air War Starts

Sergeant Major Bo Pippin, Battalion Sergeant Major

I don't think there was any apprehension on the Marines' part. They were ready to go. A little of it was the motivation to get the job done. They'd been there five months now, and it was time to get down to business. That's one of the Marines' favorite sayings: "Let's get down to business." The thing I heard a lot was "Saddam can sit around and talk the talk. We know he can't walk the walk, so we've got to get in there and demonstrate the walk."

Lieutenant Dan Henderson, Platoon Commander, Kilo Company

They knew what was coming. The Marines knew. We knew when we moved to Al Mishab that was it. We picked up our pace of training there. It's the first time I ever heard a Marine tell me he wanted to dig a hole. Once we moved up there, there was no doubt about what we were going into. We started preparing.

Captain Mike McCusker, CO, India Company

The January deadline was already public by then. So we know the Iraqis have got to do something or we're going to be kicking somebody's ass here. Our mindset had now decided that war was going to happen, and now we were just waiting. It worried me—the fact I'd never gone to war before. I think the same went for everyone. Are you going to be capable enough to do your job?

Will you perform as you should to take care of your Marines? As with everything else, you couldn't dwell upon it.

My FO [artillery forward observer] was Ivan Wray. He's a very capable person. He would say, "You know, we're going to be changed after this." I'd say, "I don't know. I don't think so. Some people are, some people aren't. My father-in-law has been to Vietnam three times and he's not a changed person. It's had an effect on him, but he's not strange or anything." He says, "Yeah, but this war is different." So we kind of talked about that. I never dwelled upon it. I had too much other stuff to dwell upon.

Late at night as I'd talk to Marines and they'd ask, "Sir, what's going to happen?" And I'd say, "I don't know." "Are we going to move on the fifteenth?" "I don't know."

They were worried, and I was constantly telling them, "Hey, you guys are good. You've proven yourself. You'll do well. Take care of your buddy." Those are the basic things that you've got to constantly tell a Marine. He'll do well, as long as he knows. So between the gunny and me, we did all that—talked to them.

At that time I received a letter from a prior India Company commander who now lives in Montana. He said India Company has always done well. He was in Vietnam. He passed some good words on. I read it to the Marines and they really appreciated it, and when I read it, it made me feel good, because here's a former company commander, who had been in Vietnam, who told about what they had done, how they'd been bombed in Khe Sanh and all that and had gone through Tet. The letter was important. I stopped everybody and said, "Listen to this." I read his letter to everybody and they were real "Oorah, Oorah!" He promised when I got back we'd go fishing at his place, and I'm taking him up on it. I think it's important.

Captain Mark Davis, Battalion Logistics Officer

The XO pulls us in about the seventh of January and said that he'd just come from a meeting and that the war was going to start on the eighteenth of February. We were sitting in a tent, and the guys who had given up smoking were firing those suckers up. If you didn't dip, you didn't chew, or didn't smoke, everyone knew. He showed us a map where the 1st Marine Division and the 2nd Marine Divisions were going through.

1st Sgt Wylie McIntosh, Weapons Company

[1st Sergeant McIntosh was one of only a handful of 3/3 Marines who had any combat experience.]

I was going around and talking to people and trying to calm them down. I'd have a sit-down and ask what was bothering them. They'd always ask what it felt like to be shot at. Of course, nobody can answer that because it is different for everybody. The second biggest question was about knowing how you would perform in combat. Of course, there is no answer for that either.

Major Craig Huddleston, Battalion XO

The day the war started we knew it was imminent, but we didn't know exactly when. One of our platoons was in the middle of a cross-training exercise with the Saudi marines. These Saudi marines had just been issued their rifles. They barely knew how to wear the uniforms. One of our rifle platoons was over there training one of their companies. In that vicinity Marine Air Control Squadron 2 [MACS2] had a large early warning radar set up on a hill right in the center of our training area. At about 1500 that afternoon, the 16th of January, the platoon commander showed up with his platoon and his stuff. I asked him why he was back. His training was supposed to go on for another five or six days. The lieutenant told me that he couldn't talk to me on the air, but the people from MACS2 pulled the radar down and told me I ought to get out of there because the war was going to begin tonight. Of course, we didn't hear anything and I didn't believe the platoon commander, a second lieutenant. Well, about midnight the war was on. In retrospect, the lieutenant made a helluva good decision, because he was in the ground target area.

I was wakened about 0030 on the morning of the seventeenth. The Combat Operations Center watch officer told me we were at war. It was like someone had hit me in the gut. Even though I had been preparing for it all this time, the cold, hard fact pretty much knocked me down. I got a little shaky, a little nervous. We all gathered in the Combat Operations Center, the colonel and the staff and myself. We had this feeling that since we were at war we should be doing something. We didn't know what to do, because it was an air war. So we finally decided to put everyone on alert. So that's what we did—we put everyone in their bunkers and holes and went on 100 percent alert. All the Marines got in their holes and bunkers and went on a full war footing, and of course nothing happened. We were listening to the radio, and they were telling us how great the air war was going and all the things they were doing. We were listening to a continuous CNN feed out on Armed Forces Radio, and it sounded like everything was going great. Along about daybreak we thought that what we were doing was stupid. Here we are, sitting here with fixed bayonets, waiting for something to happen, and obviously nothing's happening.

So we stood down and we got instructions from higher headquarters to continue as before with training. We tried to make up some of the sleep we missed the night before. It was sort of like the night before Christmas. We were excited . . . and nervous, scared, and all these emotions were wrapped into one. We were a bit drained. It was my first experience with war, and little had changed from the day before. The biggest difference was we could hear aircraft all the time, and we could hear some bombs way off in the distance. The impact on us was absolutely nothing—zero.

Corporal David Bush, S3 Driver

My feeling was that we were at war. This is it. This is what we've been here the whole time for. At least something was happening now. We were not sitting and waiting for someone to say that we were going to do it tomorrow. My thought was *If we are going to do it now, let's do it as fast as we can and get out of here.*

Corporal Patrick Sterling, Recon Team Member

When we heard that, everyone sat and thought, *Oh, no. Oh, no. It's finally started.* And then we thought we had been there since September, and it was already all the way into January, and we have been waiting and waiting and waiting. Then we thought, *Yeah! All right! Let's do it!* Everyone was waiting for it to start so we could get it over.

Corporal Allen Uskoski, Recon Team Member

We were waiting to get a shot at Hussein. But then again, no one was sure they really wanted to do it, so they talked amongst themselves to keep themselves going. They would say, "We're going to kick their butts." They were just trying to keep themselves busy.

Corporal Patrick Sterling, Recon Team Member

We were walking around, giving each other high fives and going, "Yeah, sock it to them." We were ready. We had prepared, prepared, prepared. We were ready to blow up. We wanted to fight. We really did.

Captain Joseph Molofsky, Liaison to the Saudi Brigade

When the air war kicked off, the Saudis were really stunned. The Saudis hoped, really, in the back of their minds, up until the last minute, that war would not happen. To the very last minutes their senior officer told me it wouldn't happen, that Saddam would back down. They just didn't believe there would be a war. Personally, I was pissed off, having lived in the desert out there, without a head [toilet], eating on my knees with my hands for five months, and I wanted to get the hell out of there, no matter what it took.

9 / Rockets

Less than twenty-four hours after the beginning of the air war, the Marines of 3/3 no longer had to wonder about what it felt like to be shot at.

Captain Leon Pappa, CO, Kilo Company

The next night I was up talking to one of the Marines who was awake. He directed my attention out to the northwest. We saw some very slow-moving flashes arching up into the sky. There were about seven or eight of them. He asked me what they were, and I said that I didn't know. They were too slow for tracers. About half a minute later all hell broke loose. I saw a flash that looked like a hit out by the road. I didn't hear it coming in. The second one looked like it was inside my position, but it wasn't, it was near the Qataris.

The other Marines woke up in midair with everybody diving for a hole. I remember flying elbows and assholes, legs and antennas. I was on the landline to battalion and thinking at the same time that Saddam couldn't hit us, because his artillery would only reach the causeway at Khafji. It never dawned on me that his rockets could reach us. I was trying to alert the battalion, although I'm sure they heard them too. Before I even got finished, the entire company was coming out of the dark and into their holes. It was amazing.

It was kind of neat up there when I saw the first rocket, but almost unreal. I'd seen minimal fire in Beirut, but I'd never seen anything like that. I'd never been under any kind of rocket or artillery fire. I had to pinch myself at first. But not for long.

Captain Joe Fack, FAC

I was the officer of the day, and I was getting ready to make myself a cup of coffee when I heard this whistle and all of a sudden this big explosion. I wondered what on earth we were shooting at now. Then all of a sudden I figured out that it wasn't our artillery and that it was something coming at us. I woke everybody in Lima Company up and got everyone out. The next morning the artillery liaison officer, Lieutenant Grant, and I went out there and checked the crater to figure out what it was. He said it was an Astro 300mm rocket. It hit about one thousand meters from where I was and was really close to the S4.

Major Craig Huddleston, Battalion XO

I hit the rack [bunk] at about 2200. At 2215 the inside of my tent lighted up like a flashbulb going off in there. I wasn't asleep yet. I was lying there staring at the top of the tent. The interior of the tent lit up, and then I heard several very loud detonations. My first thought was that we'd had an accident in one of our ammo dumps, or a Marine had touched off a round in nervousness. But it was a big detonation.

I got up and got on the telephone and called the Combat Operations Center and was kind of angry. I asked what was going on and what happened. They told me they didn't know; there had been some loud explosions. So I got up, dressed, and walked over to the COC. I thought I would find out what was going on, because I knew the colonel would want to know. I walked outside my tent and I saw another flash and explosion off in the distance, and then another one. One to the right and one to the left. One appeared to be up in the Qatari position, and one appeared to be in my Dragon Platoon's position. From where I was standing, they were maybe five hundred meters away.

Now I was getting even more angry, because we had had an accident and nobody was doing anything about it. I took a few steps and my knees nearly went out from under me. I nearly fell down. I don't know what caused me to think, but all of a sudden I realized that this was enemy action—that we were taking incoming. My throat went dry. I didn't believe it was possible, but my knees were actually shaking. I thought I couldn't go into the COC like this. I had to get myself together. There was a piss tube right outside my tent, so I thought that if I could take a piss I'd be all right. I stood there for about five minutes trying to unbutton my trousers and take a leak and I did, and by that time I wasn't shaking anymore and was calmed down. I was still shook up inside, but my mouth wasn't dry anymore. I lit a cigarette.

I walked into the COC and it was like a madhouse, because now reports of incoming were coming in from everywhere. I tried to bring order to the chaos by appearing to be calm, although inside I was shook. The first thing I did was to tell everybody to shut up. I told them to be quiet, that we needed to get back to being a professional organization. We needed to get on with it and we'd done it a hundred times in exercise. I asked the staff for reports, starting with the S2 and S3. I began to get decent reports. They were all pointing to incoming. An outpost reported that they had taken a large-caliber round, two hundred meters to their rear. They were about two kilometers to the front of our position. The Dragon Platoon reported taking a very large round just in front, near where the Qataris were.

Now I wasn't so sure. I thought maybe the Qataris had fired a tank round. We got on the landline with the Qatari brigade, and I asked them if they had fired. They said they hadn't. Meanwhile we reported to regiment that there was some doubt whether it was incoming or perimeter fire. We were trying to sort it out, but we had no casualties. We were relieved that no one was hurt, but we still weren't positive what had happened.

Captain Sam Jammal, CO, H&S Company

The first one hit about three clicks away from most of our position. Everybody claimed that it hit right on top of them. This included the Qataris. A Qatari officer told me that their mess hall got some shrapnel. He fell out of bed.

Captain Joseph Molofsky, Liaison to the Saudi Brigade

The Qataris' idea of a mess hall was a tent full of bags of rice and a herd of goats. They ate well, though.

Lieutenant Dan Henderson, Platoon Commander, Kilo Company

We started getting hit with rockets—300-millimeter rockets—every night between 1800 and 2200. We started taking bets on what time the rocket would hit. We called them the "Boogey Man." It got so it wasn't much, just irritation. You always went into the hole. It was the only time I ever said a little prayer before I went to sleep: "Now I lay me down to sleep . . . " Because you don't know if a rocket is going to get you and you're gone. The first night the rockets hit, my squad leaders knew where their people had to be. They already had head counts. A lot of things that I had to push for were being done without my asking.

Captain Mark Davis, Battalion Logistics Officer

I was reading a book and I hear a *wham, wham, wham, wham*. I thought that I really wish those guys would let us know when they are going to shoot out so we wouldn't be going crazy. Somebody yelled for us to get in our holes, that it was incoming rockets. So we hit the ground and got to the bunkers. One of my Marines, Lance Corporal Hartsack, he pulls up—this big old country boy. He's excited as a fourteen-year-old in a whorehouse for the first time. He said, "Sir, you should have seen them. They was mortars! I know they was mortars." I thought, *Oh shit, we're in trouble.*

Lieutenant Ivan Wray, Artillery FO, with India Company

I was lucky I was dressed. I had trousers on. I had my boots on. I was looking over my map. The first explosion just shook the entire place. That was the first time I'd been shelled. That cherry broke in a hurry. I was confused. The biggest thing was confusion. Captain McCusker, Gunny Carrington, Tim Mundy, and a few of our Marines were sitting there. We looked at each other.

The first thing on our mind was to get to the holes. We all stood up at the same time. We all turned around to get our gas masks, our helmets, and our flak jackets at the exact same time. Looking back on it, it was hilarious. It was just Keystone Cops. I don't think they could have done any better, or Buster Keaton for that matter. It was incredible. Every single person must have knocked into every other single person several times. We did the most damage in the least amount of time. I saw nude Marines with just a weapon, a helmet, and a flak jacket. I was sitting there thinking how incredible it was—all of these nude guys moving at the speed of light.

Corporal David Bush, S3 Driver

I couldn't hear anything coming in. It was about ten o'clock at night. I was in my rack, in my sleeping bag, on my cot, crashed out in a tent—and

BOOM! It was loud. We knew something happened but didn't know what. It was kind of comical looking back, because everyone was asleep but everybody heard it. They sat up in their sleeping bags and looked around. "What the hell was that?" I said, "Maybe it's artillery, and it doesn't take artillery long to adjust onto the target if they know what they're shooting at."

We had all our gear, but everything was not where it should be. It should have been ready to go and it wasn't. Everybody was running out to the bunkers, trying to get in there as fast as they could. They'd have one boot on and one off, that sort of thing. They were scared. Four or five rockets came in, and I swear it sounded like thirty. By the time it was over, it sounded like they had shot the entire world. After that we sat around not saying anything, wondering what was going on. I didn't sleep for about sixty hours after that. I didn't sleep all that night, I didn't sleep the next day. I didn't want to go to sleep. The feeling was that you could be asleep somewhere and not be able to get your gear on and get somewhere fast enough. Everybody got serious real quick. After that there was not a lot of joking, playing around and doing nothing. Everybody was serious about what they were doing. If you asked them to do something, they'd do it for you right away as opposed to before that, when they'd do it later.

I still don't know what it is to lose a good friend of mine. I'm glad I don't and I hope I never find out. That was the thing that bothered me the most.

Lieutenant Ivan Wray, Artillery FO, with India Company

I was talking to Heckler, my radio operator. If I could pick just one Marine to be with in that position, it would be Lance Corporal Harold Heckler. He was a real Devil Dog. He carried more gear than any man, the heaviest pack in India Company. I remember saying to him, "Well, Heckler, here it comes." He looks at me and says, "Oh, Christ, sir!" He was a Chicago tough guy and he wanted to see some combat. His story was like many in the war. He wanted to see some combat, but as the war went on, his ambition got lower.

Captain Leon Pappa, CO, Kilo Company

Something else comes to mind that was a bit comical, the night we were on alert, when the air war started. We went to MOPP4. We had gone from 100 percent alert back to 50 percent and then back up to 100 percent with MOPP4. Somehow the word never gets to everybody. The landline got pulled out or whatever. I had the staff NCOs and lieutenants in one tent—my first sergeant and my gunny in another one. My XO was up on the line with me. My company gunny was yelling at me. I could tell he wasn't in MOPP4 from what he was yelling. Well, he saw us and . . . he was a black Marine and he almost changed colors that night. It was three in the morning and he saw us in MOPP4. He was still in his regular uniform. All of a sudden he is airborne. Clothes were flying off him. He took off everything and didn't have any skivvies on. Then he realized that his MOPP suit was over somewhere else, so he's running around with nothing on.

Captain Kevin Scott, CO, Lima Company

The Marines were prepared. We had put them all in helmets and flak jackets as soon as we had moved up to Al Mishab. When they rocketed us, everybody became a believer in flak jackets and helmets. You'd see some of them sleeping with their helmets on and their flak jackets. I guess a prudent man would.

There were a few that wouldn't come out of the bunkers. I had to talk them out of them. I'd tell them that they couldn't live their lives in a rat hole of a bunker. They would argue that they were safer in there, and I'd tell them that if the hole took a hit they'd be as dead as if they were outside.

Then after a couple of attacks, most of the apprehensions went away. It became routine, though some were careful to not move too far from their bunkers. When they made a head call, they made it damned quick.

Captain Sam Jammal, CO, H&S Company

Colonel Garrett drove a lot of things that happened. He thought the harassment fire would demoralize our people, because the Iraqis would fire to the east and then fire to the west. We didn't know when they were going to fire down the center and hit us. The colonel was really anxious to get up to Khafji and hold it. Tactically, I agree with him, but we had the dilemma of who was in charge. Because of the political situation with the Arabs, we couldn't control our own destiny.

The rockets may have been just harassment fire—we didn't know. We didn't know if they had observers or anything like that. What we did know is we couldn't just sit here and take it, because the troops are going to start asking what we are doing about it.

We went through fear. We went through lack of sleep. I remember looking out and thinking I was a coward and then seeing a lot of people who just barely could move their legs, they were so tired. You could tell they got absolutely no sleep. At that time I think everyone reassessed things and figured out that it was normal.

We did a lot of talking with the troops and let them know that it was okay to be afraid. We told them that there was something wrong with them if they *weren't* afraid. The Saudis and Qataris showed they were afraid. Some nights I was afraid to move around.

Colonel John Admire, CO, Task Force Taro

In preparing our Marines for the Gulf War, we acknowledged that fear and apprehension would be present but that we must overcome them. These emotions are normal. It would be abnormal if they were absent. We needed to confront them and use them to our advantage. In confronting fears it is important that leaders appear calm, collected, and well-organized. This instills confidence within the unit. Leaders should be highly visible and circulate among their Marines. Their mere presence is calming and confidence-building.

Captain Sam Jammal, CO, H&S Company

I made a particularly good friendship with one of the Arab battalions, the second battalion of the Qatari brigade. The first three times we got incoming rockets, as soon as the impact was over, the colonel told me to go over and see the Qataris and see what was going on.

When we first moved into the areas with the Qataris, we moved in at night. My driver was a Marine named Sergeant Abcher, and he and I had all these excursions in the middle of the night. The first one, we were driving around in the pitch black, with our blackout lights on. A truck came up to us with his headlights on and a .50-caliber machine gun pointed right at us. They were Qataris and they were extremely vigilant at night. They had good patrols and good solid challenges. One time I got challenged and I answered back in Arabic. The guy chambered a round and I answered again in English, real quickly, "I'm an American! An American!"

They were extremely vigilant, and the reason I mention this is because when the rounds came in that first night, our Marines were scared. Some of them were saying, "Gas! Gas!"

It turned out that there was no gas, but the biggest fear that ran down my back was when Colonel Garrett sent me over to see the commander of the Qatari brigade to find out what was going on, make sure they were okay, and find out if they needed any help.

This was the night of the first attack. I hopped in the vehicle and tried to find my way. All the camps looked the same, and I couldn't find the Qatari COC. I stopped, got out of the vehicle, and asked directions. As I was going back to the vehicle, I heard the "Gas! Gas!" I was trying to figure out if I should mask or not, but the Qataris weren't masked and that made me feel better. I got back into the vehicle and made my way back to our COC. I think the colonel knew I was afraid. After a few minutes he asked if I would go out again. I was afraid and sure as heck wanted to say no, but I said, "Aye, aye, sir," jumped in the vehicle, took off, and smoked a whole pack of cigarettes in fifteen minutes. I finally made it to the Qatari COC and found out they were okay. They had no more knowledge than we did. I went back and reported to the colonel. I did that three or four more times that night, becoming more at ease every time I moved around. I think the colonel taught me; he worked with me to build that confidence and overcome the fear. He would probably say it was just coincidental, but I say he did it on purpose. Later I set up a landline, because it was ludicrous for me to drive in a jeep at night looking around. As the war went on and we moved to Khafji and all that, I wasn't as scared.

Lieutenant Dan Henderson, Platoon Commander, Kilo Company

The Marines impressed the hell out of me. They were unbelievable. My biggest concern with them was teaching them three things—first aid, communications, and calling for fire support. Every day we had classes on first aid and communications—how to talk on the radio the right way. Every single Marine, no matter what his rank, knew how to call in fire support. I figured if I was dead and there was nobody else, they could get themselves out. They knew, like I knew, the only way of getting out of Saudi Arabia was by going north.

10 / Marines in Khafji

Sergeant William liams, Recon Team Leader

I was the senior recon team leader at the time the air war started. I was woken at 3:15 and was told that the air war had started and they wanted us up in Khafji. Of course, Khafji was a border town. I got my team together. We got an S2 [intelligence] brief. We got ammo and all that stuff and took off at 0600. My mission was to go up to Khafji to observe and report if it was under siege, which it was.

On the way to Khafji I met with Colonel Garrett, who was outside Khafji at Al Mishab. Three-three had a defensive perimeter, and we weren't sure if Iraqi tanks were going to come across. As I was going into Khafji, all the Saudis left. They thought this was it, and they retreated behind 3/3. There was only one observation post and it was outside the city. The two guys there said they weren't going into town but I could if I wanted to. On the way into town we passed an oil refinery that had been hit by artillery fire, and one of the tanks was burning.

The only ones in the town were my team and some French and American journalists. I had seven people, including myself, and two Humvees. We rode around the city and found that it was completely vacant. Artillery rounds were still coming in, and later I thought the Iraqis must have an OP [observation post] in there. We stayed there for a day and a half. They wanted us in the city because they weren't sure exactly what was going to happen. We were sitting in the city when two U.S. Army six-bys came blowing by. Ten minutes later they turned around and started out. I stopped them and found two Army women were driving them. There were two [women] in each vehicle and they were all crying, "Oh, shit, we're lost. We don't know where we are at." They were crying and crying and crying. They missed their turn-off about twenty-five miles back down the road. I straightened them out and sent them on their way. The reason I mention this is because this is what happened to Melissa Neeley, who was captured by the Iraqis. Personally, I think their commanding officer should have been hung for this. It was a major screw-up.

Our recon teams started rotating in to Khafji. The problem was that the Iraqis had multiple rocket launchers coming down to the border, shooting their rockets and taking off. They were hitting Al Mishab and 3/3's area and everything else.

We would go in and go into the houses that were all vacant. We'd kick down the doors and go to the rooftops. We would watch all night long and find the multiple rocket launchers—you could actually see them take off and get an azimuth and range. We would send that back, and the A6s or whatever would come in and pound them.

Colonel John Garrett, Battalion Commander

There was a guy named Rick Barry who was the XO of the SRI [surveillance, reconnaissance, and intelligence], and they put him up into Khafji to run a network of observation posts. He could see all this happening when the rockets lit off. He was fifteen clicks or so ahead of us.

Corporal Allen Uskoski, Recon Team Member

The first time I went into the city, the Iraqis were bombarding it. They were shooting rockets or artillery or whatever it was. We ended up moving from safe house to safe house. To me it was scary as shit to have someone shooting at me. I was up on the .50-cal on the Hummer, and I thought there were eyes all around me.

It was really scary, because you couldn't see people that could be hiding in buildings. They could sit inside a room and look out and you would never know they were there. We didn't know who was friendly and who was enemy. To me they all looked the same, and the clothes were the same. Coming through town sometimes you'd see someone, but you didn't know who it was.

When you were driving through town you didn't waste any time, you didn't dilly-dally around. You had to hide your helmet so no one could easily identify you as U.S., or if you got dropped off, get dropped off and get out of sight quickly so nobody would see you being inserted into the town.

Most of the houses there had big cement walls around them. And double doors. You could jump over or go through the door. We always carried bolt cutters in case they were locked. You'd spot a side street, jump a fence, open the gate, and put the Humvee inside. And then you'd do your security. You'd just sit there for ten minutes or so listening.

Sergeant William Iiams, Recon Team Leader

The artillery raids started in the meantime. We didn't know it, but there was a Palestinian group that was still inside the city. They were watching us and the Special Forces team that was also inside the city. Then the Special Forces team was compromised and they left.

One night we'd stay in one house, the next night stay in another. We tried to move around. We couldn't go north of the city, because we found out that's where the Palestinians were. It was strange going into other people's homes. We were using their food to supplement our MREs [meal ready-to-eat]. I think that it's just because we're American that we feel bad about kicking down doors in people's houses, but it's a war. We used their facilities and slept on their beds. It was strange.

Some of the things we saw and did were remarkable. We had trouble with communication, so my guys began hooking our radios up to the copper TV antennas, and that helped. The guys were outstanding. They knew what they were doing. When I was given operations orders, everything went like clockwork. When everyone pulls together, it's amazing.

Corporal Patrick Sterling, Recon Team Member

When we first went into Khafji, it still hadn't hit me that we were actually at war. It was kind of fun for us because we had the vehicles and it was pretty much a ghost town. There was really nobody there, so we had the key to the city. You could go into anything and check it out—do this and do that. You didn't have to worry about the enemy, because it was an abandoned city. We did a lot of running around going through houses. We expected to find people in the houses, but there was no one there. We were always careful when we went into the houses. The city was pretty dirty.

A few trucks would come in from the south. They'd come in empty and leave full. When the Saudis left the city they left everything behind, and some of them came back to get their stuff. I saw one lady loading up a truck. She didn't seem worried or scared. She just wanted to get her stuff and go back down south.

did they know Saudi Army was coming in?

11 / Cross-Training

Another Step in the Relationship

Captain Joseph Molofsky, Liaison to the Saudi Brigade

The relationship that Colonel Admire, on instructions from General Myatt, developed with the Saudi Abdul Aziz Brigade and the Qatari brigade was a critical, pivotal factor in the entire campaign.

The Saudis were inexperienced in heavily mechanized warfare in the open desert. It was reinforced to them over and over again—by General Myatt, by Colonel Admire, and by me and the ANGLICO team I was located with—that when push came to shove, if war were actually going to happen, that the Americans would stand shoulder to shoulder with them and we would fight together.

The ANGLICO team's presence reinforced without question to them that American air support, which they had virtually none of, would be at their beck and call when required. We reinforced that by flying U.S. Air Force Thunderbolts, Harriers, and FAC teams right over their tents daily, to reinforce that when they needed it, the American advisors with them would provide them with air cover. And that made a big difference. We took some of their artillery officers down to our artillery shoots and got them to adjust American artillery. We did a number of aircraft flybys on a daily basis over the course of months to reinforce to them that our air was at their disposal.

I had a satcom [satellite communications] radio out there because I was kind of working for General Myatt and General Draude. I could report back to division and also to Colonel Admire. Periodically, I would get a mission to go out to some lat-long in the desert, stand by for aircraft, and then conduct tours of the forward area. There were a string of eight Saudi outposts out there starting at the coast.

I'd go into the desert and meet the aircraft. Invariably it would be the commander of the British tank brigade, or General Myatt, General [Thomas] Draude or General [Walt] Boomer's assistant, General [John] Hopkins. They'd show up with their chiefs of staff, and I'd arrange for vehicles to take them to look at what later became their attack routes. It was pretty interesting for a captain. I'd pick these guys up, we'd go up to a Saudi outpost and have some tea and look at the Iraqis looking at us. They were able to actually walk up to the breach sites they'd eventually breach and look over the berm and see the terrain they would have to cover. I think that was very helpful to them. The Saudis wouldn't allow Americans up there until Colonel Admire developed this relationship with the Saudis, and then they told us to go ahead. Because of that our general officers got a chance to walk the ground they would later attack across. I think that's damned significant.

Colonel John Garrett, Battalion CO

The Qataris had tanks and they had Renault armored vehicles. We were on foot, but we had helicopters available. We'd invite them to do helicopter operations with us, and in turn they'd bring their tanks over and we'd give classes. We had some artillery raids and they'd participate in that. At our level it couldn't have been greater as far as the communication goes.

Captain Sam Jammal, CO, H&S Company

They became good friends of ours. They would bring in tanks and APCs, and we'd practice joint raids on company outposts.

Colonel John Garrett, Battalion CO

The Iraqis did attack Khafji, which was just a few clicks up the road. If they'd continued the attack, there is no doubt in my mind that our defense would have held just fine. We could have handled whatever had to happen—we and the Qataris. We were really close to the border, and this was the end of January. Even though we thought the United States was going to attack, you never know what's going to happen. So you always had to think of your defense. Saddam Hussein is a very unpredictable, enigmatic guy.

The rocket launcher that the Iraqis had, it would start just like Washing Machine Charlie in the old television show, pop off a few rounds every night. It started the night. We tried to find them with RPVs. They were smart enough not to come out when the weather was good. You could see them going off. The rockets were scary because it's one of those situations that you don't have any control over. It's like being in the back of a helicopter and landing in a hot zone and there's not a damned thing you can do. Once you get on the ground, you can start maneuvering and firing and getting some control over your destiny. You're not completely at their mercy. When the first rocket came in, crater analysis said it was a 300-millimeter. I think all they ever hit was a white four-door Chevrolet across the road.

12 / The First American Ground Action
*The Artillery Raids

Major General Mike Myatt, Commanding General, 1st Marine Division

During the six months of Operation Desert Shield, our Marines spent a great deal of time studying how the Iraqis fight and looked extensively at the eight-year Iran-Iraq war. We learned that the Iraqi artillery was very effective in trapping Iranian soldiers time and time again in confined areas called "fire-sacks," where thousands of Iranians perished. We knew that there were over 1,200 artillery pieces belonging to the Iraqi divisions facing the 1st Marine Division. In our studies of the two obstacle belts in Kuwait and the positioning of the Iraqi artillery, we concluded that the Iraqis were planning on trapping us in at least two fire-sacks when we attacked. We also recognized that there wasn't enough ordnance in the aviators' inventory to *destroy* all that artillery during the first phase of Desert Storm. So we designed a series of ambushes [combined arms raids] to *defeat* the Iraqis before we ever attacked into Kuwait [emphasis here is Myatt's].

Colonel John Admire, CO, Task Force Taro

In response to the allied air campaign, the Iraqi army conducted supporting arms attacks into Saudi Arabia. As the most forward-deployed United States combat unit, Task Force Taro initiated the first ground-oriented attacks against Iraqi positions in Kuwait by conducting an artillery raid on 20–21 January. Arab coalition force observers were invited to participate, and subsequent American Marine instruction and rehearsals with the Arabs prepared them for the conduct of similar such raids. Thereafter, artillery raids and border skirmishes were conducted randomly and frequently.

Captain Joseph Molofsky, Liaison to the Saudi Brigade

Colonel Admire called me up and asked me to coordinate a passage of lines for artillery batteries to move through the Saudi defensive screen and move up just south of the border. So I did that. I took a couple of Saudi officers with me for them to get the experience with artillery raids, because they expressed an interest in doing the same thing once it worked out.

Colonel John Garrett, Battalion Commander

Our mission on the raids was to move the artillery up about twenty or thirty clicks from where it was. We provided flank security for that. All I had for my guys to ride was trucks, so we got the Qataris and they came with us in their Renault APCs. They would have an English-speaking officer or two with each APC. We'd put my Dragons in a truck and we'd have those APCs in front.

Major Joseph D. "Dan" Stansbury, Battalion Operations Officer

The artillery raids were somewhat disconcerting to me initially, because we had to break apart the battalion to make a task-organized artillery raid force. I did not have a good feeling about what they would do if they were engaged in indirect fire, if they were going to be able to extract themselves. My job was to make sure that they had plans so if they got fired on by indirect fire that they would pull out. I was concerned that they would run into a mechanized force with artillery pieces and TOWs and heavy machine guns. They were very mobile but vulnerable to any type of tank or heavy mech attack.

One raid had a combined Qatari-Marine security force. We were in Qatari personnel carriers.

At night, confusion between friend and foe was a potential problem. There were Saudi national guard personnel driving up and down the main road. U.S. personnel were driving up and down the MSR [main supply route], and personnel in Khafji providing intelligence to higher headquarters. U.S. advisors were going up and down the road with headlights on at 0300. We had to stop all these vehicles, because that was our job—to make sure no infiltrators got down the road.

Staff Sergeant Don Gallagher, Platoon Sergeant, Weapons Company

On the artillery raids we sat out there as security while the artillery fired off their mission. We'd heard that the Iraqi artillery outnumbered us four to one. Then our artillery guys told us that if they found us, they could take out the whole grid square. This was not good. It made us pretty jumpy.

Captain Joseph Molofsky, Liaison to the Saudi Brigade

On one raid the battery commander had his radio handset sitting down next to his compass. He was going north and talking on the radio at the same time. The handset screwed up the compass, and we drove around in circles and I was getting nervous.

We finally set up and got ready to shoot when we saw an Iraqi multiple rocket launcher on the target line right in front of us. I'm standing there at two o'clock in the morning, and we'd been driving around a couple of clicks south of the border for about two hours. We finally got set up and I saw this missile get launched, and it goes right in front to the target line. I said to myself, "Well, that's it. We fucked around. We got here, acted like amateurs, and they saw us, and now we're dead." But it went right over our heads and landed about a click behind us.

I don't even know if they were shooting at us. It was just chaos out there. Units driving around at night—Saudis, Bedouin tribesmen, Iraqi infiltrators. I'd never seen it that bad. The Gaza Strip was weird, but this was really weird.

We had to make a whole passage of lines rearward at three in the morning. The Saudis didn't know we were coming. I pulled up to a Saudi outpost, and my driver and I almost got shot up. A young Bedouin kid, sixteen, seventeen years old, stepped off the side of the road, locked and loaded a weapon at me, and I thought I'd had it. But I managed to speak in Arabic and get his officer and explain it. He called other commanders to allow us to pass through.

Major Dan Stansbury, Battalion Operations Officer

Our artillery was using M-198 155-millimeter Howitzers on the raids. I don't recall how many rounds they fired. It was around fifty. It wasn't a whole lot, but they did have some effect on targets. We did get some battle damage assessment afterward.

The raids were successful, particularly morale-wise, because we were able to counter the Iraqi barrages on us. It was part of the reason we did the raids. It was a confidence builder. It was something that allowed us to take a pro-active role and not just sit there.

Captain Joe Fack, FAC

My job on the artillery raids was to seal the back door. The artillery wanted to shoot and get the hell out of Dodge. I would come up with air in the rear to watch for tanks. The air would be on station. We used A6s and a lot of A10s. We had a bunch of A10s chopped [temporarily assigned] to us so we could use them against the tanks.

We'd drive up at night using night-lights on the trucks. They just followed each other up the road. They would get into position using a gyro-guided vehicle. They could get within one-half meter of where they wanted. They would use their equipment to get each gun exactly at the place on the earth they wanted. They would know exactly where each gun was and their azimuth to the target, and they'd figure out the range and then they'd give their guns the data, and they'd shoot. It was pretty accurate.

Major Craig Huddleston, Battalion XO

It was more of an artillery ambush. We'd position the guns and then wait for the target to appear within their range, and then they'd shoot. On the first one we supported the artillery battery with all our TOWs and all of our heavy machine guns and a rifle company. We had twenty-four TOW launchers and six heavy machine guns. When the target appeared, the battery would engage, quickly displace, and then we would follow their displacement. We were the rear guard. We went out with both the Qataris and Saudis.

The first one was supposed to last about four hours and went on until dawn, because the target didn't appear and we waited until it appeared. We engaged it and had good effect, because they stopped shooting at us that night. We were mostly shooting at their rockets.

We did a port-and-starboard routine. One night the colonel would go out with a rifle company, and the next night I would go out with one. The second time we went out, the Iraqis tried to sucker us. They were not stupid.

They shot a few rounds, and they were laying for us with counter battery. They launched a bunch of rockets at us but didn't hit anything.

We ain't stupid either. The next night we took two batteries out. After we fired our rounds, we moved out as the Iraqis fired about a dozen rockets at us. As soon as they fired, the Saudis opened up with about two hundred rockets and just clobbered them. That substantially ended the Iraqi fires. They got a real bloody nose, and after that night they just didn't feel like coming back very often.

While all this was going on, our aviators were getting much more adept at finding small groups of Iraqis. If they moved at night, air and ground fires were attacking them. It became a suicide proposition for them and pretty much ended their forays down to the border. After we'd gone about a week around the end of January without taking a round, we knew we had them on the run.

Captain Joe Fack, FAC

I only worked with Air Force A10s a couple of times, but they worked out great. The nine-line brief that we gave Marine pilots was almost the same thing that they used. They used a seven-line brief, but it was much the same. One thing that they had that we didn't was frequency-hopping capabilities for their radios. Their radios changed frequencies automatically and frequently and prevented an enemy from locking onto and jamming them. We also had a two- or three-second delay in the encrypted voice system. We'd give him the nine-line brief encrypted, but in the terminal phase of the strike we'd talk in the clear, because in those two or three seconds when the pilot is rolling in, he could be throwing a bomb at someone we didn't want him to, and that two or three seconds could help save somebody's life.

Colonel John Garrett, Battalion Commander

One day I was sitting in my tent, and someone comes in and gives me an envelope addressed to me personally. I open it and it was a letter from Rick Barry. He said, "I think we got lucky last night and took out that rocket that's been giving me fits, so you can sleep better. See you downtown. Rick." Sure enough, that was it. We never had anymore trouble after that.

Captain Joseph Molofsky, Liaison to the Saudi Brigade

The joint operations with our artillerymen and the Saudi artillerymen backed up the idea that when push came to shove, our artillery would fire in support of them. Those initiatives and a number of others created in the minds of the Saudi leadership on the ground there was a sense of confidence that really encouraged them to go ahead and retake Khafji. I am not sure, if we had not been there, that they would have reacted in the way that they did. They went up there because they knew the Americans would back them up. Colonel Admire is in large measure responsible for that.

13 / The Alarms Go Off

Major Dan Stansbury, Battalion Operations Officer

We were tasked to go up and provide a defensive position in Khafji. There was apprehension on my part about whether or not we were capable of defending Khafji with a company-size force. I felt we were not. Having been up there before, we did a recon. We know Khafji is mostly brick buildings in close proximity with each other, heavy walls, metal gates, some homes with steel bars on the windows, courtyards, and very narrow streets.

We were tasked to go up with a platoon of Qatari personnel carriers to go up and put up a defensive perimeter there. Unfortunately, the Qataris could not get permission to go, so we went with the forward command element and Kilo Company and put in a defensive position and take some action to see what was going on.

We put the company in with his fire support cell and did a reconnaissance but never really occupied the city, because we could not find a good location for our Marines where we could control access to Khafji from the north.

Captain Leon Pappa, CO, Kilo Company

We were getting a lot of intelligence saying that Saddam may attempt to push across the border into Khafji. I was given a warning order, late one afternoon, to be prepared to insert Kilo Company at night into Khafji with assist from some light armored vehicles that would screen to the west and northwest of the city. They would clear through the city first, and then I would go in.

I was apprehensive about going in, because we had not talked to these guys who were in there, like the recon teams, or SRI, or ANGLICO, or any of the spooks we heard were up there. I talked Colonel Garrett into letting me take a patrol in there first. I took a small headquarters with my forward air controller, my artillery forward observers, that kind of thing. I had a heavy gun vehicle and a Saudi vehicle with an interpreter.

By the time I got out of Khafji, the company was waiting for me about two kilometers south, where there was a gas station. The battalion headquarters group was there too. It was about three o'clock in the morning, and I wanted to go back into the city. Now that I had seen it, I wanted to go back in with a patrol during the daylight, pick out some spots, and leave some guys. I badgered and badgered the S3 but was turned down.

From north to south, Khafji was about three kilometers long. From east to west maybe two kilometers wide. The buildings, even the detached buildings, could have been mini-fortresses. They all had walls around them. If the Iraqis really wanted strongpoint locations in the city, it would be difficult to dig them out.

The night I went in with the patrol, we did a lot of moving back and forth. If one street didn't work, I'd try another one. On one street, I ran into some construction that wasn't on the map. I found the fire station. That's something I remembered from Amphibious Warfare School. If you go into a built-up area, look for the fire stations. It was the fire stations that had the good maps. We found the fire station even though there were no fire trucks. We broke in, with the permission of this Saudi lieutenant who was with me, to look for maps. I found them, took about ten copies, and brought them back to the battalion. They showed a lot of detail, the projected construction, and other things that our maps didn't have.

Major Dan Stansbury, Battalion Operations Officer

I recommended that if we were going to defend Khafji that we move the entire regiment into the city. The reconnaissance teams up there were reporting artillery and rocket fire into the city nightly.

Colonel John Garrett, Battalion Commander

Not too long after that the Iraqis attacked Khafji, and we thought they were going to continue the attack down to us. We were getting ready for some offensive operation, and the Iraqis meanwhile just waltz into Khafji. We thought sure they were coming on down and thought, *Oh, oh, here it comes.*

Major Craig Huddleston, Battalion XO

An outpost, which was centered around some TOW vehicles, called in. They reported forty to sixty armored vehicles on the road headed south. I called them back and talked to the platoon commander, Captain John Borth. I asked him what kind of vehicles and to identify the type. There was a pause, and everyone was standing around the loudspeaker when he said they were BTR50s, which is an Iraqi-type vehicle. My estimate at the time was that we were taking incoming in preparation of an attack.

We started moving people, heavy machine guns, and TOWs into a position to interdict the road. We called the Qataris and told them what we knew, and they told us they had observed the same thing. About the same time, we got a call from the regiment, which told us to prepare to repel an attack from the sea. There were reports coming in that barges or small craft were approaching Al Mishab. This happened at the same time we got the report of forty to sixty vehicles heading down the road, so we thought we were really into it.

I think this was the proudest I've ever been of the battalion, because when we heard what we were facing, these guys set their jaws and just dug in and said, "All right. If you want a fight, we'll give you a fight." There were a few high-pitched voices on the radio, but people were giving professional reports. There appeared to be no stress. I think everybody recognized that they had to get hold of themselves and calm down, because we were facing a very serious threat, a threat to overrun us in a heartbeat if we weren't prepared. People got ready—very calm, very orderly. In retrospect, I expected it to be a madhouse, but after the first few rounds everybody calmed down. We prepared ourselves.

Captain Joe Fack, FAC

We had a lot of reports that there were tanks coming down the road. The Saudis had a V150, which looked a lot like a BTR50, the Iraqi armored vehicle. They were running up and down the road. And we got a lot of alarms that tanks were coming down the road and stuff like that. Captain Shamin, who's the other FAC, was helping the A10s coordinate.

Captain Michael McCusker, CO, India Company

We were told that the Iraqis actually entered Khafji. We were up on the lines, and in my CP area we moved up below the cul-de-sac because the enemy was coming from that way. The CP group was set up with all the radio nets and everything else in a bunker.

The next thing we knew, we got a report that they'd gotten by us. A platoon commander called in and said, "They're by us—twenty-eight BTRs. We thought, *Jesus Christ! How the fuck did they get through town?* We're behind the TOWs on the highway. We were told we'd have to turn our defense around 180 degrees. I thought, *Yeah, right, there's a HAWK missile battery right behind us and another company back there. They might as well shoot me in the back.*

Lieutenant Ivan Wray, FO, India Company

So the enemy is right behind us. The CP was now in front of everything. Tim Mundy was saying, "Wait a minute. We're right in front of everybody." I wasn't laughing then. I said, "Holy shit. Let's all get down in case everybody starts firing. Just get the hell down."

Major Craig Huddleston, Battalion XO

It turns out that these were Saudi vehicles. Because we had reached the point of calming down, we didn't shoot at any of them. Not one round went out. They'd been identified as enemy, and the Saudis couldn't account for them. It would have been easy for the Marines on the line who were cleared to fire. But they took their time and made sure of the identification. They let them get well within range. We could have engaged them at 3,500 meters with the TOWs, or the Qataris could have gotten them at about 2,000 meters with their tanks, but they held fire to see what we would do. We let them get to within about 1,000 meters, and then we could see that they were six- and four-wheeled vehicles. The Iraqi BTR50s had eight wheels. Then we could see the Saudi flag, which they tended to fly at night, as they got even closer. So we passed the word to hold fire, it was friendlies coming in. It was a Saudi brigade withdrawing. I don't know why, but they were.

About that time we took some more incoming. One was an airburst, which set off a chemical alert, so we went to full MOPP gear and stayed that way for quite a while.

Captain Mike McCusker, CO, India Company

We went to full MOPP4, and that was as scared as I'd been in my life. We had rockets going off behind us, everyone's in MOPP suits, and we had to do our mask-and-monitor drill. That's easy to do in training. You have a Marine take his mask off, and you use him to test to see if there is any gas in the air. I was pretty positive there was no gas, because birds were still flying around, but it was still a hard decision to make—to tell a man to take his mask off— because you were putting that man in danger of losing his life. There were two Marines in my CP group who volunteered—Lance Corporal Francis, who was my 81 FO, and Lance Corporal Spinks, who was a clerk. Francis said, "I'll do it, sir." I said, "No, you won't. You're my FO. You can't do it, so just shut up." Spinks said, "I'll do it, sir." Spinks was my scrounge. I said, "Okay, Spinks, give your weapon to the Doc." We had a very competent doctor, Doc Collier. We went through the entire process. Mask off—so many seconds of breathing. There are numerous steps you have to go through. It turned out that there was no gas, but it was a very brave act on Spinks's part, not knowing what is actually there. He's a character, but a good kid. That morning I drove through the lines and made sure that everyone and everything was okay. They'd been through the mask procedure, and I was checking to make sure it had gone properly.

In the morning we got several calls telling us that it was all clear. A wave of relief came over us as we took off our MOPP gear. I was laughing with relief when I got out of it. There was definitely fear out there.

Ivan Wray said it all when he said, "Fuck Saddam. Nuke him." We'd been rocketed and subjected to the fear of being gassed. We said, "Fuck him and everyone who put him in power. Nuke them all and turn his country into a sheet of glass."

At about 0200, about four hours after the initial rockets came in, we calmed down enough where we got out of our chemical equipment and went back to 25 percent alert. We anticipated it would be a long night, so I went back to my tent about two-thirty. I decided to sleep on the decks below this berm I had around my tent.

No sooner had I laid down than we took one more rocket and the whole process started over again. They were 300-millimeter rockets. We wanted to send a team out to do a crater analysis to determine for sure what was shooting at us, but we didn't want to do it at night. There were too many people moving around in front us—Saudis, everybody. We had to consider anything that moved as potentially enemy. This went on until about six in the morning.

Colonel John Garrett, Battalion Commander

It was a wild night. We were getting reports that there were up to two hundred vehicles. As it turns out, they were all friendly. The people who saved the day were the Marines who were manning the TOWs in my position and the Qataris who were out there. The guys had enough sense and courage to just not shoot at the first thing that came barreling down the road. It was hard to tell the difference between the Kuwaiti BMTs and the Iraqi BTRs. It was dark, and how can you tell?

Major Craig Huddleston, Battalion XO

By the time it got light we were drained physically and emotionally. That set a pattern for the next nine days. On a good night you would get about three hours sleep. We were up and down all night with various alerts. The Iraqis rocketed us nightly for the next five nights or so.

It wasn't serious after we got used to it. We were all scared, but after about the third night when we saw what they were doing, which was harassing us, we got to the point where at dusk we'd go to our holes, our bunkers, and go to sleep down there and sleep through it. Most Marines, myself included, got to the point where when the rockets came in we'd feel pretty secure.

We never took one casualty. I attribute that to Colonel Garrett. He had us so spread out and so deep that it would have taken a lucky shot to get us. They didn't have anything to shoot at. My hole was about eight feet underground. That was just for me, a one-man hole. The ones where they had a whole squad working on bunkers were real deep. They could have taken a direct hit. We didn't really worry about it much anymore. The only people I know who were really upset were the Qataris, and that was when the rocket took out their field mess.

It was shortly after that that we found out that Saddam launched the Scuds against Israel. That's when we were the most nervous. We wondered what was going to happen and we quickly went over to the Qataris. The colonel went over himself, and I called the major on the phone and asked now that Israel had been fired upon what would happen to the coalition. We'd never asked that question before, because we were a little afraid to. Once it happened, we asked them what they were going to do about it. They were incredulous and told us that they knew who the enemy was, that he had just fired on them. They said that Israel wasn't the enemy. Perhaps after this war it would be, but not now.

We were nervous while we waited to see what the Israelis were going to do. We kept our fingers crossed and hoped they wouldn't do anything. We knew if Israel got involved it would be a real mess. We were worried about the Syrian and Egyptian force. We were pretty sure of the Saudis and Qataris. When Israel decided to not do anything, we were pretty happy.

Every night Scuds were being launched, rockets were impacting around us, and we were trying like hell to kill these guys with various means. The intelligence forces we had forward would identify their movement, and we'd try to roll aircraft in on them. We did all sorts of things trying to hit them. They were quick. They'd get their missiles off and their rockets off and move, but they weren't very accurate. They weren't hitting anything.

14 / The Battle for Khafji

The battle for Khafji was Saddam Hussein's attempt to draw U.S. forces into the ground war prematurely and inflict a great number of casualties on them. If he could stun American willpower by filling up Dover Air Force Base with hundreds, if not thousands, of U.S. dead, he expected America to weaken and leave him to his adventures in the Middle East. In furtherance of this aim, he launched a multipronged attack across the Saudi-Kuwaiti border, hoping to isolate the Saudi border town of Khafji.

One Iraqi tank brigade crossed about fifty miles inland and clashed with the light armored infantry battalion of the 1st Marine Division. In was in this fight that a light armored vehicle and twelve Marines were mistakenly killed by U.S. aircraft. A second tank brigade ran into the light armored infantry of the 2nd Marine Division about twenty-five miles closer to the Gulf, where its attack was stalled and then repulsed.

The third prong of the offensive attacked Khafji from the west and was immediately engaged by the Qatari force screening the city. An Iraqi mechanized unit got by them and entered the city itself.[1]

Captain Joseph Molofsky, Liaison to the Saudi Brigade

There were these eight Beau Geste desert forts strung out along a line from the coast. On the evening of January 29th the Iraqis launched a three-pronged attack across the border, where an LAI [light armored infantry] company commanded by Captain Rock Pollard bumped into a convoy of fifty tanks and lost twelve kids. They had gotten a report that one of the outposts, with a Special Forces A Team, and an ANGLICO team, and some Saudi special forces, had been overrun. They ran into these Iraqi tanks and destroyed most of them with air.

OP 4
29 Jan
13 LAVs
7 LAV w/ TOW

Captain Pollard, commander of Company D, 3rd Armored Infantry Battalion, arrayed his force around OP 4 on the twenty-ninth of January. He had thirteen LAVs [light armored vehicles] and seven LAVs with TOWs mounted and covered about a four-thousand-meter front around a basin to the front of the outpost. At 2000 hours, members of the reconnaissance platoon at the station observed about thirty Iraqi vehicles through their night-vision devices. The enemy was moving toward them. They called for air support and began to withdraw after telling Captain Pollard that the enemy was attacking. A furious firefight erupted in which Captain Pollard coolly and continually shifted his forces under fire to meet the changing situation. At one point he had to lead a counterattack on the outpost to permit the reconnaissance elements to withdraw. Air Force A10 Thunderbolts came in to help and killed several Iraqi tanks and other vehicles. However, a miss-dropped flare by one aircraft caused another to mistakenly fire on one of Captain Pollard's LAVs, killing seven of the eight crewmen aboard. Another four Marines were accidentally killed by one of their own TOW missiles. Hammered badly by Company D and the aircraft, the Iraqis finally withdrew.

Company A, 3rd Light Armored Infantry, commanded by Captain Michael Shupp, arrived to relieve Captain Pollard's Company D. Captain Shupp's company had no sooner arrived before the Iraqis attacked again. The fight continued well past sunrise and, backed by air, Captain Shupp's Marines again pounded the Iraqis. The Iraqis again withdrew under fire after being outmaneuvered and outgunned by the Marines. *✗*Twenty-two destroyed Iraqi tanks were later discovered in the position.

Captain Joseph Molofsky, Liaison to the Saudi Brigade

OP 7

Another prong was at outpost seven, where Captain Doug Kleinsmith was with an ANGLICO team, a Special Forces team, minus, and a force reconnaissance detachment. They used air, shot up a bunch of Iraqi tanks, and did not get overrun, but some of the tanks bypassed them. They had tanks on both sides of them, so they withdrew and got back to Colonel Turki's command post the next morning.

I was at division headquarters about a hundred miles away. I got woke up in the middle of the night, told the Saudis were going into action and "to get my ass back up to Colonel Turki." He was west of Al Mishab, which is where his command post had been since August 4th.

Colonel John Garrett, Battalion Commander

The Iraqis occupied Khafji, just clicks up the road from us. We were in the defense just south of there with the Qataris and preparing for an attack. Nobody was too excited about Khafji. They were, but they were determined to not fall into the trap of forgetting about planning for the main objective, which was the important thing.

Captain Sam Jammal, CO, H&S Company

Khafji started like this: I was told to report to the COC. The reports were that there were thirty-one tanks that penetrated the border right above Khafji. I asked the colonel what he wanted me to do, and he told me to get over to the Qataris and tell him what was going on. I no sooner got ready to leave than another flash report comes in. "The Iraqis are surrendering. They have their turrets turned the other way." Khafji started that way, with the tanks coming in with their turrets reversed and reports of the tanks being a surrendering unit. So I was sent out with the Qataris. I drove up to the Qatari commander, who was all excited. They already had a platoon of tanks and some antiarmor weapons up forward. We took off along the road to get there. We got to the first checkpoint and the news changed. The Iraqis had turned their turrets back around and were engaging the Saudis. The Saudis are trying to destroy them, and they were not having an easy time doing it.

I stayed with the Qataris until we reached a checkpoint where we had some troops and some heavy machine guns. I was told to see Mr. Quinn. Mr. Quinn was a strange egg. He had a Chevrolet Blazer with about a million dollars worth of communications gear in it. I am sure he could have told me who he was could he have killed me after. He was that kind of guy. Whether he was a mercenary employed by the Saudis, CIA, or whatever, it didn't matter to me. The guy had a lot of control over the Saudi unit that was there.

Captain Joseph Molofsky, Liaison to the Saudi Brigade

Quinn was a member of the Dinnel Corporation. They had been big in Vietnam. Now they are a civilian contactor that advises the Saudi Arabian National Guard. They are mostly retired U.S. Special Forces types. Quinn was a retired Special Forces colonel and had been there for a couple of years.

He had a relationship with the Office of Program Management for the modernization of the Saudi national guard, an active-duty Army organization which also advises the Saudis. They work for an active-duty major general. Who Quinn really works for I am not sure. In any case, Colonel Quinn and I lived together out there at the brigade headquarters. He was Colonel Turki's advisor, and I was Turki's liaison with the 3rd Marines.

I lived with him for several months. Just before the war started, he went back to the States. When he returned he brought enough high-speed communications gear in his vehicle to talk to Washington. He was an interesting guy. He had three tours in Vietnam, Ranger, and Special Forces. A pretty interesting character and an eccentric wild ass.

Captain Sam Jammal, CO, H&S Co

We thought it was going to be a surrender, so there was only me, my Humvee driver, and the assistant S4, Lieutenant Schooner. Schooner was a hard-charging son of a bitch who wanted to come along and witness the surrender. He wanted to see POWs. Everybody got kind of excited.

Major Craig Huddleston, Battalion XO

We were put on alert. It looked like several Iraqi divisions were crossing the border and invading Saudi Arabia. I cannot overestimate the value of those first ten days or so when we understood that we weren't all going to die when they shot at us. We learned that we could function, no matter what the situation was. It was a much different battalion by the end of January, after two weeks of being shot at. When the word came down that the Iraqis had penetrated Saudi Arabia, it took us about one and a half hours to deploy forces to backstop the Saudis again. That's when the battle of Khafji started.

Captain Joseph Molofsky, Liaison to the Saudi Brigade

The Saudis hauled ass out of Khafji during the night. The only people that were there—they'd evacuated the city of civilians a couple of weeks earlier— were Saudi marines, and they ran like hell. They got in their little Toyota machine-gun-mounted trucks and got the hell out.

So the Iraqis occupied the city. There were two six-man reconnaissance teams from the 3rd Marines that were occupying OPs inside the city. They get woke up in the middle of the night and they see Iraqi APCs going down the street, so their orders are to stand pat and report what's happening.

While this is going on, I'm back at division headquarters and get ordered to go back up and find out what the hell is going on. So I go up there and check in with Colonel Turki. He's running around like he's lost his mind. The Saudi officers are putting on their gas masks and then taking them off. Everyone is in a high state of agitation. I figured nothing was going to be found out there, so I get in my vehicle and link up with an ANGLICO team that's northwest of the city, where the Qataris are involved in a tank engagement with Saudi armor.

I found a Qatari tank broke down on the road on the outskirts of the city. I got the crewmen off the tank, and one tells me that the tank's broke and there are Iraqis in the city. He doesn't know what to do, so I put him in my vehicle and we go find the Saudis. This was about 0800.

I think the Iraqis must have entered the city around 0100 or 0200 in the morning of January 29th. Several hours later I'm up there with a bunch of Qatars, the ANGLICO team, and the commander of the Qatars is in his Land Rover roaming all around the desert at sixty miles an hour. He's got all the windows down. The staff's in there and they're screaming at the top of their lungs, "Do this! Do that!" Just riding back and forth. There are tanks burning in the background. I walk up to this group of Arabs and asked them what was going on. I asked them what was going on and found that they were all Iraqi prisoners—the first I'd seen.

I called on the satcom radio and I'm trying to report what's going on. This Iraqi APC comes up over the hill about a thousand meters away, and everybody just goes bananas, jumps in the vehicles. Tanks are roaring, APCs are going, and I've got satcom out in the sand trying to get communications up. This enemy APC starts coming toward us. Our guys throw the Iraqi prisoners in the back of this pickup truck and they hightail.

This was the first Iraqi APC that I'd seen. The driver and me have the satcom radio, which has got crypto attached to it, which is something that can't be compromised. We jump in the vehicle and we're running like crazy too.

The vehicle with the Iraqi prisoners in it comes under fire from a small group of buildings. The fire flattens the tires, so the prisoners jump out with this sixteen-year-old Saudi kid with a rifle guarding them. We go past and they're yelling, "Pick me up, pick me up." I said, "Later, Bub," and kept on going, because I couldn't take a chance on compromising the crypto. I never saw them again, and I think the Iraqi APC stopped them.

We fell back to the battalion, which was on a stream just south of the border. They have reports of an Iraqi brigade massing to cross the border. So I report that back to division and to Colonel Admire and decide that I need to get back to the Saudi headquarters.

Major Craig Huddleston, Battalion XO

Colonel Garrett has always been real good about reconning. If we had the time, we went up and did the reconnaissance. All of the key staff members and company commanders had been in and out of Khafji several times. We anticipated it might be either an area we'll have to go through in the attack, or we may have to fight through it, so let's go up and look at it. We were pretty familiar with the layout of the city.

When it became clear that the Iraqis had in fact invested Khafji, it didn't shock us too much. First, it wasn't occupied. Secondly, we had about a thirty-click buffer that allowed for all sorts of things. They penetrated some Saudi forces, but the Saudi forces stayed pretty much on the border. What we believed was that about a reinforced battalion had entered Khafji and was surrounded as soon as they were in there.

Colonel John Admire, CO, Task Force Taro

Prior to sunset on the day the Iraqis captured Khafji, we conferred with the Arab coalition force leaders to develop plans for a counterattack. We advised Colonel Turki, the Saudi brigade commander, and the Qatari commanders of proposed actions. We explained that two of our reconnaissance teams had remained in Khafji to continue their intelligence collection and to engage the Iraqis with artillery fire and air strikes. We told them that the Marine teams could remain undetected for thirty-six to forty-eight hours, after which their positions would be compromised or jeopardized.

Personally and professionally, the battle of Khafji was one of the most difficult decisions I've ever had to make. As a leader of Marines, one waits for the opportunity to execute a major counterattack, to recapture an enemy-seized objective, to validate months of arduous training and preparation. I believed in my Marines. I was confident of their capabilities. But it was also an opportunity for us Americans to demonstrate our trust and confidence in the Arab coalition forces.

Therefore, with General Myatt's concurrence and support, we deferred to the Arab forces. We encouraged them to be the main attack and accepted the secondary role as the supporting force. Khafji was in the Arab area of operations, and for us to have preempted them with an American-dominated attack would have been counterproductive to the four months of cross-training we had accomplished with the Arab forces.

Task Force Taro planning, then, focused on the Saudi and Qatari forces conducting the main attack and mechanized forces. American Marines would support the assault with antiarmor weapons systems and infantry security forces. More importantly, we would also provide the supporting arms fire—artillery as well as the critical air support.

The plan agreed to, Colonel Turki proclaimed two of the most important words of the war. Although political and military factors contributed to the counterattack decision, we sensed Colonel Turki's respect and concern for the recovery and the safety of the Marine recon teams when he very directly and simply stated, "We attack."

Major Craig Huddleston, Battalion XO

There were a couple of things that complicated our decision. Right away we found out that a U.S. force was not going to liberate a Saudi town. The Saudis would liberate Khafji and we would help. Then there was the question of when we were going to do it. Should we let the Iraqis just stay in there and let them die on the vine and keep shelling them, or do we go right away? Finally, would our ground war commence with the counterattack? Right away the first consideration was solved. The Saudis were going to attack, and the Marines would provide fire support, direct fire support with heavy weapons, and assist in planning. It would be a combined attack.

Captain Leon Pappa, CO, Kilo Company

We first thought that we would attack Khafji ourselves. We were prepared to go into Khafji at night with all three companies. We looked at maps and discussed areas of responsibility. I was most familiar with Khafji. I had taken a patrol all the way up to the northern part of the city two or three nights before the Iraqis attacked.

Captain Mike McCusker, CO, India Company

When the Iraqis attacked the city we went on 100 percent alert. The colonel called and I went to the CP. Kevin Scott, who had Lima Company, and I were to take our companies up there and attack back into Khafji with the Qataris. So Kevin and I came up with a plan.

Captain Kevin Scott, CO, Lima Company

Mike McCusker's India Company and Leon Pappa's Kilo Company were forward. The company commanders were called into the CP and told about the recon teams inside the city. We were to go in and get them, and we were to use two companies. They decided to not use Leon, because he was protecting the road, the major high-speed approach, and he had the capabilities to engage armor and protect the road. So Mike and I got the warning order to prepare to do an entry into Khafji. We were supposed to go at night. Mike and I looked at each other and thought, *Oh, boy, here we go.*

It appeared that we would have to cross a bridge on the western side of Khafji to get into the city. The information we had said the city was very fragmented. The alleys weren't American-style. They'd go off in one direction, and then they'd turn. There would be a little house, and then there'd be another alleyway and then the street. There were all kinds of alleyways, passageways, and streets.

It would be difficult to coordinate boundaries between Companies I and L inside the city, let alone across the bridge. We didn't know what kind of defenses they had. So we talked about it—how we would set the city up, which way he would go and which way I would go, and what we would do when we got our initial foothold. We decided that Company L would come in and take the western side, and Mike would take the eastern side with Company I and go to the east and secure that. We wanted to wait until morning came to give us time to do a visual reconnaissance of the urban terrain. I went back to the company after the warning order and started preparing as best we could.

Captain Mike McCusker, CO, India Company

We had all the ammo, the whole nine yards, for the attack. We were ready to go. This was a big thing because it was MOUT [Mechanized Operations in Urban Terrain], and you know how difficult MOUT is. There could be a lot of casualties. As much as you didn't want to lose anyone, you knew you were going to lose *someone* to the war. You didn't really want to lose them to a city that belonged to the Saudis.

Captain Kevin Scott, CO, Lima Company

Sometime later we were called back and told we were not going to go.

Captain Mike McCusker, CO, India Company

The Qataris impressed me. I worked with one of their tank units and we did cross-training with them. They drove over our bunkers to test them. They had a good attitude and wanted to kill the enemy. They were there for a reason.

We had dinner with them one night—ate lamb and rice and sat on the ground. Sam Jammal took us over. We had a real nice time and learned some of their customs; we did it all that night. It was really good, and we felt together as a fighting force. We knew that we might have to fight along with them, and it was fine with us and fine with them. I was impressed with them.

I wasn't that impressed with the Saudis. We'd gone out to a training practice with them, and we'd trained them with one of our platoons. Lieutenant Schaeffer trained the Saudis and did a real good job of it. He said they were motivated and wanted to do a good job but their experience level was very minimal. That was the Saudi marines. The Saudi army used to drive by, and I was more worried about *them* shooting me because they didn't know who I was or because they were too scared. It is sad to say, but we called them the "speed bumps," because all we thought they would do was slow the Iraqis down.

But the big reason we didn't go and take Khafji was because it was decided

✻ that it was their city and they should take it. We assisted with TOWs and other fire support and planning.

Major Craig Huddleston, Battalion XO

Colonel Garrett took his CP group as far forward as he could get it, and they ended up having to displace about four times as a result of enemy fire. But they stayed in there and made coordination with the Saudis for a night attack. The Saudis put it off at first and decided not to go. We felt secure because the two recon teams were reporting everything the Iraqis were doing.

1st Sergeant Wylie McIntosh, Weapons Company

I was sitting there in the COC listening to the jabber come over the radio—you know how things get garbled—and we got this report. We got about five different stories and couldn't put anything together. Colonel Garrett's group called in and said they were taking enemy rounds, and then the radio went dead. I assumed the colonel in his Hummer had been wiped out, because that's where his radio was. They came back on the air in a while, and we found the incoming wasn't directly on them. They took a few .50-caliber rounds that didn't do any damage. They had some heavy guns with them and silenced a sniper up in a tower. They were the only Marines actually putting out some rounds that night.

Colonel John Garrett, Battalion CO

To complicate matters, we had two recon teams that were tied in with Rick Barry's guys. We believed they were in reasonably good shape and didn't require an emergency extract yet. We wanted to make sure that if the Arab forces attacked they would not interfere, compromise, or injure our Marines that were still in the town. So I went up the road to see what I could do to find the Qataris who were left.

Colonel Admire was on the scene, and we started talking about the attack. We concluded that we should try to help the Saudis if they were going to make this attack—to provide some supporting arms and command-and-control communications and be there so our recon teams would be okay as the attack progresses. Colonel Admire thought that Bob Blose, who commanded 2/3 and was further up the road at a filling station, at Checkpoint 67, about two or three clicks south of the city, would get involved too. He told me to stay there and to coordinate with one of the Saudi battalions. He would go up and tell Bob Blose to go with whatever Arab battalion was going to be the point, attacking into the city, since he had some folks up there anyway. So off he went.

I told my fire support coordinator to go back and get the rest of my forward command group. Meanwhile my S3, Major Stansbury, and I stayed to look for this Saudi battalion that we were going to go with.

About that time a U.S. Army lieutenant colonel comes rolling up, and he had some Saudis with him. He said that he was bringing a battalion up, that he was an advisor. He said he needed intel. He appeared to be sort of a loose cannon. He was running around, not really knowing exactly what he was doing or why. It appeared to me that they were going to launch some attack here shortly, and he was going to be right in the middle of it.

I told him that I really didn't have any intel and told him what I knew about Khafji and what our recon teams had been able to gather. Other than that, nobody was quite sure of the magnitude of the Iraqi force and what their intentions were. So he bounced off down the road, and I thought to myself that I was glad I didn't have to have anything more to do with him that day.

15 / With the Recon Teams in the City

Two recon teams were in the city when the Iraqis attacked. Corporal Alan Uskoski was with one of them, and Corporal Patrick Sterling was with the other.

Corporal Allen Uskoski, Recon Team Member

We got our order to go in and had picked a house the time before. We knew which one to go into and thought we could get in without anyone seeing us. There was hardly anyone in the city. We didn't see anyone in any of the houses or anything, and everything was fine. We were expecting to stay in there maybe two or three days. We ended up staying a couple of days longer than that.

We'd gotten resupplied with batteries. Why we got so many batteries as we did, I don't know, but it's a lucky thing we did. We talked to our headquarters on the radio. They gave us a street and street number. They told us that there were three garbage cans on this road and the batteries would be in the second yellow garbage can, in an MRE box. We went and checked and brought them back. At the same time, we got water because we were out of water. That was a good thing too, because we didn't go in with supplies to stay long. Everything was okay. Each night there would be rockets shot up, and we'd get the azimuth of where they came from and try to figure out the distance so we could tell headquarters.

Most of us were sleeping when the Iraqis attacked. At least one or two guys were up that night, and I came by waking everybody up. "Hey, get up, they're raiding the city."

We didn't know if they were enemy or friendly yet. That night, we'd heard the sounds of a big firefight in the very northern section of the city. We kept calling the rear and telling them that we needed air and artillery. They already had missions written up. We looked at our maps, figured out the grid square, and drew up the missions. We were sitting there watching it. I'd keep telling them that we needed air and artillery, and they kept asking me if we had a definite ID. We didn't have a definite ID, because it was dark.

The Saudis were shooting and the Iraqis were shooting. Our platoon commander wanted to pull us out that night, but the colonel said, "No, stay, we need them there." So the platoon commander got on the radio and told us we could pull out at our own discretion. We didn't think we were in any danger yet. That's when we bedded down with two guys on watch. In the morning we were woke up with "Hey, they're in the city." The Saudis were retreating, and it was the Iraqis.

They did have uniforms but not uniformity. Some were wearing big heavy coats, some weren't. Some were wearing combat boots, some weren't. Some of them were wearing hats. Some of them had beards. Some had long hair. Some you could see with no weapons.

We got on the air and started hollering for fire support. We asked for air and for artillery. We told them that we had a definite ID and they were Iraqis. They told us to lay low and asked if we could evade and escape. We told them no.

Our team leader got on the radio and screamed for artillery until he got it. He got it and told them to fire for effect. We spotted movement up in front of us too, and we called artillery on that because we had definite ID. We could see it hit. I don't know how many rounds from our first strike hit. We had just moved up on the rooftop and were looking around this wall. Then we saw rockets coming over our head and we ducked. We found out it was from friendlies. They fired rockets over our heads and they starting hitting. After the first strike we didn't get anymore artillery. Our radio was screwed up. We were trying to get it working. We got two adjust rounds and then communications broke down and we lost communications and couldn't get anymore rounds.

We were looking over the city. There was one built-up road that stretched across it. There were trucks, and that's where the Iraqi APCs had come down. The trucks stopped by a water tank, and that's when we started calling artillery on them. The troops were walking along the road up there. You could see them walking, and that's what we were trying to fire on.

The Iraqis were passing on the road two blocks away. They were piled on APCs, just like a hayride. They started disembarking from their APCs and scattering around. They were a lot closer to us when they started disembarking. A few of them might have been patrolling, but most were standing around. We kept observing, but we couldn't get good radio contact. Our 104 [portable radio for talking to aircraft] was what was reaching out in the distance, and we'd get broken-up communications now and then. It would come in and then go out.

Corporal Patrick Sterling, Recon Team Member

We were inserted by vehicle at approximately two hundred meters from the first building we went into. They dropped us off and we stayed there for the night. Before light we moved to another building about two hundred meters to the south.

There were two of us on watch. Me and my radio operator started getting messages about troops massing on the border and moving south. We looked at each other and discussed whether to wake our team leader. We decided not to, because we were always getting messages like that but nothing really happened. The same time this was going on, artillery was flying overhead. You could hear it going by to our east. We were thinking that before Iraqis went into a city they would use artillery. We were watching the horizon and checking things out. We got a message saying that they were already across the border and they're coming down the road towards us.

We woke the team leader. He said, "Okay, yeah, yeah," and went back to sleep. Then we saw red flares going up on the horizon, which was our signal that there's danger. Something was wrong. Maybe they were coming down. Then we heard the rifle fire, the firefight. We saw the tracers shooting up in the air, people firing. When I was looking past the edge of the building, it seemed like the Saudis were just driving south and firing at nothing in particular. I saw one vehicle with people piled on top of it firing into the air. They weren't firing at anybody. This was the Saudis leaving the city. When we saw that, we figured the Iraqis were actually coming through the city. We told everyone they were coming and that the Saudis had left.

Army Special Forces and some SEALS were up there. They had these black jeeps, and the next thing we saw was them leaving. They left early in the morning. When we saw the deuce-and-a-half trucks they used to move their gear leaving, we knew they were running.

So we were up there by ourselves. There wasn't anybody else in town. That morning when the Iraqis started coming in, they came down the MSR. Our building was right next to the road. You could tell they were Iraqis, because they looked different. There was something about them. They looked ragtag and were lollygagging around, and they had Iraqi vehicles.

The first few were on trucks. They'd drive around and people would pile on the truck. Not all of them had weapons. Some of them had these big coats, the beards, the long hair, no hats. They had to be Iraqi, because there was no one else up there.

They turned at this intersection and stopped right in the middle of the road. They didn't take cover or anything like that. They had a few civilian vehicles, small four-door Japanese vehicles. They had dark green uniforms and white turbans. They were going into buildings. I don't know if they were stashing ammunition or taking things out of the buildings. They went into these buildings and came out and put stuff in the trucks and left.

Then more vehicles started coming down, tanks and stuff. That's when we started to call in artillery. We were all up on the rooftop, and we knew that the artillery we called was a "danger close" mission. This meant we were in danger from the effects of the artillery. There was something that looked like a shack on the roof, but it was actually a cover for the stairwell that went down. We took cover inside there and called in the artillery. We called it in on the road intersection where we had the exact grid, so they didn't have to adjust. We called for a fire for effect.

All the way down the stairwell were tinted windows, so we were able to view north while still taking cover. They warned us that the artillery was going to be coming in and told us to take cover until the mission was over.

I was looking out the windows, and out of the corner of my eye I could see out of the door up in the sky. I could see the DPICM.[1] I saw them and thought, *Oh, no, they're too high*. But it was just the airbursts I saw, and that they were still going to bounce down and then explode again. I immediately looked down at the tanks. There were still people walking around down there. They didn't know anything. They were still sitting in the tanks. I looked at the ground and you could see little puffs, and then everything was just a cloud of smoke, of dust. Everything was covered about ten feet into the air. The road was all smoke. You couldn't see anything. It was devastating. You'd feel the force of the blast, and the adrenaline's going because you're looking right at the enemy. You never know if he'll see you. It was a constant adrenaline flow.

When all the dust cleared, there was nothing. There was nothing but two Iraqi 531 APCs in the street. There were no dead bodies. There was no blood. There was nothing in the streets at all. Then all of a sudden these two Iraqis come running down the street. They each jump into a separate 531, start them up, spin them around like they're really scared, and went back north.

After a while the Iraqis moved back south again into a building. We called in Cobras [helicopter gunships]. They couldn't come any closer than two thousand meters, so we had to guide them in. We were trying to tell them to come in closer, but they wouldn't do it, because they didn't want to put themselves in danger. They were firing at the buildings where the Iraqis were. The TOW missiles would hit, and you'd see the roof of the building fly fifty feet into the air. That was a good feeling, because we were so alone. The Cobras didn't have that great effect, because they were too far away.

After we called the Cobras in, we called some Harriers. They did a few strafing runs and some bombing missions across the street and down maybe two hundred meters. When the Harriers came screaming in, we didn't know if they were coming in on top of us or next to us. They didn't really hit the target. If they'd been much closer to us, we'd have been dust. The RTO [radio telephone operator] and I happened to be looking out of this one window that had no glass in it when the first bomb hit. There it was, but we felt it rather than saw it. It blew dirt and debris in our faces. My eyeballs must have been huge. And then the second one hit close to the same spot.

Then we got the word that 2/3 or 3/3 was preparing to come get us out, so we thought we wouldn't be there much longer. We waited and waited. When it started to get dark, they told us again that the Marines are going to come up and get us out, but they never came. What finally came was Qataris and Saudis. I didn't know what a lot of their vehicles were. A lot of APCs came, Saudi APCs. We were telling them that we were all right. They had 50s [.50-caliber guns] and TOWs. There were a lot of them, and they just kept coming and coming.

Corporal David Bush, S3 Driver

The recon teams were adjusting artillery on a group of about ten or fifteen Iraqi APCs. The teams were whispering on the radio: "We've got Iraqi APCs and we have to be quiet, really quiet." They adjusted artillery—about sixty rounds fell on top of them and the Iraqis scattered. After a few minutes, the recon guys whispered, "They're coming back. They're going through the buildings." They were trying to find out who was adjusting artillery on them, because nobody could see anything from outside the city.

1st Sergeant Wylie McIntosh, Weapons Company

Listening over the radio, I didn't think we'd see them [the recon teams] again. It sounded like the Iraqis were walking into the building on them at their last transmission. I figured we'd lost them. They had been giving us some good information. They did a fine job spotting, putting in some artillery, killing some Iraqi tanks, some APCs. Over the radio they sounded calm and like they knew what they were doing. I was really impressed with them, and I never met them.

Major Craig Huddleston, Battalion XO

They were well hidden. They felt pretty secure and they were able to report. Colonel Garrett brought his CP group back and decided to send me forward to solve things, or at least see what was going on. I decided to go up without a CP group, just with some communications assets that allowed me to talk back to the battalion headquarters, and also to deliver hot chow to the Marines up there.

We had hot chow every day up until we invaded Kuwait. I think this was great. These Marines were out there on the line taking incoming artillery, rockets, and some direct fire all night. The weather was cold, windy, and rainy, and the sun comes up, and here come the sergeant major and the XO with eggs and bacon and hot biscuits and coffee. Our cooks and mess men put up with the same alerts, the same defensive measures. They got rocketed and everything just like the rest of us did, and they kept on cooking. Man, they were great Marines.

While we were up there, we went around and saw everybody. The TOW platoon commander told me that he had a problem with one of his two-vehicle teams. He sent them forward and they hadn't come back yet. And he couldn't talk to them on the radio. I said, "Geez, I hope they didn't get lost up in Khafji. We'd better go find them."

So we went off with about four or five vehicles, heavy gun vehicles, my vehicle and the platoon commander, trying to find these guys. We went all the way up to the southern gates of Khafji; sitting in the middle of the road was a Qatari tank. They were blocking. They were the first coalition forces south of the town.

We went up and talked to this tank commander, and he spoke English. He said, "No. I haven't seen anybody. They haven't come by me. Everything's going pretty well. We're taking some fire, but it's nothing to worry about. Just small arms occasionally. The Iraqis are sniping at us." He said, "It's not a big deal. They haven't hit us yet. They've taken a few rounds off the tank, but we're just waiting for a target." So we decided, "Let's get out of here." So we took off and went back. We eventually found the TOW platoon guys. In the meanwhile, two batteries of 1/12 were in position behind us, and they were firing into Khafji while this was going on.

Captain Mark Davis, S-4

The Marines up there needed fuel. We took a refueler and went up the road. As we drove up this road, it was getting darker and darker. There's nobody at the Saudi checkpoint. We drive a little further and saw these Toyota pickup trucks with .50-cals mounted on the back of them. We go back two or three miles down the road. We can't find 3/3 anywhere. The bad guys are in Khafji.

We found out where 2/3 has got a heavy machine gun section there. We asked the question, "Where the fuck is everybody?" They asked how far we'd gone, and I told them three or four miles, maybe five. "Shit, sir, we got word that the Iraqis had captured a bunch of four-wheel-drive Toyotas from the Saudis, and now they're driving down the road and firing people up." *Holy shit. What am I doing? How stupid can you be?*

As we were there waiting, I didn't know that Bravo and Charlie batteries of 1/12 were laid out. They cut loose and I hit the deck. Everybody else knew that those guys were there. "Hey, sir, you're new around here, ain't you?" About thirty seconds later the artillery unloads again, and this time they all hit the deck. I went, "Hey, you guys are new around here, ain't you?"

Major Craig Huddleston, Battalion XO

So the scene is, we had some outposts scattered across the desert south of Khafji, we just had a hot meal, our artillery was firing, the Iraqis were returning some small arms fire and an occasional four or five rounds of mortar fire. It was relatively quiet, and the Marines were up there taking it like it was just another day at the office. They were under cover, they were ready to fire, and they were anything but nervous. I hesitated to say they were battle-hardened veterans, but it was going to take something to scare them. There were rounds laying all around us. Artillery was shooting behind us. We'd hear an occasional small arms crack overhead.

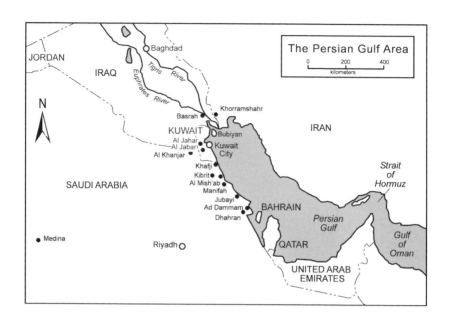

Another day begins. Painting by Charles Grow. USMC Art Collection.

Left, Captain Mike McCusker, CO, India Company, with Captain Joe Fack,
Forward Air Controller. Just inside Kuwait. Courtesy of Joe Fack.

Lieutenant Ivan Wray, Artillery
Forward Observer with India
Company 3/3. Courtesy of
Ivan Wray.

Christmas in Kuwait. Sergeant Major Bo Pippin as Santa Claus. Courtesy of
Bo Pippin.

Colonel John Admire meets General Colin Powell. Courtesy of John
Admire.

Captain Kevin Scott, CO, Lima Company. Courtesy of Kevin Scott.

Captain Joe Molofsky, third from right, standing, and some of his Arab trainees. Courtesy of Joe Molofsky.

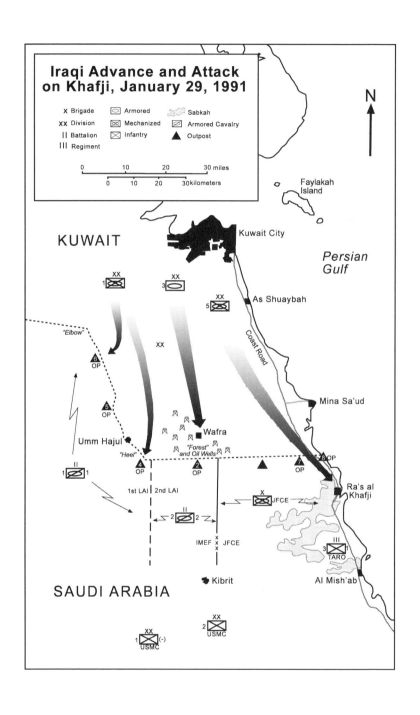

Iraqi Advance and Attack on Khafji, January 29, 1991

X Brigade
XX Division
II Battalion
III Regiment

Armored
Mechanized
Infantry

Sabkah
Armored Cavalry
Outpost

0   10   20   30 miles
0   10   20   30 kilometers

N

KUWAIT

Persian Gulf

Kuwait City

Faylakah Island

As Shuaybah

"Elbow"

Coast Road

6 OP

5 OP

Umm Hajul

"Heel"

Wafra

"Forest" and Oil Wells

Mina Sa'ud

OP

OP

1 II 1

1st LAI 2nd LAI

OP

2 II 2

IMEF JFCE

Kibrit

SAUDI ARABIA

8 OP

OP

Ra's al Khafji

X JFCE

III
3   1
TARO

Al Mish'ab

2 XX USMC

1 XX (-) USMC

Sergeant Major Bo Pippin briefs the company first sergeants the night before the breach. Courtesy of Bo Pippin.

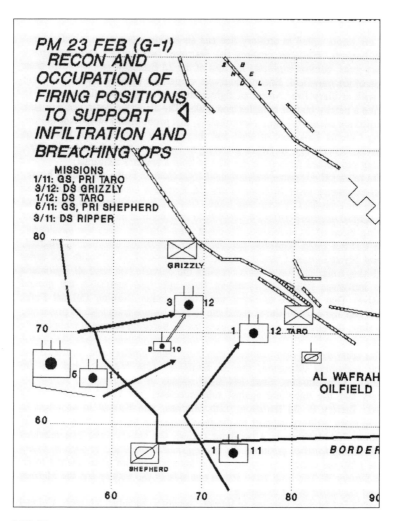

USMC map.

Lieutenant Colonel John Garrett with abandoned Iraqi vehicle. Courtesy of John Garrett.

Hawaii homecoming. Courtesy of John Garrett.

Hawaii homecoming. Courtesy of John Garrett.

Colonel Garrett hands over the colors, passing command of 3/3 to his successor, Lieutenant Colonel Golding. Photo by author.

16 / Melissa and Friends

Colonel John Garrett, Battalion Commander

This was the same day those two soldiers got captured. Craig Huddleston, the XO, went on a rescue attempt, which went in with Humvees and heavy guns, and they ran into Iraqis, screeched to a halt, and spun around. The Iraqis were probably doing the same thing. My guys got out and called in the Cobras, which killed the Iraqis.

Captain Joe Fack, FAC

On about the twenty-third of January I got chopped to TOWs to make sure that the road was secure. They had a position where they put a depth charge on the road right where two *sapkhas* came into the road. A *sapkha* is kind of a muddy swampy area, which was generally impassable for vehicles. The charge in the road could be detonated remotely, cratering the road and slowing down an attempted mounted attack through this position. There used to be a Saudi checkpoint on this road, but once the Iraqis attacked, the Saudis got out of there.

This was at a place called Battle Position 20, which was right south of the Saudi border. I was with TOWs and Captain Borth, the TOW commander. I was with him when Melissa [Rathbun-Nealy], the woman soldier, and a guy named [David] Lockett were captured in Khafji. They got lost. They'd come down from Abu Kadre, where the road goes straight into Khafji. They were supposed to turn west, but they kept going north. They had two semitrucks that had just come out of rework, and they were supposed to deliver them to the Army up here somewhere. One of them came back to our battle position. They didn't know where they were and didn't have a map. I asked them if they knew where they were, and they said no, they didn't know. I asked them if they'd ever heard of Khafji. They said that they had heard about it on the radio. I told them that the town they were in was Khafji.

Major Craig Huddleston, Battalion XO

We were trading shots back and forth, nothing major, when I got a panicky call from a platoon commander who told me that a very large Army truck just showed up at their position and it was shot full of holes. The soldiers were okay but badly shaken up. The problem was that their buddies were in another truck that was still in Khafji. They didn't wait for them, because they were getting shot at, and the other truck appeared to be stuck, so they didn't try to rescue them. They just left. I said, "Well, we better go and get them."

Captain Joe Fack, FAC

Major Huddleston turned to me and told me what had happened. The other truck went up to the arches at the entrance to Khafji and got shot at with small arms fire. I believe Lockett was driving. He panicked and tried to wheel the truck around and hit a cement wall and got stuck. When we got up there a half hour later, the rear wheels were still turning at full force.

Major Craig Huddleston, Battalion XO

I tried to call battalion but for some reason couldn't reach them, but I did reach regiment. I told them the situation—that we had two MIAs in Khafji, two soldiers in big trouble. We didn't know what they were doing, but they took some fire and one truck got out, but the other was still up there. I was looking at my options. About that time Captain Jammal called me and told me that one of the soldiers was a woman. That's what put me over the edge. I thought, *There's a woman up there. We can't allow her to be captured.* I just wasn't going to let that happen. The sergeant major was in the vehicle with me. I told him that I thought we had to go get them and asked what he thought. He said we didn't have any choice. I called the platoon commander and told him to organize a TRAP [tactical recovery of aircraft and personnel] and I would be there in ten minutes. I wanted the patrol ready to go. I wanted to be mobile. I wanted to go in and get those folks out, or at least try to find them.

I couldn't talk to the battalion by radio and tell them what I was going to do, and I had strict instructions not to leave our area, but we decided to go. The patrol was organized by the time I got there. Captain Borth had done a great job. He had these guys lined up and ready to go. We had four heavy guns and six TOW vehicles. There was a total of about thirty of us.

From our last manned outpost to where we thought his vehicle was, was about thirty-five hundred meters over the ground. We dropped vehicles off along the way to provide overwatch. As we got up to this last outpost that was manned by 2/3, the battalion commander happened to be there, Lieutenant Colonel Blose, and we told him what was going on and asked him to provide covering fires if we needed it. He said, "Sure, you bet."

We also had a FAC and an FO with us. As we were making this coordination, the FAC, Captain Fack, came up to me and said he'd like to get some Cobras to go with us. *Great idea. Why didn't I think of it?* I told him to do what he could, but we couldn't wait any longer. He called right away, while I briefed the 2/3 folks on what our plan was. It couldn't have been more than three or four minutes before we took off. We raced into town. The last two vehicles, the two that were to go into Khafji, were the platoon commander and the one gun vehicle covered by me. We were going to search the truck and for the two soldiers. I planned to park my vehicle behind a burned-out Qatari tank.

Staff Sergeant Don Gallagher, Platoon Sergeant, Weapons Platoon

We moved up into the gas station area that was a quarter mile outside of Khafji. Captain Fack briefed us on the plan, where we'd take the vehicles and start dropping them off in pairs, to provide cover. Major Huddleston was in one of the last ones. The first one was dropped three hundred meters past the gas station. About every few hundred meters or so we dropped another vehicle. The last covering vehicle dropped, and then the one I was in went in another fifty meters. We were maybe twenty meters from the Army truck when I stopped and got out. It was a big, heavy wrecker truck. It had gone through a cinder block wall, the wheels were still spinning.

In my vehicle there was me, my driver, and the gunner up in the turret.

They covered me with the .50-cal when I jumped out, sprinted to the vehicle, and ran around it. It busted through a wall and there was a big courtyard inside. Buildings surrounded it. I looked in the courtyard and didn't see anything, so I ran to the vehicle. There was loose gear thrown everywhere. There was no blood and no weapons. So I ran around to the other side of the vehicle. All the time I'm yelling, "U.S. Marines! U.S. Marines!" I ran around to the driver side, and there was nothing there either. I was walking along this wall that was about five and a half feet tall when I saw a vehicle move. I thought I better get out of there. The vehicle was sand-colored. Reports were coming in that there was nothing in front of us that was friendly, and it looked like an Iraqi APC, one of the four-wheelers. I couldn't get a really good look at it, but it didn't have a turret on it or anything. All I caught was a glance. I went running back, yelling to my vehicle driver to turn around, that we were leaving. As I came running out, two Cobra gunships showed up. As we wheeled around, I could hear them engaging that vehicle. It all happened so fast.

Captain Joe Fack, FAC

Our mission was to try and get these guys out of there. We didn't know if they were still there or not. At the gas station right up there at Battle Position 67, we told our people what we were going to do. We went up there, and there was a disabled Qatari tank. The tank crew was still there. Before we went up, I called for as many Cobras as I could get. They didn't get there until we were on our way out.

We went past the Qatari tank and got up to the wrecked Army truck, and all of a sudden there were two Iraqi soldiers that came out. One guy came straight out to the middle of the road. I told the gunner that if he shot at us to let him have it. He was fifty meters or less away. Then I saw what I thought was a BTR50 or one of the Chinese-made PRC63s. I identified it as a PRC63, and there were two of them with a lot of Iraqi soldiers dressed in green standing around it in spit-shined boots. I don't think we got shot at. At the moment we saw each other they were as surprised as we were. But they were Iraqis, and we told the guys that if anything happens, shoot them.

Once we got in there, Sergeant Gallagher went to the semi vehicle, went around, and looked in the cab. The soldiers' sleeping bags were still there, but their M-16s were gone and the soldiers were gone. Once Staff Sergeant Gallagher did that, we decided to get the hell out of there. He was screaming "U.S. Marines" at the top of his lungs.

Major Craig Huddleston, Battalion XO

My vehicle pulled in behind a Qatari tank, and I jumped out and I was going to ask their tank commander what he had seen and where the Iraqis were. I went around the tank and looked up to talk to the commander. They were all dead. The tank had been shot and had burned out, and the whole crew was lying out of the hatches, dead. I thought to myself that this was not good, that the Iraqis had heavy weapons up here and we're exposed.

I looked over to where our two vehicles were searching, saw an Iraqi soldier walk around the corner. I don't know why I didn't shoot him. He would have been about a two-hundred-meter shot for me, but I was shocked. It was my first eyeball-to-eyeball look at the enemy. I looked at him, and he saw me and jumped back around the corner of this building. I looked back to where our two search vehicles were, and they were already coming back. They whizzed past me as fast as they could go. I stuck my thumb up and the platoon commander stuck his thumb up as he went past, and I thought that they had the Army soldiers and we could get the hell out of there.

Staff Sergeant Don Gallagher, Platoon Sergeant, Weapons Company

I got together with the captain and he asked what happened. I told him there was nothing there, no blood and from what I could see, no weapons. The personnel just weren't there. I had no idea where they were. He said, "Okay," and they pulled us back.

The vehicles started moving off and I told the other vehicles to follow me. There were some Iraqi vehicles moving into an open field and setting up a 360-degree perimeter. As we were moving out, they fired an RPG [rocket-propelled grenade] at us. We were out of its range, but they were definitely firing at us. I told my gunner that if he came out again, to let him have it. About thirty seconds later, the RPG gunner fired again. My gunner froze and I had to yell at him to get him firing. He let loose a few rounds.

1st Sergeant Wylie McIntosh, Weapons Company

One of the drivers, Lance Corporal Graff, was in his vehicle waiting for Captain Borth to come back when he saw this Sagger [a Soviet-manufactured antiarmor missile] coming. He backed the vehicle up, and the Sagger passed right in front of him. It bounced on the ground right in front of him, came up, and kept right on going. He said, "That's it. I quit. I want to go home." He has made corporal meritoriously since then.

Staff Sergeant Don Gallagher, Platoon Sergeant, Weapons Company

The firefight kept going off and on. It was funny because we'd be behind a Saudi vehicle and there'd just be a hand sticking out and a .50-cal pointing straight into the air. Rounds would be ripping, going nowhere. TOW missiles were bouncing off the ground.

Major Craig Huddleston, Battalion XO

I looked back one more time and I saw a BMP2, an Iraqi infantry fighting vehicle. It was about seventy-five meters away from where we were, and I said, "We've got to get away. We are in no way, shape, or form prepared to fight these guys right now. Let's get out of here."

We re-formed the patrol back at the last checkpoint, where 2/3 was, and that's when I found out that they didn't get the soldiers. They found the vehicle all shot up—no weapons, no bloodstains, and no soldiers. They hollered and hollered. Captain Borth asked me if I had seen the BMPs. I said no, I only saw one. He said there were two of them up there and about two squads of infantry. I asked how close he was to them, and he said about fifty meters. I asked who shot at who. He said that no one shot—they just kind of looked at each other and we ran away.

I told him that we would kill them with the Cobras. We lost radio contact with the Cobras and by waving our arms got them to land. Colonel Blose ran out to the lead helicopter with one of the armor identification books. He pointed at the picture and pointed on his map where they were. The pilot nodded and took off. They killed one of them and missed the other.

We counted heads. All of our Marines were there. We hadn't taken any casualties. The press was there and trying to interview us. I was in a strange situation and didn't realize how emotionally charged up I was. Once I realized that we had failed to get the soldiers, that we'd come close to being wiped out next to the Qatari tank, I got the shakes all over again. All these things were running through my mind. *Did I jeopardize these Marines for no good cause? Did I accomplish anything, or did I fail? Should we try to go back and get these folks?*

About that time Brad Willis from NBC sticks a microphone in my face and starts interviewing me. I told him what I knew, and while I was talking to him I was trying to decide what to do. I decided that we couldn't go back, because the Iraqis had moved significant forces to the southern edge of the town, and if we went in there with anything but armor we were going to have trouble. So we left and I went to the CP, and the colonel relieved me up forward.

That night we watched as the Qataris launched their first attack in the town, ostensibly to rescue the recon Marines but really to try to retake the town. They never really made it into the town. They took enough fire that they felt that they had to back out.

Captain Sam Jammal, CO, H&S Company

We went out beyond our checkpoint to try and find Mr. Quinn. I drove north towards Khafji for about five hundred meters. Then I went west towards what looked like an old storage area, some kind of rock quarry with a structure around it. I was told that Mr. Quinn operated out of there in an underground position. I hate to stereotype it, because he was a Vietnam vet, but he looked like something you'd see in a movie.

He was about fifty and there was nothing funny about him. He wasn't running at the mouth. He wasn't very show-offish. At the same time, he wasn't quiet either. He was proud of how the Saudis ran their attack. We went looking for him, couldn't find him, and went back to the checkpoint and reported that we could not find him. Shooting was still going on. When Major Huddleston came up at that point and he took the unit and went forward, I moved back with the Qatari battalion commander. We hooked up with Colonel Garrett, and Colonel Garret decides he wanted to link up with Mr. Quinn.

Somehow it turned out that we had coordinated support for the attack. I wound up taking the colonel and the forward CP and some heavy machine guns up north towards the gas station and looking for Mr. Quinn. Columns and columns of armored vehicles, which we later learned were the Saudi national guard, were moving up and setting up approximately two to four thousand meters away from the entrance to Khafji.

We found Mr. Quinn. It was a big gathering. In the middle of the night we had a meeting. We found out that the real reason the Saudis were there was to pull out the recon teams which were cut off when the Iraqis entered Khafji and held it.

We're sitting up there in the parking lot, and people are talking. There are two gentlemen who were advisors to the Saudi national guard from the U.S. Army. They were starting to train them.

I talked to one and found out that he felt a little shaky about their capabilities. The willingness to fight was there, but the capability wasn't. He wanted to send the Qatari tanks in. Since I had been educated at the Amphibious Warfare School, I knew there was something wrong with pushing tanks in to establish a foothold in a city. Tanks will get eaten alive in close quarters.

I told the Qatari commander that the tanks would never make it inside the town. I tried to put it humbly, but I was pretty sure you shouldn't go in in a tank. He said he agreed but said that was what the Saudis wanted them to do, to send in his tanks. He asked me to please ask Colonel Garrett, who had more influence with the Saudi commander, to please convince the guy to at least wait until daylight, which I didn't think was a bad idea. My advice was to wait until it's almost daylight, make your movement two thousand meters under the cover of darkness, and when you fight, fight in the daylight. Mechanized operations in urban terrain are very complicated, and these guys did not have the training. We had plenty of training and *we* wouldn't try to do it at night.

Colonel John Garrett, Battalion CO

Meanwhile Quinn roars up in a white Blazer. It looks like something you'd see in Southern California. We had tried to get tan paint for our vehicles so we wouldn't be sky-lined, and here we are, potentially in the first ground action of the war, and our vehicle turned out to be a white Blazer, with white tires.

Anyway, the Blazer stopped and Quinn gets out. He is sort of tall and blond-headed, and I had no idea who he worked for. He looked like a character out of the movie *Air America*. He seemed to know what he was doing, and he had credibility with the Arabs. I told him what my intent was and what Colonel Admire's was, and he said that was okay and he could help me get hooked up. So Dan Stansbury and I get in this Blazer and off we go for his compound. Then he gets a radio call from somewhere up front and said, "Okay," that he knew who we had to see, and took us up to Checkpoint 67.

As it turned out, Bob Blose wasn't there and neither was Colonel Admire, but I was because Quinn had just brought me up. Guess who the guy was he was going to hook me up with. It was the Army lieutenant colonel who had been running around looking for intel. As it turns out, this guy was the advisor with the lead battalion going in to attack Khafji. He came over to me and Quinn pointed us out to each other, and he told us that they were going to attack to rescue our teams. I told him that the teams didn't need rescuing and that we just wanted to coordinate with him because he was going to attack to drive the Iraqis out of Khafji. He said, "No." So I asked him why he was going to attack, and he told me he didn't know. I didn't know either, so I went back to talk to our people.

17 / Khafji Retaken

Colonel John Garrett, Battalion Commander

About this time the recon company commander comes walking over and he said he just talked to the teams and now they need to be rescued. So I agreed to do it. The Saudis show up, and we're just about to start getting our language straight and the Saudi commander said he was going to attack in fifteen minutes. I told him that if he would wait about twenty-five minutes, I could give him some artillery and maybe some air, probably some Cobras. I told him that he had some thin-skinned armored vehicles going up against BMPs. It was getting dark, and I told him we should go for a combined arms agreement. He agreed.

Captain Joseph Molofsky, Liaison to the Saudi Brigade

At that point, a whole bunch of Saudi armor, V150s from the King Abdul Aziz Brigade, come roaring up the road. I asked Colonel Quinn where was their assembly area, and he said that this was it.

The 7th Battalion, King Abdul Aziz Brigade, was ordered to recapture the city and rescue the Marine reconnaissance teams. It is still light, about 1700. Colonel told me to go find Colonel Turki and tell him that we would support his attack. I drove up to the gas station at Checkpoint 67, and I found Colonel Hamid Moktar, who is in command of the 7th Battalion. He had orders to attack the city.

We're all milling around. We've got all these command vehicles in one huge mass, with about forty APCs and the Qatar tank company shows up. Nobody has radios that are inter-operable. There are three languages being spoken. Nobody has any idea what the hell is going on except that Colonel Moktar has been ordered to attack the city immediately.

There is no ANGLICO team either. They're all out on the northwest side of the city getting ready to line up with their respective battalions to fight the Iraqis out there. So we get the FAC from 3/3, a good man named Joe Fack, and a lieutenant artillery FO. The night counterattack on Khafji is planned on the hood of a Humvee in about three languages as it gets dark. The Saudi commander was just going to drive up the road into the city. We talk him into artillery prep.

The American artillery doesn't want to fire unless it's got eyes on the target. You just can't shoot artillery into a city. The discussion goes on and on. The plan changes a bit, attachments get made, and minor coordination is made between the Qatar tanks and the Saudi brigade, but nothing really gets firmed up—just a bunch of guys milling around this huge assembly area in the middle of this open road in direct observation of the city. If one Iraqi could have gotten some indirect tank fire or some artillery, we'd have all been killed. We're standing around and it's getting dark. We are waiting for the artillery prep, which keeps getting put off, and finally Moktar says that if it doesn't happen in ten minutes he is going to attack anyway.

He's got a Special Forces lieutenant colonel with him named [Michael] Taylor, who's assigned as Moktar's advisor. Colonel Taylor, quite frankly, ran the battalion counterattack on Khafji. If he hadn't been there, it would have fallen on me, I suppose, to help the Saudis. Colonel Taylor deserves tremendous recognition.

Moktar said we're leaving in ten minutes, so the artillery FO, Doug Stilwell, called up the artillery and told them to just shoot the damn thing because they're going to attack without it if they don't. So they shot it. At about 2200 the battalion lines up, the tanks go forward to provide cover, the APCs drive into the city. Nice plan, huh?

Major Dan Stansbury, Battalion Operations Officer

At that point the recon team in Khafji controlled the prep. The prep went and the tanks didn't go. They waited about five minutes into the prep. Then when the tanks went, they started shooting from the get-go.

Captain Joseph Molofsky, Liaison to the Saudi Brigade

So we get up there, and it's kind of nerve-wracking. The tanks are on the side of the road, not up where they are supposed to be. We go up there; half the company gets into the city. I am right behind Moktar and Taylor, who are in his vehicle.

Captain Joe Fack, FAC

We never did get past the arches into the city, because when we got up there, I identified, through my peepers at night, ten APCs just sitting there, and we were under fire from these guys—plus there was a sniper up in the tower right on the arches themselves.

Captain Joe Molofsky, Liaison to the Saudi Brigade

We got to the edge of the city. My vehicle gets to the edge of the arches, and we get caught in the counter-mech ambush. We have a main gun, the APC main gun, .50-cal, and we're just sitting in the middle of the road. All this shit is coming straight down the road from the Iraqis. They opened up first.

Initially, the Saudis didn't do a thing. We're sitting in the middle of the road. I told my driver to pull up around the side of the colonel's APC to get a little cover. He finally pulls off the road. We're milling around in a field outside the city, and the whole place just blows up. There was a really intense level of fire. The Saudis still didn't react, until one of them finally opened up and then they all opened up in every direction—up in the air, down in the ground. The truck that the two American soldiers had been captured in earlier was stuck to this concrete wall, with the rear flashers blinking. The TOW gunner next to me fired three missiles at the truck, all of which went over by thirty feet. I told him to stop shooting at the truck, that it was an American truck. The Iraqis didn't open up until half the company had gotten into town. Then they opened up on the rest of the column. The rest of the column pulled up and then moved off to the left-hand side of the road into a big open field and just started milling around and driving in circles.

Major Dan Stansbury, Battalion Operations Officer

It looked like the best Fourth of July you'd ever want to see. There were .50-cal tracers in the air everywhere. The entire sky was lit up with tracers. Also you could see rocket fire. You could see RPG rockets coming out and going towards the vehicles.

From our position, a vantage point right at the gas station, we began to receive friendly fire, .50-cal fire, and either tank fire or some type of rocket fire. About fifteen minutes into the attack I turned to Colonel Garrett and told him it was time to get the hell out of there. We had received friendly fire, and we were starting to receive some type of rocket fire at our position. So we moved back to Checkpoint 20. Our movement back was hurried. I felt we weren't doing the right thing tactically, because we didn't have our Marines up there. We were just advisors with a small security element, and we weren't in control.

Captain Joe Molofsky, Liaison to the Saudi Brigade

There were only a few Americans up there. Most of the 3rd Marines were back at Checkpoint 67, five clicks to the south. We had two heavy gun vehicles for security. We had one vehicle with the reconnaissance relief team, Captain [Dan] Baczkowski, and a couple of his kids, and my vehicle.

Captain Joe Fack, FAC

Our scheme of maneuver was to get in through the town to try to penetrate through the Iraqi force, and then Captain Molofsky, the recon relief team, and myself were going to find the recon guys. That didn't pan out very good, because we never got into the city that night. I talked to their partners—one black guy and one white guy from recon—and they were very concerned with getting those guys out.

Captain Joseph Molofsky, Liaison to the Saudi Brigade

We spent from about 2200 until about 0400, dawn actually, driving around in that field and trying not to get killed. Nobody was in control. The Saudi battalion commander went into shock. He was sitting in his APC staring straight ahead. Colonel Taylor was in his ear trying to get him to do something.

Major Dan Stansbury, Battalion Operations Officer

Colonel Taylor fought the war for Khafji. The Saudis planned, but Colonel Taylor would bump them and say that they needed to do this or that.

Captain Joe Fack, FAC

There was a soccer field that all the Saudi guys went in. First the Qatari guys went up and tried to get into the city and then came back. Then the Saudis went up with their V150s. They had missile launchers and heavy machine gun stuff. They got on that soccer field in a 360-degree perimeter and started shooting at anything that moved. There were three Humvees from 3/3 involved in this. Staff Sergeant Gallagher was in one of them. Staff Sergeant Nugent and Lieutenant Johansen were there also.

We got on the soccer field and these guys started shooting all over the place. We identified an Iraqi machine gun nest, which we started taking fire from. There were also RPGs going off all over the place. One went right for one of the heavy gun vehicles not two feet away. I was in the backseat yelling, "Oh, my God, let's get the fuck out of here." In the vehicle I felt more vulnerable than if I'd been outside and running. Inside, all you could do was sit there.

Captain Joe Molofsky, Liaison to the Saudi Brigade

So we spend from about 2200 until about 0400 in the morning in this field. There were at least four major engagements, but who was shooting at who is unclear. At one point the Qataris, who don't have communications with the Saudis, leave their position parked on the road and go roaring down the highway south and scare the pants off the Marines at Checkpoint 67, who thought it was an Iraqi counterattack. This was around midnight.

The Qatari tanks get oriented and they come roaring back up the road. They mistake us in the field outside the city for Iraqis, and we start taking tank and .50-cal fire from our rear. So the Iraqis are shooting from the front, the Qataris are shooting from the rear, and every one of the Saudi vehicles is firing TOWs and .50-cals. There was total and complete lack of fire discipline; nobody in control. There are Saudi APCs roaming around the city and shooting.

The recon kids get caught in an ambush and pulled off the side of the road. I'm concerned about them now, because they are cut off. They're on the other side of the road in a row of garagelike buildings and are really cut off from us.

Sergeant William liams, Recon Team Leader

I was part of the recon rescue force. I don't know how it happened, but for some reason we ended up in the front of the column. We were with the Qatari tanks. We got to the arches of the town, and the lead Qatari tank took an Iraqi round, which killed it. We pulled off to the right, right outside the arches. In my Humvee were myself; Lance Corporal Bara; Corporal Radcliffe, who was the radioman; and Captain Baczkowski, who was our platoon commander; and a Kuwaiti officer who was along as interpreter. The Kuwaiti was a college guy who'd come back from college and they told him he was an officer. He had a brand-new M-16. He'd never fired it.

As the firefight started, the Saudis were firing indiscriminately at every single building—throwing missiles at buildings. The Iraqis, on the other hand, were very well disciplined with their firepower, their grazing fire. I thought that we were in for a good one. Someone was shooting at Corporal Radcliffe and me. I fired a magazine into a building, and it stopped. There was also a firing position in front of me. I threw a hand grenade into the firing position, and that was silenced. There was a wall, and I looked over it and saw an Iraqi BTR60. The Saudis were firing at it. Captain Baczkowski grabbed a LAAW [light antitank assault weapon], went over to the wall, popped the LAAW open, threw it over the wall, and it wouldn't fire. He forgot to take it off "safe." So he takes it off "safe" and tried to fire it again. It still wouldn't fire. What he'd done was take it off "safe" and put it back on "safe." This was in the heat of battle, and everyone makes those foolish mistakes. He got it off "safe" and shot it at the BTR60 and knocked it out. After that we fired some more rounds, and the Saudis went back to the open field and we were left by ourselves. The Qataris turned around and just left. Captain Baczkowski and I went around and looked inside the BTR60. It was on fire and there were a couple of weapons lying around. Next to that was a vehicle that had a radio inside, and the radio was still on and operating. So we fired up that vehicle with a couple of more rounds.

The building that was there was completely locked up. But someone had taken the air conditioner out of the window and they had used cinder blocks to get inside. I wasn't going to go in and clear that room. Captain Baczkowski wasn't going to go in and clear the room. We didn't know how many

Iraqis were in there, so we both grabbed hand grenades and threw them inside the building. Once the hand grenades went off, the Saudis started firing at us. They thought we were firing on them. At that time the Kuwaiti officer went into shock and started throwing up. He was totally delirious and was pointing his weapon all around. We had to take his weapon away from him and treat him for shock right there.

Captain Joseph Molofsky, Liaison to the Saudi Brigade

Our heavy guns located a couple of targets, shot and suppressed the targets. We take RPG fire; a rocket goes underneath one of the heavy gun vehicles. The Saudis are just depleting all their ammunition. A couple of episodes like that, and the Saudis say they have to have a resupply column—they've used up all their TOW missiles. This is after about two hours. They were shooting straight up into the air, and I am yelling at the gunners to stop shooting in the air.

The relief column comes up the road, but the Saudis didn't put a guide to the entrance to the city. The relief column goes right into the city and it gets ambushed. A truck with forty TOW missiles on it gets its tires shot out. The crews all jump out, and they had eleven missing in action. Nobody knows what happened to them. I still don't know.

At one point, about 0200 I feel like we're really going to get killed. Nobody's in control again. I got tracers that found our vehicles and were actually trying to hit us. We do this little start, stop, start, stop thing. When the tracers stopped, we drove through the area and linked up with the recon team. Then we kind of cooled our heels. Nobody has any idea what the fuck's going on.

Sergeant William Iiams, Recon Team Leader

The Saudis tried one of these last-ditch things. They sent DP105s into the city and they got ambushed. Two vehicles went in, and one came out. We got the word that some Iraqi tanks, T72s and 60s, were heading our way. So Captain Baczkowski and myself grabbed some AT4s [shoulder-fired antitank weapons] and went all the way up to the arches, and we were going to engage them when they came out.

There was still someone who was shooting at us. So we sat there for a little while. I looked at him. He looked at me. I said, "We've got two AT4s each.

Do we really want to engage these tanks?" We decided, "No, let's not. Let's not get into this." So we went back. We got everyone in the vehicle and we took off to where the Saudis were. They got in another humungous firefight.

As we were sitting there, the Qataris came back up the road. They saw all this firing going on, and they engaged the Saudis. The Saudis turned around and engaged them. They were having a complete firefight, and the Americans were saying, "This is ridiculous, let's get out of here."

The Arabs wouldn't cease fire, so we got in our vehicle and took off. The two guys in the back of my vehicle were screaming their heads off. I didn't know why. Someone had fired a missile, and it had a lock on us and was headed this way. Between the missile and us was a chain-link fence. It hit the fence and blew up.

After that, the tracers starting beaming at all the vehicles around us. We were getting a little worried about this whole thing, so we took off. Somehow the Arabs called a cease-fire. They got all the groups there to chill out. It was about three-thirty or four o'clock in the morning by this time. We decided to get out of there and regroup.

Captain Joseph Molofsky, Liaison to the Saudi Brigade

It was pretty chaotic, and I thought sure I was going to get killed. About 0500 the sun's getting ready to come up. The Saudi battalion commander makes a decision that there is nothing to be gained by staying there. So he decides to withdraw to the Saudi national guard compound, about three clicks south of the city.

There is a fence there that runs perpendicular to the road. We get an APC, pull the fence down, and rally back there. I got out of the APC. Nobody's had any sleep, and everyone's kind of nervous. I walk over to the Saudi commander and ask him what he's going to do. He said he was going to attack again in forty-five minutes. At that point, I said, "You've got to be kidding. Give me a break. Attack *what* with *who*? *Why*?" There was no plan at all. They just drove up there.

I drive around the side of the national guard compound, and the Saudis have now all withdrawn and rallied at this point. It looked like a scene out of the 1820s, except that instead of camels there were APCs. The Saudis had all parked together, fender to fender. They'd gotten out of their vehicles and put on their cloaks. They were lying on the ground or sitting around little fires, brewing tea, smoking, and sleeping, just kind of sitting around. It looked like something out of the Civil War. I suppose it never changes. A soldier is a soldier. They were preparing to get back up and do it again. That's what actually happened. The 7th Battalion attacked the west. The 5th Battalion attacked the east. They went through the city that morning and pushed the Iraqis back out. This was from about eight until noon.

Staff Sergeant Don Gallagher, Platoon Sergeant, Weapons Company

That day when we were sitting outside Khafji, just about five minutes before we were ready to go, there was a goat herder, a Bedouin, who had a herd of about 120 goats. The aircraft are bombing, and he's trying to get his flock out of town. He's coming right down the middle of the road through town.

He turned around and was yelling at the planes and then was yelling at us. There was a huge puddle on the side of the road. The goats were all drinking from it. He comes up, drops right down with them, drinks out of the damn puddle, then up and away he goes. I couldn't believe it. I wish I could understand what he was saying.

Major Craig Huddleston, Battalion XO

Colonel Garrett and his folks helped the Saudis and Qataris replan, and at first light they attacked from a different direction, with our support from weapons and artillery, and they carried the town. It was a very successful attack. They killed a couple of hundred Iraqis and captured over five hundred of them and destroyed about forty to forty-five vehicles in the town. I mention that because there was a lot of second-guessing going on, probably at the headquarters level, about these guys having what it takes to launch an attack. Clearly they did. We knew they did. They just didn't know how. The will was there, but they needed some help. They got the help. They got a pretty good preparation fire—about a fifteen-minute artillery prep from 1/12—and they went in there and really kicked ass. They killed a lot of Iraqis. They did a good job of it.

Colonel John Garrett, Battalion CO

And then who shows up but four or five reporters who were lost. We were up there in our vehicles, and they were in a rented gray Honda four-door sedan, just about to drive into the attack. I stopped them and told them to stay with us, so they did.

The artillery prep went down and the Saudis attacked. My guys were with them. We got caught in the crossfire and had to pull back a ways to get out of that. My guys are looking at me and asking me what we were going to do, because we weren't supposed to be there. The only mission I had was verbal. So we pulled back a little ways, and I told them we had to pull back up because we're supporting these guys. We went back to the filling station.

Sergeant William Iiams, Recon Team Leader

The Saudi attack didn't stop for anything. There was just vehicle after vehicle after vehicle. We went with the second wave. They were firing at everything. The Iraqis, after they fired off two or three magazines of stuff, were just throwing down their weapons and giving up. Their own troops were shooting some of them who were trying to surrender on the spot. When they started surrendering in masses is when they didn't shoot them anymore.

At that point is when Corporal [Chuck] Ingraham's team finally had a chance to get away. I was in a Humvee and blew into town with the Iraqis still firing at me. The team was on foot running down the street from their building. I pulled up and they all jumped in. All of the guys were pretty shook up. A couple of them looked like they were ready to cry. They were very relieved to see me. We came back and had a quick debriefing with the Saudi colonel. We told him where the tanks were and everything. Sergeant [Lawrence] Lentz's team didn't get out of there until later on in the afternoon. He came out with the three flat tires. His engine was completely trashed from shrapnel. His team did a really outstanding job and kept their cool—they kept their heads about them. They were in a pretty safe place, a safe house, although they had Iraqis going up and down the streets.

Corporal Allen Uskoski, Recon Team Leader

When our team heard the Saudi attack, we thought it was the 3rd Marines to help us get out. All these rounds started flying all over the place—they were TOW rounds. Once you have heard them, you know exactly what a TOW round sounds like, and you could tell a .50-cal. We were wondering what the heck these guys were doing. The rounds would bounce off the buildings, fly over our heads. We were told to get out the minute the rounds started coming in. Our platoon commander came on the radio and said it was time to E&E [escape and evade], get ready to go.

We opened the gates of the area we were in. The rounds were impacting everywhere out there, just bouncing off everything. We were all of us crouched down next to the Hummers and thinking, *We're supposed to go now? No way in hell.* If we'd gotten in those Hummers and taken off, we'd have all been dead. There was just no way we'd have gotten out of town. Fire was everywhere and TOW rounds were coming by the house.

Then we found out it wasn't the Marines moving in. It was the Saudis. We thought we were going to get out that night, because they said they were going to come and get us out. We were ready to go. Nobody slept that night. We were on top of this roof. That was one of the coldest nights I have ever attempted to sleep through. It was raining and wet. We were on a concrete roof and there were many mosquitoes. Plus there was the thought that we were surrounded. You couldn't really sleep. It was a long night. During the night there were small firefights. The next morning they told us again that they were going to come get us out. The minute the sun started coming up we could hear the Iraqis coming in with massive quantities of those 531s [an Iraqi APC] and a couple of tanks.

We got on our radios up with the roof antenna. We didn't have call signs, because we were in there longer than we were supposed to be. We were just talking on the radio. My team leader was standing there. I was sitting there next to him. He was talking and talking because all we saw was thirteen more APCs and a couple of tanks come in.[1]

Corporal Patrick Sterling

The Iraqis were in the building next to us. When I looked down the spiral stairway, I saw them walking underneath. I thought they were going to come up the stairs, but they just walked underneath. They went to the bottom of the stairs, and they knew we were there because they'd fired at us. We knew they knew we were there. I was imagining that they came to the bottom of the building, then looked at each other and said, "Should we go up there? I don't know, they're Americans. Nah, let's leave." So they left and went away talking. I don't know what happened to them.

Early that morning Corporal William called in another artillery mission, a DPICM. I was watching again out of that back window. Directly to the north, a few rounds hit on a building maybe a hundred meters from us. I thought that that was pretty close. Then, all of a sudden, four or five rounds hit on top of the roof. I saw this concrete flying here and there on our roof. Corporal [Jeffrey] Brown, Corporal Immerman, and Doc Allen were all there next to each other. They ducked down and blew in the door. Corporal Immerman came in first, and then Corporal Brown ran in holding his leg. "I'm hit! I'm hit!" We took a look, and it was like someone shot him with a BB gun or something. It was just a little tear in his cammies. There was no blood or anything. So we told him to put on a bandage or something and didn't think much of it.

Corporal Allen Uskoski, Recon Team Member

They adjusted the firing. They kept hitting all around us. Then they'd move over a little farther and hit right on top of us. There was shrapnel flying through the building. Sergeant Lentz was sitting on the window, looking directly south at the artillery. I was shriveled up in a ball in the corner. I guess I was lucky I was wearing my flak jacket and helmet, because a piece bounced off me. I thought, *What was that?* It was shrapnel. I picked it up and it was hot, so I dropped it. Sergeant Lentz was yelling on the radio, "Check fire, check fire, check fire!"

When we went out we found that we had two flat tires on the Humvee— one on each side. There was a hole in the gas tank and one in the radiator. The house was wiped. There was stuff gone everywhere on the vehicle. Chunks just fell out of it. It scared the shit out of us.

We kept talking on the radio. The best feeling was to know that someone was on the other side of the radio listening to you. About that time we started getting sniper fire from the building next to us, so we had to be especially watchful for the open window then. We couldn't really take a vantage point too close to the window because of a possible sniper. We saw the sniper moving around and popped some shots at him, but I don't think we got him. It was pretty close to E&E time when we fired him up. We weren't going to risk going in there to get one guy.

Right after the artillery happened we all moved inside the building and we dug out everything we had. We had machine gun ammo linked together. We had two AT4s, two LAAWs, and an M-60 machine gun. A squad assault weapon and a grenade launcher. We all had sectors of fire. Everyone was spread out throughout the house. All we did was watch the walls. We thought it was the end. There were tanks going by the house. Rounds flying everywhere. It wasn't safe to step outside.

We could only get communications now and then. We just decided that this is it. A bit earlier that morning, after the artillery hit and after we had no idea if anybody was coming to get us, we didn't know what was going on. We started looking at a map and looked for whether we could do this or that. Could we get a helo? We looked at the map and decided that there was no way we were getting out of there without a fight, so we decided our best bet was to stay right there inside that cement house where we were and just take up positions and fight with all the rounds we had left. So we moved everything up, and we sat there and waited.

Corporal Patrick Sterling, Recon Team Member

We were all up on the rooftop looking at all the holes in the roof and going, "Whoa, check out this shrapnel." We thought we were so lucky that the rounds didn't do more damage than they did. We weren't able to get any battle damage assessment on the enemy. We were all huddled inside the doorway because the rounds hit so close. We weren't able to tell if our rounds hit anything. After that, we moved up on the rooftop and were observing again. Corporal Ingraham had the muzzle on his radio. It looks like the thing that you see pilots wear in the movies. He had to whisper into the radio because they were so close.

Corporal Allen Uskoski, Recon Team Member

The morning when arty [artillery] was called in, our team got the arty on the radio. Corporal Ingraham, on the other team, did the artillery adjustments because he could see the enemy. He was whispering in the radio, and our team was catching it and passing it off because we could talk.

Corporal Patrick Sterling, Recon Team Member

Corporal Brown came running in again. This time he was holding his head. This whole time there's rounds going off. The Qataris got into it now. An occasional TOW missile would hit something. Or some bomb would hit somewhere. They were firing at each other. Corporal Brown was observing over the wall. He was looking down at this vehicle, and they got the

Iraqi tanks down there with their 12.7-millimeter machine guns. Corporal Ingraham was right next to him. Brown was looking over the wall and he says he seen a guy wheel the gun around, point it straight at him, and fire as he went down. The round went through the wall and it sprayed the back of his head with concrete. So that's the second time Brown got hit.

So we knew that they knew we were there. We were thinking that they would be up there any second. We had two claymores on the stairway; one was on the fourth floor, and the next one was on the fifth or sixth floor. We had the clackers [detonating devices] in one hand, grenades in the other. We were waiting for them to come up. That's when we seen them. They were downstairs and were walking around.

I was looking out that window again, and there were four or five tanks out in the middle of the road. Guys were just walking around in the street, sitting on the tanks. All of a sudden, this guy came out. I assume he was an Iraqi officer, because he came out to the middle of the street and started giving directions.

The next thing you know, the tanks are spreading out more, going off to the side. I was watching, and these two Iraqis came from behind this building. We were on top of our building and looking out on the street, and from across the street to our east, two Iraqis came running from behind this building and jumped up on this berm with their rifles.

They were sitting there, about thirty of them. Some of them were walking in the direction of our building. They didn't look like they were coming to get us or anything, but they were coming in our direction. Maybe one or two of them had a weapon. None of them had any deuce gear [field equipment] or anything like that. They were just walking around in the middle of the street or not doing anything. It was like they didn't care who was there or if anyone was going to fire at them or anything. They weren't ready to fight or anything.

Later the Qataris came. They would drive up to the south entrance of the city. They'd draw fire, then they'd turn around and pull back out. I guess that's how they'd find out where the Iraqis were. We were near the south side of the city and we got word that the next time the Qataris came up, we should try to either run out of the city or jump into the vehicles and get right out of there. We dumped all our gear and took only the mission essentials, the radios, the weapons, and the ammo. We left our rucksacks and sleeping bags. We left all this gear in the stairwell and went downstairs because we saw the Qataris coming back up. An APC came up and we had orange air panels, the friendly sign. They came up from about three or four hundred meters south all the way to our building. A Qatari saw us and waved. We started coming towards him, and he waved us back. He wheeled his gun around and fired at this one building across the street. It was like he was telling us there was someone over there and we should go back. Then he turns around to leave. He got maybe two hundred meters down the road and an RPG hit his vehicle. We ran back upstairs to the top of the building. The APC was smoking all day and rounds were going off inside. We thought, *There went our only chance.* We decide that if we're ever going to get out of there, we are going to have to make a run for it. We were three or four hundred meters from where the Qataris were in a safe position. We went back up to the rooftop and called back on the radio and told them that we were going to run out of this place—that we were getting out of there.

Again, we reorganized. We got all our stuff together and psyched each other up. Then we went back downstairs. There was a road that came straight down all the way to where the Qataris were. We just got all our gear, ran downstairs, ran to the west, and then ran all the way down south to where the Qataris were.

Our platoon commander and Sergeant Iiams, the first team leader, came driving up in the Humvee, coming at us at about a hundred miles an hour. We saw Captain Baczkowski, our platoon commander. Finally, we're out of this place! They were telling us to get in, get in. We're getting out of here. So we all piled in the vehicle. There were six of us, and we took off south. We got to where we were going, about a half-hour drive.

When we got there the sergeant major came out and was climbing in the vehicle, and was shaking our hands. Our platoon commander was hugging us. We were saying, "What did we do? What did we do?" Everybody was looking at us like we were heroes or something. We told them that we were just doing our job.

Corporal Allen Uskoski, Recon Team Member

We thought it was the Alamo. We thought it was the last stand. We had the radio going. We heard that there is a column of APCs coming through town. We can't see anybody. It was horrendous. Maybe it was, "This is the one."

This time it was daylight and you could see who it was. It was the Saudis again. There were so many of them. There were four-wheel APCs, TOWs, with large orange panels on them. So we got on the radio and told them, once they came towards the city, that Iraqi tanks and APCs were driving right by the house we were in. We had ATs and LAAWs, but the platoon commander told us to lay as low as we could, not to be firing anybody up.

So we loaded up all our ammo, our weapons. We came around the last corner of the city, observing everything. I've never been so wired in my life as the days we spent doing that.

Sergeant William Iiams, Recon Team Leader

The dangerous thing about the whole battle of Khafji was that there was so much indiscriminate fire that we could have actually killed our own troops. I was scared about that, and Captain Baczkowski was really upset. There was one point where we really thought we were going to lose Corporal Ingraham's team. For a young leader, he kept his head about him. They got all the right stuff. They burned the crypto. They got rid of all their deuce gear. Probably one of the biggest factors, besides Corporal Ingraham, was a guy named Doc Kevin Callahan, their corpsman.[2]

Staff Sergeant Don Gallagher, Platoon Sergeant, Weapons Company

My first combat experience was pretty hairy. I thought it was a major cluster fuck. I understood the Saudis had never been in a major battle but they had a general idea what they wanted to do. Probably to them they did a good job, and I thought they did pretty good. If we had an interpreter, somebody that spoke the language, somebody coordinating, they'd probably have taken the town that night the first time. But they got ambushed and the plan went out the window.

Colonel John Garrett, Battalion Commander

By about 1400 that day we had the recon teams out of the city. The press said the first Saudi attack was botched; it was failure the first night. But the attack was sort of a reconnaissance by fire. The Saudis went back and revised their plan, and they attacked again the next morning. How can you say the attack is a failure until it's over and you evaluate the results? The results were the Saudis had retaken the city and the recon teams had been safely rescued. Both objectives were accomplished. My point is, it's a little discouraging to give the press every benefit and to have them do a sloppy job of reporting. On top of that, they come back later and whine that they didn't have access. They weren't all like that, just a few were, but one or two like that is enough. So, anyway, it was a success. That was our big participation in the battle for Khafji. We had the command group involved, plus heavy machine guns and TOWs.

So far, 3/3 had done two things. We were taking enemy fire before anybody else with those damn rockets, and we had been involved in what we thought was a heavy attack on the Iraqis. The lads had proved themselves well in terms of discipline. The fact that we didn't fire on any friendly vehicles the night they attacked Khafji was pretty damn heroic itself. Of course the other thing we did that nobody else had done at this point in the war was participate in that battle of Khafji, which was the first ground action of the war.

Captain Joseph Molofsky, Liaison to the Saudi Brigade

The significant factor about Khafji, with a couple of other very rare exceptions during the ground war, it was just a slaughter. It was almost murder in some cases. The Saudis just rolled up on the Iraqis and destroyed them. The first night, the outcome was in question. Nobody really knew yet—not General Schwarzkopf, not the Saudi commanding general, not Colonel Admire, not Colonel Turki—nobody really knew how capable the Iraqis were at the operational level. After the first counterattack at night, my feeling was it was going to be one helluva long war, because they whipped our ass.

The Saudis were successful on the second attack, because even though they might be inept and unorganized and not really adept with their equipment, there can be no question about their courage, their decisiveness, and their willingness to die for their country. Without orders, without any good plan, with every indication that they would get killed, they went up there anyway, and some of them drove their APCs right into that ambush again because they were told to do it. For that reason, with my limited experience with them, although I don't really feel comfortable with the Arabs anymore, I'll always respect them, because when push came to shove, they fought and they died well, and I'll never forget it.

I got the figures from the Saudi brigade headquarters afterward. Aside from their decisiveness and their courage, the reason they won at Khafji was because of allied air. The ANGLICO teams had been up there since the beginning of the war, controlled Cobras and Harriers and FA18s, and really destroyed the lion's share—maybe 40, maybe 50 percent—of up to ninety-three Iraqi vehicles that were later reported as destroyed.

In addition, Marine artillery from Task Force Taro fired about seven fire missions and got a great deal of BDA [battle damage assessment]. I think it was the cooperation, the competence inspired by Colonel Admire's initiative that had direct impact. The Saudis saw the air, the Iraqis saw the air, and the Saudis saw the artillery; the Iraqis felt the artillery and that's what broke their back. The Iraqis fought hard initially, and then they lost heart because they saw that it was a combined effort that had tremendous violence potential, and they quit.

By noon the outcome of the battle was decided. There were nineteen Saudi soldiers killed and thirty-six wounded, a number of them double and triple amputees. Six hundred and six Iraqi prisoners were taken. There were eleven Saudi MIAs. Ninety-three Iraqi vehicles were destroyed. I don't know how many Saudi vehicles were destroyed.

Colonel John Admire, CO, Task Force Taro

To understand the significance of the battle of Khafji, one must appreciate the circumstances. At the time Colonel Turki courageously announced "We attack," the Iraqi army was the fourth largest in the world. It was reportedly the most combat-tested, veteraned, experienced military in the world as a result of its eight-year war with Iran. Furthermore, in the vicinity of Khafji, intelligence analysts estimated the Iraqis had four to six times the tanks we had and six to eight times the artillery pieces.

Meanwhile, the Saudi military had minimal experience in conventional battles in modern times. The Qataris, to our knowledge, had never deployed from their sovereign borders to participate in combat. With American Marine support, the battles succeeded admirably, and from that point on there was absolutely no question regarding the courage and conviction of the Arab coalition forces. The consequences of the battle for Khafji were profound. First, the confidence and morale of the Arab coalition forces were enhanced immeasurably. Second, we concluded that the Iraqi army had no resolve.

We debriefed the division commander, General Myatt, that if we hit the Iraqis hard and fast, they would quit and quit early. Consequently, General Myatt decided to pull battalions off the line and to assign them the primary task of prisoner collection and control. This would contribute to a rapid and unimpeded attack by Marine forces without the administrative and logistical burdens of prisoner-of-war processing and welfare.

Thirdly, the Arab coalition forces requested a major modification to the ground campaign scheme of maneuver. The previous scheme focused on the U.S. Marines attacking north in the eastern and central portion of Kuwait. The U.S. Army, British and French forces would also attack north from positions in the west. Meanwhile, the majority of the Arab coalition forces would follow in trace of the attacking Americans and Europeans. The American Marines would then encircle Kuwait City and secure all entrances and exits. At this point the Arab forces would conduct a passage of lines and clear the city by house-to-house fighting and door-to-door fighting.

But after the battle for Khafji, the Arab command advocated that they attack as equal partners with the Americans and multinational forces. This resulted in the Arab forces attacking north in the eastern avenue of approach that focused on the coastal road. The American Marines shifted their attack to the west and were now able to concentrate their forces for a rapid and massed assault directly at Kuwait International Airport. This, in turn, permitted the remainder of the allied force to displace further to the west to conduct what General Schwarzkopf, the commander in chief of Central Command, termed the "Hail Mary" or end-around flank attack. The genesis of this victory was the cross-training with the Arab forces; the friendships, trust, and confidence that developed; and the combined operations that characterized the battle of Khafji.[3]

Major General Mike Myatt, Commanding General, 1st Marine Division

Up until that point in time the Iraqis had been painted to be ten feet tall—by DIA [Defense Intelligence Agency], by everybody—and then all of a sudden, we had the one force that we were not convinced would fight on our side defeat the elements of this very experienced division of Iraqis who had been painted to be so potent.

That reverberated through, I know, all the Marines. We thought, *God, this is great. We know what we've got.* And it just kind of changed our . . . About a week before this happened, they brought an issue to my division of ten thousand body bags. I had a twenty-two-thousand-man division, and they were saying the casualties were going to be so horrific. . . . You talk about a sobering feeling when my G4 reported to me that we had just been issued ten thousand body bags. The predictions were that once we got into these obstacle belts, that we would be trapped in these fire-sacks and we would be annihilated the way they did the Iranians in their eight-year war.

I don't think it [the battle of Khafji] was really recognized for what it was by the people in Riyadh, the CentCom folks. Because it should have told all of us that it was going to be different than the slug-out that they had predicted. Can you imagine the commander of the [Iraqi] 5th Division . . . ? Can you imagine how he had to explain to his Corps commander that the Saudi Arabian National Guard had driven his brigade out of the town of Khafji? I think it was a significant event.

What I think happened, and it is the thing that we always teach never to let happen, and that is to never fall in love with your plan. Because you're gonna have to change your plans. Once we had that plan set in concrete in December, we never modified it until after my division had been more successful than Schwarzkopf thought it could be and we were actually through both those obstacle belts the first night. He realized that unless he accelerated the 7th Corps schedule that we weren't going to be able to defeat the Iraqi Republican Guard, that we wanted to. So, between the time that the plan is approved until G-Day [Ground Attack Day] plus one, my guess is that there were no main adjustments made in the plan. And for a force of that size, in today's world, it seemed to me that we needed to be a bit more agile. Your plan has to be able to adjust quickly. I think they learned that lesson, and I'll tell you that the way CentCom fought in going to Baghdad this time was much more agile, as far as their planning, their understanding, their adapting to what the enemy is doing in reaction to what they are doing.

When John Admire called me and said that Colonel Turki had been successful in getting back into Khafji, I can remember people giving each other a high five. We had expected another outcome.

We were all saying, "If the Saudis are not successful, we can't leave that Iraqi element there." And the psychological damage we might do to that Arab coalition on our right flank by having to come in there to take the

Iraqis out of there . . . We were counting on the Arabs to be the ones to go into Kuwait City, because we thought it should be Arabs liberating Arabs and not these westerners. So we were really pleased.

Major Craig Huddleston, Battalion XO

While we were training in Khafji, we were told that there were some new coalition forces. They were in tents right next to Khafji. They turned out to be about fifteen hundred, soon to be five thousand, *mujahadins* from Afghanistan. These fellows were the scariest people I have ever seen in my life. They were otherworldly. It was like you'd gathered up fifteen hundred Charlie Mansons and put them in one place. They all had a vacant stare, a grid-square stare, and beards. They had no weapons but knives, but you'd talk to them and you knew they were ready to go whether they had rifles or not. They were going to go in with knives and rocks if they had to, to help out their Muslim brothers. I don't know if they ever got into battle, but if I'd been an Iraqi, that would have convinced me to stop right there. They were so scary. They were like a horror movie. Just sitting on the ground, sticking their knives in the deck, absently swatting away flies, the sunken hollow eyes, always beating their chests and talking about Allah's will as we go and punish the invader. Man, if they'd been turned loose, they would have punished somebody. I know why the Russians got out of Afghanistan. I've never seen anybody so scary.

Captain Mike McCusker, CO, India Company

We were out there one night with our first platoon—Lieutenant Folger's platoon—and this shepherd came down the middle of the road with his sheep. We didn't know who he was or what he was doing out there in the middle of the night. You'd swear there was no one there. We didn't trust anybody, because we had been told that the Iraqi special forces were infiltrating down. So we check this guy out and found that he was just a legitimate sheepherder who found himself in the wrong place in the wrong time.

Right after that is when we got ready to move west; we did some helicopter operations during that time, still doing a lot of operations training, preparing for the war.

At that time I became very proficient with my peach cobbler. I could make the best peach cobbler there was. It was the envy of the platoons. They'd have a meeting in the evenings, and the guys would come up and ask, "Hey, sir, can we get some peach cobbler?" I'd make some for them.

We baptized three or four of our people as Christians, which was amazing when you thought about where we were. You couldn't show that in the paper, because it was against the Saudi beliefs.

We were constantly doing battle skills tests, getting people up to par, prepared and ready to go.

Major Craig Huddleston, Battalion XO

One night we were told that the Iraqis were coming down in force. They were coming back with about 150 or 200 vehicles, multiple divisions. I was again stuck out there with one rifle company and couldn't go anywhere. I figured we'd fight in the city. We thought we were taking incoming. We heard this tremendous detonation not too far away. We ran down to the basements in the buildings and got under cover. Then nothing was happening. The whole sky was lighting up. The naval gunfire officer got on the radio and told us it was the battleship *Wisconsin*. She was firing on the Iraqis. So we ran up to the rooftops to watch the battleship fire. It was so exciting, because it wasn't far away. When she fired, you could just see the ship's silhouette, all nine guns going off. It just raped those Iraqi forces coming down, just raped them. It was my only time seeing a battleship fire, and it made a believer out of me. It was beautiful, wonderful! There were 150 to 200 vehicles coming down, and they were not only stopped, they were pretty much wiped out.

18 / Movement West to Attack Position

Captain Joseph Molofsky, Liaison to the Saudi Brigade

The Saudis, after Khafji, were confident that they could fight and confident that they could win. As a result of that confidence, they insisted on a change of plans which caused the 1st and 2nd Marine Divisions to shift west and for the Saudis to move up along the coast on about a forty-kilometer-wide path and to have an active full role in the actual invasion of Kuwait.

Until just after Khafji, in late January, the plan was for the 1st and 2nd Marine Divisions—from the coast out to the elbow, the bend in the border, and around—to attack up and circle Kuwait City. Once they had done that, Saudi forces would follow behind, penetrate our lines, and actually do the hand-to-hand fighting in the city. As a result of Khafji, the Saudi general insisted on his own sector on the coast. He was given that, and it changed the whole array of forces.

Colonel John Admire, CO, Task Force Taro

As the Kuwait and Iraq assault plans were prepared for execution, Task Force Taro received orders to displace approximately one hundred kilometers to the west to rejoin the 1st Marine Division for the first time in nearly two months. Prior to executing the movement, Task Force Taro Marines bid farewell to our Arab comrades in arms. A letter was personally delivered to Colonel Turki from Major General Myatt. The note congratulated Colonel

Turki for the superb Khafji victory and thanked him for assisting in the recovery of the two Marine recon teams.

The letter was delivered to Colonel Turki the evening prior to our departure. As was his custom, Colonel Turki had assembled his commanders and staff in his Bedouin tent for the evening meal. The meals were always characterized by talk and laughter, similar to any family evening meal. But Colonel Turki's presence always made them special. He was a proud, authoritative leader, who encouraged all present to have a good time.

As Colonel Turki opened and read Major General Myatt's letter, it were as if everyone present sensed a subtle mood change amidst the many conversations in the tent. Colonel Turki read the letter, looked up and around, reread the letter, and quietly folded it and returned it to its envelope. By then the tent was totally silent with anticipation.

Slowly, Colonel Turki searched the faces of his commanders and staff; then, in total control, he solemnly said, "General Myatt has congratulated us for our heroic victory in Khafji. General Myatt has also thanked us for safely recovering the two American recon teams." After a momentary pause, Colonel Turki added, "We appreciate the congratulations; the thanks is unnecessary. The professional and personal friendships we have developed, we Arabs and you Americans, cause me to believe that if it had been Arab recon teams in Khafji, you would have safely recovered us. For now we are brothers in arms, Arabs and Americans. And we fight as one, and for one another."

Colonel John Garrett, Battalion Commander

Shortly after that we picked up and moved west. We moved in these big multicolored civilian buses and our Humvees. We were quite a caravan to behold. We'd been in the desert for about six months. The Humvees were dirty. They ran great, but they had all kinds of antennas all over them. There were all kinds of modifications. It was really a sight to behold.[1]

Captain Mike McCusker, CO, India Company

Every night we'd listen to Armed Forces Radio and they'd go through the briefings of what was going on in the war, how the battle was coming along. It was amazing to hear what they were saying as compared to what we knew was actually going on. They talked about Khafji and they talked about the woman being captured and how that happened. We knew that they were so out of whack that it was unbelievable.

Another very interesting thing was the Super Bowl. They showed pictures in the paper of people in Saudi Arabia watching it on TV. We had no Super Bowl on TV. We had a radio, and even then it didn't come on until two o'clock in the morning. I'd just finished checking the lines, came back to the CP, and woke everybody up. I told them to get up, it was Super Bowl time. We cooked some popcorn and some soup. The game never came on. We kept getting some guy saying there were technical difficulties. We waited until about three or four o'clock in the morning, waiting for the game to come on. We were really pissed. It was a letdown.

Captain Mark Davis, Battalion Logistics Officer

We went to this place called Al Qaraah. We took a helo trip over there, flew around, got out, and looked around. The site was good. The chow hall was there.

We did a motor march down that road—a thing called the Miracle Mile. There were all these different things on that road—all the MREs you'd want were stacked on the road, a post office, a chow hall, a mini-PX, these type things. We sent the battalion in about three sets of convoys. One would go, and two hours later someone else, and then two hours after that I went.

We set up in the middle of the night in the dark. It was an eerie feeling, because now we're getting closer and closer to war. There was a feeling in the battalion that something was going to happen. We didn't know exactly what, because at that time we still had a helo mission. We were still putting our heads together about how we were going to pull that off. What if we could only get six helicopters? We were going through the motions and really thinking hard on that.[2]

Captain Leon Pappa, CO, Kilo Company

We moved out to Al Qaraah sometime during the second week of February. At this time we thought we had the heliborne mission to seize Al Jaber airfield. The general consensus of the company commanders was—after the head shaking went away and the wiping of the brow—was if we could get on the ground, we could take it. Of course there was the normal fear of flying in.

We were briefed that Saddam had five artillery battalions that could range Al Jaber, plus he had some serious antiaircraft capability. In fact, at one point we got to see a film from an RPV over a flight during the BDA mission of an air attack the night before. I saw one Iraqi lurking and then running into a bunker. When the RPV pulled up real high, you could see the layout of where the antiair units were.

Our attack was supposed to be, I heard, made up of as much as the entire regiment, a minimum of two battalions, and we were told that 3/3 was going to be the first. All three companies would go in on the first wave. I was supposed to take the northern part of the airfield and establish a blocking position. Lima was to take the southern part, and India was going to take the center and the terminal buildings.

We were concerned about the plan. We couldn't tell anybody, so holding it inside didn't help. I think the lieutenants caught on, because all of a sudden we were starting to pick back up on helo team organizations, landing zone drills. They couldn't understand why it was necessary to get out of the landing zone in a minute and a half. We'd drill every night. We were very relieved when that mission went away.

Captain Joe Fack, FAC

We moved over to Al Qaraah and I got chopped to India Company. We still thought we were going to do a helo insert into Al Jaber. That never panned out, because they put it in the war computer and it predicted 80–90 percent casualties, so they thought they wouldn't do it. Al Jaber was one of the biggest bases there. A lot of the air defense was around this area. The whole regiment was supposed to go there.

Captain Sam Jammal, Commanding Officer, H&S Company

Ground Attack Day, G-Day, was now inevitable, but the date was still to be determined. We ended up staying at Al Qaraah a little longer than we thought.

Initially we thought we were going to do a heliborne raid on Al Jaber airfield. I thought that was one of the looniest ideas that we could have. But as a captain, I didn't have any say-so on the plan or how we executed it.

Cooler heads prevailed. We knew it would take seventy or eighty helos to insert us and none would be returning, no medevacs by air. We would fly over the axis of the main attack, which kept changing, and no reinforcement would be available until the next day. Mobility by helos is great until the unit gets on the ground, and then there's no place to go. There was an estimate that we would lose 10 percent of the aircraft, which is a lot of casualties. To me it wasn't a risk worth taking.

Captain Kevin Scott, CO, Lima Company

The turn-around time to get another battalion in there was something like two and a half hours. We looked at an RPV tape of Al Jaber. There were a lot of tree lines and trenches all over the place. Companies I and K were to go into the built-up area. I was to go into the southern side.

Major Craig Huddleston, Battalion XO

About four days prior to the commencement of the ground attack, they came down and told us to forget about the heliborne mission. We were disappointed that maybe we would be left out of it and not have a mission.

Three-three got a new mission, which was to infiltrate the barriers on the Kuwaiti-Iraqi border and anchor the flank for the entire U.S. attack. The remainder of Task Force Taro would come through the breach behind them. Securing the left flank of the Marine forces was Task Force Grizzly, which was tasked with breaching the obstacle system at the same time 3/3 went through on the right. Once the flanks were secure, Task Forces Ripper, Poppa Bear, and Shepherd would carry the main attack through the space between them.

Colonel John Garrett, Battalion Commander

General Myatt had this meeting. The battalion and regimental commanders came over to his place, where they had this tent dug out. They had chow for us and we all ate. We kind of joked around, and they took pictures of us all, all the commanders. Then we went back. Three-three's new mission was to go through the obstacles and minefields and the Iraqi positions and secure the right flank.

While we were at the meeting we looked at maps and had a sand table brief. General [Royal N.] Moore came. He had the 3rd Marine Aircraft Wing. At the sand table brief he said he was sorry that he couldn't tell us what was down there because the sky was so black from so many burning oil wells.

While we were doing our sand table exercise, General Moore was there in his flight suit, saying that if we needed to have some grids hit from the air to let him know and he'd take them back and work them. It was like at a nightclub and we're giving the band our requests. People were giving him little pieces of paper with requests.

The main attack had to be protected. That was our job—to try to sneak through, neutralize whatever resistance was there, and anchor the right flank so that at first light our armor attack could come through the center.

Captain Mike McCusker, CO, India Company

We thought it was really asinine, crazy, because here we are, a foot-mobile unit infiltrating across the desert, attacking the enemy's flank to set up a block position. Everything you read in Rommel and everywhere else said that foot troops were a waste in the desert. You couldn't do anything—it was too slow.

So it was kind of scary to see that was our mission. We'd gone over the plan for this attack and looked at how big the minefield was. We were like, *Holy shit! How are we ever going to do this?* There was barbed wire, fire trenches, long rows and rows of mines—this was a formidable thing. We coordinated arms, artillery, B52s, and all that would help us. Then we got something new. It was a pack that you put on your back and it shot a minefield clean. It was a great piece of gear that we'd never seen before. But it weighs fifty pounds and someone had to carry it on their back.[3]

We started training on this thing because I was told that India Company was to be on point. Once we were through, Kilo would be on the right and Lima on the left. Headquarters would be behind us with everything else. We were going to go in early.

I explained to the company that we were going to go in two days before the ground war began. We would be an advanced force to get behind the enemy and block the route to the east, so when the main blow comes, we've already got the flank, and the main attack just can keep on going. We only had a few days to prepare for this new mission.

The whole time we'd been preparing for something else and now we got this. I know it was hard for Colonel Garrett to give me this mission, and it was hard for me to go down to the company and tell the Marines. Some of them thought we had lost our heads and it was suicide.

It was not the best of missions, but it was the only mission we had, so we trained to go do it. I was lucky because I had trained in infiltration before this, so I knew what I was doing, but taking a battalion across a desert was awesome when I thought about it. So now we had to pack up and rush and move up until we were right on the border.

We had done some advance reconnaissance, actually gone up and seen it. A dead T62 Soviet-made tank was up there. Here we are, Doug Stilwell and I, getting our picture taken standing beside the tank. It was the first sign of war we'd seen besides being rocketed.

So we move up on the line up to right where the two berms are. This is just across the border. We hid in there and now we're ready to go, given a day or so. The bulldozers start coming up to cut a hole in the berm. We're walking through our final rehearsals, preparations, and everybody's real jittery, but we're ready to go.

Colonel John Garrett, Battalion Commander

Nobody had been through these obstacles. Nobody really knew what it was going to take to get through the obstacles and minefields. We had to move up on about G-Day minus three or four. There was a great big berm, a double berm. Inside of them were burned-out Iraqi BMPs and all kinds of war trash. The berm was a protective device, built along the vastness of the Saudi border, protecting their defenses. The problem is, not only is it hard for an enemy to get through, it's also hard for us to get out if we're trying to launch an attack.

We moved up just short of this berm. We went on a recon. It is so amazing in the desert. I was three years at Twenty-nine Palms. General Hopkins made the best comparison. He said, "This place makes Twenty-nine Palms look like Aspen, Colorado." Just the vastness. But it was beautiful.

Major Dan Stansbury, Battalion Operations Officer

The berm was like an ominous wall, the sand wall. When we finally got up to it, it was a double berm, which was, I'd say, approximately twenty-five to thirty feet high with about twenty yards of distance between the two berms.

When we got up there, though, we found that the berm had been penetrated by the Iraqis and also by U.S. reconnaissance teams.

When we got up for our recon we saw a destroyed Iraqi personnel carrier in between the berms, and we saw exactly how they had moved down between the berms. There was a broken-down part of the berm, so it was not an insurmountable barrier. Initially we thought there was a large ditch in front of the berm that would have to be filled in, but that wasn't true. So bulldozers were brought up, and it took half a day to flatten enough of the berm to get a good passageway.

Captain Mark Davis, Battalion Logistics Officer

The berm was about fifty kilometers away, so we motor marched up there. We pulled in south of the berm after having motor marched at night, and it's pouring down rain. Unbelievable! There's a stop whenever there is a halt in movement, and the minute the trucks stop, the drivers did what drivers have always done since there have been trucks—they fell asleep. So you have to get out and knock on the doors and wake them up.

We finally get there at about the crack of dawn. We were in the middle of nowhere. If you've ever gone deep-sea fishing, you know how you see that pretty royal blue forever. Now, everything I see is beige and it goes from horizon to horizon. I tell you what, if we hadn't had GPS, we'd have been in a hurt locker. It's a lifesaver.

We go up to the CP, and they tell me that I'm going to have to go back to the old position and pick up some more stuff. I didn't have enough trucks to lift the battalion all at once. Troop-wise I could do it, because they gave me enough trucks to bring all the troops, but I didn't have enough to lift the rest of the stuff. We moved the battalion aid station. The trucks with ammo would beat feet back to where we had maybe two hundred antitank mines with a lance corporal sitting on top of it or some pallets of MREs. The loading and unloading had to be done by hand, because I didn't have a forklift in the battalion.

So we get to this place. The colonel is very calm, cool, and relaxed. The XO is doing what the XO should do, which is ask us all about how we're going to handle this or that. The medevac procedure is being refined a little bit more. He likes the idea of me taking the battalion aid station with me and sending it out in the ambulance with the forward CP with a medical officer in it and do a triage right there, so maybe he can keep things going a little better. So now the companies would not bring casualties straight back from the field. They'd bring them into the forward CP, where they'd be looked at and then sent back down the road.

At night a helicopter flies by, and it is playing Iraqi songs and telling their guys they should give themselves up. We're thinking, *Oh, shit. Are we that close?*

We were told that anything on the north side of the berm we were free to fire at. The commanding general of the 1st Marine Division was out there looking at this thing in some type of vehicle. Lo and behold, we picked up a target out there. We cleared to fire at it from the regiment and division. I think we shot a TOW at him that malfunctioned. Then they started calling in the arty. So the general gets in his vehicle and drives off. There was hell to pay until they realized we had done the steps we were required to do.

Lieutenant Ivan Wray, Artillery FO, India Company

The 3rd Marine TOWs called Lieutenant Dave Harris out that morning. He's called out there and he's looking at an Iraqi tank. He's doing some fire missions, then someone calls me and said, "Why don't you go out there and see what's going on with Lima Company?"

So I drive out there. I didn't have a map even of the area. He says, "I think it's over this way." I had a laser-based range finder with me, so I estimated how far it was, like nine thousand meters. It plotted inside of Kuwait. There was a police station out there. There were vehicles all around it.

He starts adjusting fire. I'm sitting there looking, going, "Wow." I see smoke coming out too. I'm thinking, *Wow, he's doing something. He's kicking some butt.* He gets called back. The clearance for the mission had gone all the way to the division level and back down. We were right here on this elbow and Task Force Grizzly [2/7 and 3/7, under the operational control of the 4th Marines] was moving out in a northern direction, so they wanted to make sure we wouldn't hit Grizzly at all.

We moved up a little bit further up to the border, almost where engineers had dug some revetments. I see a convoy coming up. It was the 1st Marine Division commander. He gets out. All these guys get out. They were mighty upset. "Who the hell was firing those rounds?" I said, "Well, sir, he's not around here right now. Can I help you at all?" "Yeah, you can help me. You almost killed the division commander." At that point my heart just sunk. General Myatt pointed out to where he was. I guess he had some TOWs out there with him. There were some bulldozers, from what I understand. That was the smoke we saw. That was the confusion of it all.

I get back and talk to our liaison chief, Staff Sergeant Williams. "What the hell is going on? They just shot at the general." He says, "No, no, no, Lieutenant. The general was in Kuwait. If he wanted to die, that's his own business." He was laughing. "If he wants to go up there nosing around and not telling anybody about it first . . . "

1st Sergeant Wylie McIntosh, Weapons Company

Some Marines said this is why 3/3 had to walk across the barrier.

Captain Mark Davis, Battalion Logistics Officer

The guys were concerned about the infiltration. They were coming up looking at the gunny, they were looking at me. "What do you think? Do you think we're going to make this, sir?" You had to tell them, "There are going to be some tough times, but I have faith in you and you have faith in me, and we're gonna work this thing out. We're gonna do it."

The companies leave to move up and I leave with them. The field train came up and set in inside Kuwait. We sit there for a while, for a day. We set up a big sand training map on the ground with grid squares, and we rehearsed how we were going to do it. A company commander would get up— "I'm doing this. I'm doing these types of things." "Okay, field train, where are you at?" "I've now just left where we're at right now." We walked this thing all the way through.

The sand table was twenty foot by twenty foot. It represented grid squares— we set them off in foot squares. One foot represented a grid square [1,000 meters square]. You could actually walk out on it. When I walked out, I represented the field train, that company commander represented his company. We rehearsed the whole breach.

That evening, after we did that thing and came back, the Colonel says, "We're going into MOPP 2. Here's what we're going to do." We started breaking down the camouflage nets. The BAS sets up. They hung out the instruments, they hung out the IVs. They were ready. I had to walk back and tell them, "We ain't there yet, boys. We need to go." So we had to take that down.

Captain Mike McCusker, CO, India Company

That night the colonel came up and said, "Are you ready to go?" I said, "Yes, sir." We had waited until about 2000 when we stepped out. We knew it was going to take us all night long to get there, to get to our first attack position, which was fourteen kilometers into Kuwait, before the war even started. We were kicking off the ground war before anyone even realized it.

We were carrying anywhere from seventy five to a hundred pounds—full combat load. Every man had at least one rocket, or two LAAWs, or one AT4.

Captain Mike McCusker, CO, India Company

Our mission there was to infiltrate up, get to the attack position, then infiltrate through the minefield and block in case mechanized forces came from the east. So what we're going to do is tell the Iraqis, "Hey, they're coming," shoot as much as we can, and then hide in a hole, get down in the holes so we can destroy as much of them as possible as they come blazing through us. The battalion's front would be about three clicks wide.

Major Craig Huddleston, Battalion XO

We'd been led to believe that their defenses were formidable. All the intelligence we had said they were going to be tough.

So what was going through our minds at the time was *Well, we've got to do this one right,* because visions of the sea wall in Tarawa were dancing through our heads. We thought once we were discovered, which was inevitable, we would become a lightning rod for the Iraqi forces. So we had to figure out how to get in as fast as we could, get underground as quickly as possible, protect the division's—actually the U.S. forces'—right flank, and at the same time hold on for dear life, and all in a matter of a couple of days. This had to be prepared, and we were going to have to do it on foot. So that meant a lot of our loads were going to have to change, our logistics plans and schemes were going to have to change, everything changed.

Colonel John Garrett, Battalion Commander

I figured we could bang our heads against this minefield thing for six weeks. But when we had been back at Cement Ridge, at that defensive position, there was an operating quarry there behind it. The workers had to get in and out with their Mercedes trucks full of rocks that they would bring back in there and crush, or the reverse going out. We set up a checkpoint. We gave them ID cards. It was a weak spot. We said, "Let's try to find a weak spot like that in the minefield that we can exploit and infiltrate." This is about G minus three. We know that we're going to infiltrate, and I'm trying to find a good place to come through.

Sergeant William liams, Recon Team Leader

I had been given the mission of going to the first obstacle. There had been a recon patrol from Force Recon who had gone there prior to that. They had seen the minefield and said, "It's not that heavily fortified." They said they heard some people sleeping in the bunkers.

I was then told to go to the 3rd Battalion, 3rd Marines. I was given the entire scheme of maneuver on Ground Attack Day and all that good stuff, I was told to link up with 3/3. They were going to be there to let me know the EEIs [essential elements of information]. I found out what Colonel Garrett wanted.

I went in G minus three. I went in eighteen kilometers from the berm— Sergeant Lentz's team and myself. Corporal Ingraham went to secure the staging area where 3/3 was going to be at. Sergeant Lentz was going to go up to the minefield, but he was going to act more as security and I was going to actually go through it. Sergeant Lentz and myself, we first had to walk through Al Wafrah oil field. It was on fire. And we had some problems with carrying a little bit too much gear.

When we finally got up to the minefield, it was about 0200 in the morning. I had Corporal Knies and myself. We were in two-man teams. Sergeant Arellano and a guy named Lance Barron were in another team. I told them I wanted them to go and see if they could find lanes through the minefield. Kilo Company was going to go through one lane, and I was going to take India Company through another one. Sergeant Arellano and Barron veered off and didn't find the minefield. Knies and I found it. We also found bunkers that had cases of stuff from Jordan in them.

We went up to the fence. There were these little toe-popper mines outside the fence itself. We were wearing night-vision goggles, which are just awesome. We went up to the fence itself, and I looked around to make sure there were no trip wires on it. We were all issued Leathermans, another great tool that has pliers on it. I took my Leatherman and went *snip, snip* for fifty meters on either side of the fence, and it just fell down. I thought that was not too bad.

We went into the minefield for about ten or fifteen meters. We were side by side, shoulder to shoulder, because that's how we figured to clear a lane, me and Knies. We got up to the first real big clump of mines. They were the Italian kind, with the clusters on top and trip wires all around. We tried to get through them, but they were just too thick in that one area. On the way back, Corporal Knies grabbed me. I looked down and I had stepped on a mine. Luckily it was an antitank mine, which requires quite a bit of pressure to set it off. I was kind of relieved.

We came back. In the meantime, the two other Marines on my team started to dig the team's hide. Our hide consisted of an oil pipe to act as some sort of cover and a big ten-by-ten piece of burlap, which we mixed in with the sand. We just made a low berm and put the burlap over it, and that's where we'd sit all day and just observe.

The 3rd Battalion, 3rd Marines was already in their staging area behind us, and I was going to link up with them. Later that night, I found an actual path through the minefield, through observing. I just saw what looked like an opening. We saw a bunch of barrels and concertina wire, and Corporal Knies and I went down there and practically walked through it. There were some antitank mines on the ground.

20 / The Breach

Captain Joe Fack, FAC

The first night we went up to a place called Casino. The next night we were supposed to go through the breach. We left about 1800 and it was dark out. About 0500 we got there and started digging in. Our job was to stay under cover from the Iraqis. We got word that there were Iraqi forces in the area. We wanted to skirt around them and then get into the breach site.

I was talking to an OV10 [aircraft] that was doing clear runs for us. We got the word that we had air support at Al Qaraah in seven and a half minutes if we needed it. It was there and they would run in and do their stuff.

Corporal David Bush, S3 Driver

There was always doubt. You always doubted, always wondering, "What if?" To tell you the truth, I was scared. I didn't know what to expect out there. Nobody else knew what to expect out there. I didn't know if we were going to come on a minefield and there was going to be two-hundred-thousand people and all we had was our battalion. There were a couple of Iraqi battalions up there, and they were mechanized with APCs and so on. They could have given us a helluva fight. Who knows how many people we'd lose.

It was strange. It was definitely a stressful time for me. I wanted to get in. I wanted to get it over with, but I didn't want to talk to anybody about it at all. I kind of kept it to myself, because I just kept thinking about what I had to do—*what do I have to do now, what do I have to get ready*—you'd just kind of figure out things you had to do so you don't sit there and think about it. I didn't know what to feel. Everybody kept busy. Everybody had something to do. They kept checking their gear.

Major Craig Huddleston, Battalion XO

We knew we hadn't been discovered, because the next day we started seeing Iraqi forces moving around. They didn't know we were there. As all this was going on, the 3rd Marines moved up. All the 3rd Marines moved up and established themselves along the border.

Concurrent to this, what was called Task Force Grizzly, centered around the 4th Marines, was doing the same thing further to the west. They were going to infiltrate on G minus one and protect the west or left flank of the Marine expeditionary force. So what we had is two regiments up on the border with a fairly large gap in between.

Back about thirty kilometers from the gap was Task Force Poppa Bear, consisting of two infantry and one tank battalions; Task Force Ripper, also consisting of two infantry battalions and a tank battalion; as well as all the rest of the 2nd Marine Division and the Army's Tiger Brigade.

So we were feeling pretty lonely up there. We were dug in as well as we could make it. Sure enough, on that first day, along about evening on G minus two, we started seeing Iraqi forces moving around in front of us.

We engaged the first Iraqi forces we saw, which we believed was an artillery reconnaissance unit—a small armored personnel carrier and a rocket launcher. We engaged them with artillery and killed the rocket launcher at a range of about three thousand meters from our position. The armored personnel carrier left. We didn't take any incoming that night, but there were a lot of things going on around us. We could hear things. We didn't really know what it was, but there was some shooting off to the east and also off to the west, two-way firefights going on. We found out later that it was Iraqi forces that were out posting these police stations or border patrol stations. They were mixing it up a little bit with the Saudi and Qatari forces and some of our reconnaissance people and some of our light armored infantry. There was nothing that directly affected us.

The next morning, one of our outposts reported this APC coming back to the same area we'd shot at the night before. This guy must have been stupid. He came back and parked real close to the burned-out rocket launcher.

We engaged him with a TOW and killed him. We blew him away and burned up the APC.

About the same time, we observed some Iraqi APCs—two of them—and an Iraqi tank off to our west, very close to our border with another unit. A bunch of things were moving around there, smaller vehicles moving around.

We went though a long process of getting clearance to fire. Finally we engaged them with artillery and then TOW missiles. It turns out that they were dead Iraqi vehicles. They'd already been killed. We'd shot at some Marine TOW vehicles too. Luckily we didn't hurt anybody. That was shaky and we were pretty nervous about that.

Sergeant William Iiams, Recon Team Leader

I came back in from across the barrier with sketches of the area. I got a quick debrief by Colonel Admire and others.

Captain Leon Pappa, CO, Kilo Company

For the night movement into the breach, we made our money with Sergeant Iiams. He had the ability to be able to get back that night and talk to us. It was very reliable intel. He told us that he didn't think the enemy was there, and if they were, there were very few of them.

Major Dan Stansbury, Battalion Operations Officer

We had gotten back the teams that had gone forward to recon our route through the belt. The teams came back, and still no one could answer the question about exactly what this light was that was lighting up the barrier belt and making this noise. It was a tremendous noise. The recon guys thought maybe it was a giant generator of some sort, maybe with some sort of spotlight that was putting light along the barrier so we couldn't cross it without being seen. This was ominous. We imagined the Iraqis had some sort of spotlight system, that they'd electrified the fences, the whole nine yards. None of that happened. When we got up there, we found it was a burning oil well.

Colonel John Garrett, Battalion Commander

The recon guys come back and say that they'd found it, a weak spot. The good news is that there are about six points we could probably get through without a whole lot of effort. But we'd have to be careful. We're still talking about fifty or sixty meters of all kinds of mines, plus obstacles. There's that and then there's the defensive positions that could cover the minefield by fire.

Worse was the idea about the fire-sacks, the preregistered artillery concentrations. Even though I was trying to find a weak spot in the defense, the downside was that the weak spots were probably covered pretty heavily with artillery, which is exactly what we had done with ours.

Recon found this place and it looked real good. You know how things always fall into place on the map and you can really just say, "This is how the attack should go." And you draw in your little arrows. I decided to not go through the weak point, because it is probably a fire-sack. I wanted to go down and find another, less obvious point and go through there and attack the positions in the rear on the other side. When I briefed the regiment, they thought it was a great plan. *Red Cell*

My intel officer was looking it over real good. He went over it with a fine-toothed comb. He says, "Sir, the grids they gave us are wrong." I said, "What do you mean they are wrong?" He said that it wouldn't work, that the grids we had been given didn't match up on the map. So now I have significant doubts about this. I agonized for two days. The key to the whole damn thing was finding the correct place for us to go through. We couldn't do the infiltration any other way.

So now it's all up in the air, but the show must go on. We were supposed to move out on G minus two, which we did. We had to cut through these berms. The enemy had tanks and this was pretty scary. We walked out of the womb, crossed those berms, and at 2059 on the twenty-second of February we crossed Phase Line Black, which was the Kuwaiti border.

Captain Mike McCusker, CO, India Company

We finally moved up there, got in about 0300 in the morning in the first attack position, which is still ten clicks away from the actual minefield, and set in.

Then we were told that the recon team, which was already up there and looking at the place and taking pictures, was coming back. That was the first time I met Sergeant Iiams up in that vicinity. He came down, and I tell him what I want, the reconnaissance I need to have. We've already got pictures and photos that are over a month old, which I didn't think was too current. We should have had the most up-to-date stuff in the world and we didn't.

I told him that there were six breach points that we are looking at, numbered A-1 through A-6. I wanted A-1 or A-2 as my primary and A-3 through A-6 as alternates. I told him to find a breach point for me to go through. So he went off and did his thing while I am in a defensive position, getting stuff ready to move the next night. We were inside Kuwait. The enemy's there. *Holy shit, if anything is going to happen, it's going to happen right here.*

We moved all night long, and it was a tough move. The sun came up again, and now it's G minus one. Iiams comes back. It must have been around 1930. I had an NBC news team attached to my company because we were up front, and they were going to stay with us.

We did a final walk through the sand table, went through the whole thing. We practiced and rehearsed going through it all. We were ready to go do what we had to do. I went back to my company position making sure the Marines were getting ready, were putting their MOPP suits on, because we were going in in MOPP2—suit on, mask and boots off. We were all set, ready to go.

Colonel John Garrett, Battalion Commander

We marched by foot through an area, which had been set when our planes were flying through looking, and there was so much antiair stuff coming up at them that there had to be at least a battalion out there. It always looks like more at night than it really is.

My point is, with all the sophisticated means that you would hope that you had, we were walking into I don't know what. Supposedly an Iraqi battalion was patrolling where we were walking through, and on the other side there were up to two or three brigades. That's what we were expecting. There was supposedly an armored mech battalion on patrol out there. We're out there. I don't know if they were there or not. We go by them. We went about fifteen clicks. This was G minus one.

On G minus two the B52s had dropped on this area where the weak spots were. The drop was so powerful that here we were, about some twenty clicks away from the objective, and I'm lying on the ground sleeping and bouncing off the ground.

The problem now is it is daylight and there's nothing to hide under. The only thing that provided us with any concealment was the fact that now the airplanes were dropping on our objective area, and so whatever enemy or observation was there we hoped was either on the run or keeping their head down and couldn't look at us.

Major Craig Huddleston, Battalion XO

It was a pretty nice day too. It was warm and sunny, and after a long night march in enemy territory the Marines relaxed. I thought it was pretty good to see they just dug fighting holes, lay down, ate, and drank water.   → Def.

Meanwhile, the staff was refining the final plans for that night's activities. We'd been told that we would commence the ground attack by 2000 that night. At the same time, what was going on, we knew from news reports, was a strong diplomatic initiative by the U.N. trying to gain a cease-fire and get the Iraqis to withdraw.

> A few hours before the commencement of the ground war, Major Huddleston told his staff, "If we get the word, we'll cross the line of departure in about two hours. We said, 'Get out of Kuwait or else.' Well, you guys are the 'or else.'"

Colonel John Garrett, Battalion Commander

We were plopped right in the middle of nowhere. It was like being in Amarillo, Texas, before the city was built. We dug in and had a final meeting before the attack. The problem was I still didn't know precisely where this point was that we were going to go, and I don't know how we were going to find it, but we had to keep moving.

We got a last minute "hold," so I told everybody that I wanted an hour by which we had to do this, because if I can't get there before first light to do what I have to do, I would have to wait another day. So we all sort of estimated and I got everybody's recommendations. My estimate was that if we didn't get to move by 2330, then we'd have to wait another day because I wouldn't have the time. I told Colonel Admire that and he said, "Okay."

Right after sundown, we're all staged and getting ready. Everybody said, "This is it!" Damned if something, it was probably friendly, didn't just come screaming out of the sky and BAM, right in the center of this American radar, took it out. There were flames and people screaming. It killed I don't know how many. Some of the guys got out. Some didn't. We thought it was enemy. I thought, *Holy shit. Wait until they fire for effect.*

Captain Mark Davis, Battalion Logistics Officer

That's enough to get your heart going at a hummin'bird rate!

Captain Mike McCusker, CO, India Company

I said, "Well, that's it. We're going to have a major battle right here, right now." The next thing I know is I have a hundred enemy troops out in front of my company position, and I have patrols out there also. The OPs are still out. I have them watching and scanning and looking and looking. We can't see anything; someone said, "We have a hundred people trying to surrender out there." I had a CIT [counterintelligence] team that was in the area who came up to try to get them to surrender. As we started to get that going, we're all lined up and this all happens. I think, *Shit, we've been discovered. We're inside their territory. Our surprise is gone. We're going to get rolled over.*

Lieutenant Ivan Wray, Artillery FO, with India Company

Recon comes back with the colonel. The colonel lays down the map. We're all around him ready to move out. The Marines are getting up, standing by in the little staging areas before they moved out. That's when the missile hit. Later we found out it was our missile. At that time we thought it was an Iraqi arty or rocket attack. It takes out counter-mortar radar in 1/12 killing, I believe, two.

We just dived for the holes. You know atropine, which is a nerve agent antidote, has a real sharp needle? I jump into my hole. What had happened, my atropine needle had come loose out of its protector. I feel a real sharp jab in my left buttock. I did not want to get all excited and scare everybody. Someone said, "What's up, sir?" I pull out this needle. It's nice and thick. I've got atropine all over me. He goes, "It doesn't look too good." I wasn't laughing at that time. It was pretty serious. I got shot with atropine so I was pretty pumped up.[1]

Captain Joe Fack, FAC

"Oh, shit, here we go." We thought we were dead. We didn't know what to expect. We thought that the Iraqis found us and started shooting at us. We had word that there were people in front of us just walking, trying to surrender, but I don't know what happened to them.

We had all the S2 guys with the microphones and the Iraqi interpreters and all that stuff up there to find out what the hell was going on.

Captain Sam Jammal, CO, H&S Company

Just out of nowhere, *boom*. I didn't hit the deck. I just looked at it. I remember Sergeant Masters saying, "Get in the holes." I jumped in the hole only to laugh and feel silly, jumped back out, ran towards the vehicle to see who got hurt. And I wasn't the only one. There were plenty of people who jumped in a hole.

Major Craig Huddleston, Battalion XO

It was a helluva noise—a whistling noise, *boom*—and the whole desert lit up with vehicles on fire. There were people running around screaming, magnesium was burning, ammunition was cooking off. The same thought went through all of our minds—"We've been discovered. They've caught us."

Just about that time somebody reported in about helicopters landing, but we couldn't raise them, didn't know who they are. So the same thought raced through everybody's mind. The Iraqis are going to try to raid and hit us and prevent us from advancing.

So we quickly found positions, got down and got ready to fight, and it calmed down. It turned out that the impact was a HARM [high-speed antiradar] missile, a U.S. missile, and it had impacted on our artillery radar on 1/12. It took about an hour and a half for the fire to die down. The helicopters were in fact an army psyops [psychological operations] unit that had been up broadcasting surrender appeals, dropping leaflets, and just happened to overfly our position and didn't even know we were there. It was entirely unrelated to our mission, but it happened at the same time and we thought, *This is it*.

Fortunately, again, the discipline of the Marines came through—nobody was shot. The Stingers, the antiair teams, were ready to fire and they held off until they could visually identify the targets, and they said, "They're friendly." I was real proud of them.

Colonel John Garrett, Battalion Commander

That was rather sobering. Whatever confidence and bravado we had worked up during the day sort of just went down the toilet when that happened. Everybody kind of worked through that in their own way. And we waited. And I still didn't know what we were going to go through. Finally, at 2000—and it's good thing we did wait—the recon teams showed up, who'd been out there again, and they said, "Sir, we found them." And I said, "Great! What have you got?" They said, "Well, we found the weak spots and we know exactly how to get there—that's the good part. The bad part is we don't know exactly where we can go through like you want to and attack and then hit the position from the rear rather than go through the main opening."

Major Craig Huddleston, Battalion XO

Then we were told to delay, and that really put a crimp in our plan, because we had to be through those minefields before first light; we anticipated that our drop-dead time would be 2200. In other words, we had two hours now to get moving.

I gathered up all the main players, the logistics train, and all the people who'd be following the infiltration. We talked about the plan and what was going to happen; I tried to encourage them. I gave them a little talk about, "You're good men. You're going to do a good job. If you're afraid, you probably should be afraid, but don't let it overcome you. You're doing the right thing for your country and for this country—Kuwait."

Everybody was pretty serious. We were pretty grim. Then I called Master Sergeant Cater forward, who was the ops chief, and I told him to brief in detail the order and the time schedule for moving out.

Colonel John Garrett, Battalion Commander

We were starting to run out of time. We didn't have a whole lot of time to go down and look again. My big decision at this point was *Do I go through the obvious opening and run the chance of being blasted to smithereens in a fire-sack, or do I try to take the time to find somewhere else?* I decided to go ahead and go for it and go through the main opening.

Captain Leon Pappa, CO, Kilo Company

The night we went through the breach, we were waiting at 2100, then it was delayed until 2200. My headquarters group—again it amazed me the things they'd do—my headquarters element was standing in a circle, holding hands, and saying the "Our Father." They asked me to join in. I admit at first I felt a little uncomfortable with that, but then I felt *Why not?* I saw a different side of them—even though I lived with these men for all these months, plus Okinawa.

Major Craig Huddleston, Battalion XO

Right at 2200, now the Marines were asleep in their holes. Just at that time we got the order to move out. "Commence your attack." So I walked around waking everybody up, myself and Captain Lehenbauer, the S3A. He went in one direction and I went in the other, waking people up. I told everybody the same thing: "Wake up. It looks like we're going to war."

So they got up, fired the engines up, and the battalion moved out and off we went. By that time it had gotten dark. I mean not just nighttime dark but dark, dark; cloudy, very windy cold, and it started to rain. As physically uncomfortable as that was, we were all pretty happy to see that weather, because it was ideal weather for an infiltration. The visibility was cut down, even with night-vision devices, to about two hundred meters, and it was very windy. You couldn't hear anything. There were strong winds, up to thirty kilometers an hour, and it was cold. So we were thinking that *If those guys are in those trenches, they're down at the bottom trying to stay warm and dry and they're not going to be paying any attention to us.* So off we went. We monitored the situation on the radio. The colonel was up forward with the lead companies with his CP group, and I was about fifteen hundred meters behind him. As we approached the Iraqi minefield, we stopped about one kilometer short of it. We held up the entire battalion. The company commanders and Sergeant Iiams and his people went forward for reconnaissance to find out where we were going to penetrate. It was very successful. It took them about an hour to do it. They found a good place, came back, issued the order, and in we went.

Captain Mike McCusker, CO, India Company

We had to be through by 0600 and set up before the sun came up the next morning, or we'd be stuck out in the open. We stepped out and now we start going towards the position. Prior to this, Sergeant Iiams had come back and said, "This is what I found. We can go through here. I haven't seen too many people, but this is where the minefield is. We're going to have to go through the minefield. There's barbed wire here and here and here." The colonel told me I could go through either A1 or A2. At A1 there are mines. At A2 there were no mines, but there was a road I would have to cross. I decided I'd rather fight my way across the gap than deal with the minefield, so I decided we'd take the chance that there would be no one there.

Sergeant Iiams said he didn't see anyone up there, so that was good for me. I decided to go with what he saw. I was with Iiams with my first point element, Lieutenant Forbes's team. He was my first platoon commander by then. He didn't join us until two days before the war started; he was a brand-new, fresh-looking lieutenant. We're going towards our next position, which we called a gathering center because all the oil pipelines came together there. We were to stop there, do a final reconnaissance of the area, and then try to infiltrate.

Colonel John Garrett, Battalion Commander

This place we had picked was a weak point. It was covered with mines and so forth but not to the extent that the other miles and miles of it were. You could conceivably get through there on foot.

We moved the 81s up into position. The company commander [McCusker] and the recon guys went up and did their final recon. They walked all the way through the minefield. The company commander himself went through the final obstacle, which was a piece of barbed wire. He thought, *So far, so good.* "Should we go to the other side?" We said, "Why not?" This is where the Iraqi brigade was. When you cut barbed wire, you are supposed to hold both sides when you make the final cut and then let it go real easy, checking for trip wires. He forgot. *Twang!*

Captain Mike McCusker, CO, India Company

You could hear the bombs going off. It was kind of awesome when you saw what was going on, when you saw what you were doing. We stopped just outside the gathering center. Everything there is black. You could see the burning oil well fires. It was all red on the horizon. It's a pretty eerie sight and we're walking towards it.

We stopped just outside the gathering center, which is where all those pipes come together. We still have about two or three thousand more meters to go. Captain Pappa comes up with me, Sergeant Iiams, Corporal Knies, plus our radio operators and security personnel. We stepped off to go forward with final reconnaissance.

At the gathering center, we see a fuel line that's burning. It's illuminating the whole place. We're on night-vision goggles, looking around on the ground for mines. These Italian mines looked like little trees, with little branches sticking up out of the ground.

There is this big Texas oil rig, a real pump-type of thing. That's where A1 is, where we're going to go through. We're moving towards that. We stop at one of the pipelines, scanning, looking. This is two or three o'clock in the morning.

Iiams, Knies, and myself and Captain Pappa stopped at that gathering site, left our radio operators there, left our security personnel, and then only the four of us went forward to do the final check, because there were just too many to take to where we were going to. So we moved in and finally get to this gap. We went all the way up to the barbed wire and to where the actual minefield is. By this time we're scanning the ground. Iiams and Knies are right in front. We're right behind them. We were stepping in each other's footsteps to get up there.

Here comes the barbed wire, and you can see these mines laid on the road, on the tarmac. You could see the minefields extending left and right as far as you could see. You don't really know what else is there, because you figured they buried the antipersonnel mines.

We got through this. Iiams had already been in the minefield and realized he'd have to back out of there. We're going through there and there's this barbed-wire cross-obstacle thing. Some barrels and obstacles, a real makeshift job. You could see these mines scattered all over the place, like they put some in purposely and the rest they kind of threw out there anywhere. That worried me.

So we stopped by these barrels. There was barbed wire stretched across the top. I thought we'd just cut this thing so we didn't have to worry about it afterwards. I looked in each direction with my night-vision goggles and didn't see anything. You are supposed to grab both sides and clip. I thought someone else had the other end. I clipped this thing and it just went "Ping" down the line. It scared the living shit out of me. I thought, *Well, we're not dead yet,* because it didn't go off and must not have been booby-trapped.

As I was moving forward, I was really paying attention to the ground because of the mines. I thought that this was not the way I wanted to go in here—walking down the middle of the night up to some position and have some guy shoot me. We were so out in the open it was unbelievable.

There was an oil well fire behind us that lit us up. We couldn't get away from it. We couldn't go all the way around the thing, because we knew there were only so many gaps in the minefield, so we had to go through this area to find what we needed.

I was trying to pay attention to what was going on here right under my feet. They had so many mines stuck underneath. Some were on top. Some weren't even opened, weren't even set, but we didn't know that at the time.

We found a different route back, because we had to find a better way to come in with the vehicles. We walked down this pipeline. For all we knew, this could have been mined also. We were tiptoeing through this, back into that burning area. I leave Iiams and Knies there, and Pappa and I go back to pick up the companies.

By this time I knew there was nobody there, and I felt a helluva lot better that there was no enemy there that I could see. I knew then I could get the company through, get to the other side without being detected. We went back and picked them up and told them, "Okay, let's go. Give me the MOPP team right behind me, and I want you to stay right in line. I'll walk in front and we'll just go." So that's what we did.

We turned right around and took off and walked back to where Iiams and Knies were. We cut through the fence, went through that, went down the pipeline. We started marking with red and white markers so people could follow us. We got to the actual minefield, and Iiams and I were placing red and green markers on either side. Green right and red left.

My company comes behind me. I have them in blocking position, and I come back to find one of the other companies has gone off toward the minefield in a different direction and they were just about to step into the minefield. They missed one of the turns, so I had to stop them and pull them back.

Captain Kevin Scott, CO, Lima Company

I wanted to get the company through as fast as I could and get them dispersed, get them deployed. When we came through, Mike McCusker went to secure the left portion of the defense line in the minefield area. Leon Pappa was supposed to turn to the right to clear that way. I was supposed to kick out farther forward and angle off to the north-northeast and continue to move. I just wanted to get the company through as fast as I could, get them deployed in a formation, separated as much as possible because of the indirect fire possibilities. We came through. We hadn't gone very far when we started getting reports that there were mechanized forces coming from the northwest.

Lieutenant Ivan Wray, Artillery, FO, with India Company

The biggest thing with fire support is target location. I had to know where the hell I was and where everything was in relation to me. That was the biggest thing on my mind. If I let those Marines down, I don't think I could live with myself. I was all business that morning.

Colonel John Garrett, Battalion Commander

My estimate was that I needed to get the men through there, because they had to push two or three clicks out in order to secure the flank. My mission was to do that. They would move slower than the vehicles. So I had to get them through first and get them on the move toward where their mission place was; then I'd have time to get the vehicles up. Besides that, before I got the vehicles up I had to bring up this tank plow that we had, to proof the minefields, so that the vehicles could safely drive through, because it is a different story walking through compared with driving.

The Marines did just great. It was about five in the morning, and it was just starting to get light. About six or seven hundred of them went through in each other's steps without blowing a mine, without falling down, without attracting any attention or making any noise, were through and on their way out to the block positions, and then it got daylight and we started taking fire from something. I don't know what it was, a recoilless rifle, APC main gun, or whatever.

Sergeant William Iiams, Recon Team Leader

We actually went through, get them up into the minefield, went through the minefield, went on the other side of the minefield. I was expecting, personally, that this was a big trap and we were going to get the shit shot out of us.

We cleared the area. We put chem lights on all the antitank mines. We all came in and just starting filing Marines through. Captain McCusker went back to do his leaders' recon. He said to bring all the Marines all the way out and expose them. Corporal Knies and me cut a hole in the fence that was used as a little oil holding-tank facility. They went through there and straight up.

The next thing you know, as the Marines were filing by I looked over and the sun's coming up. That is how everything happened. It was totally exhausting. I had been up for two and a half or three days now.

I linked up with 3/3. It was really just an amazing thing, because as we were moving out, I was the point element. We were heading out. You could see the oil fields. I turned around and looked back. I didn't realize how much my mission would impact on so many men. I looked back and there were probably two or three thousand Marines, plus artillery, plus vehicles, and it was a big responsibility on my shoulders. I didn't realize it until I looked back and all I saw was jarheads for miles. This was it. They were going for bear.

> About the breach, General Norman H. Schwarzkopf, commander of all U.S. forces in Desert Storm, said, "It was a classic, absolutely classic military breaching of a very, very tough minefield, barbed wire, fire trench-type barrier. The Marines went through that first barrier like it was water. The brought both divisions streaming through that breach. Absolutely superb operation—a textbook—and I think it will be studied for many, many years to come as the way to do it."[2]

Sergeant Major Bo Pippin, Battalion Sergeant Major

The battalion commander was up with the forward company; it was India Company. The remainder of the battalion was back where I was located. They made the initial breach, and the remainder of the battalion was brought up.

We were doing something right. I was amazed at how calm and controlled people stayed. I mean the Marines really kept control at all times. There were no outbursts of Marines saying that they couldn't take it or they couldn't handle it. The Marines, the sergeants and below, they were so damn loyal. They were great guys.

It kind of gives you time to sit around and wonder what your real capabilities are. I can't say I was totally surprised at what the outcome was. I was amazed at times at what I saw. These Marines did a superb job. I can think of many, many times when those young sergeants and corporals took responsibility and wouldn't back down from it.

Major Craig Huddleston, Battalion XO

We penetrated the minefields. We just walked through the mines, marked the mines. It turns out that most of the mines were surface laid, so in we went.

Before first light, probably by about 0515 or earlier, the bulk of the battalion was through the minefield and on the enemy side with no contact, and we reported that to higher headquarters. It was unbelievable. We were through and moving up to our blocking positions, and the only thing left on the other side was our vehicles, our heavy weapons vehicles. We had one tank and two assault vehicles with line charges. The tank was a plow tank. We had our supplies, our fuel trains, and my CP group.

Captain Joe Fack, FAC

It was probably the longest walk of my life, because you didn't know what to expect. I was about twenty feet in the back of Captain McCusker. He's known for being very, very . . . they call him the Tasmanian Devil because he spins up a lot. Me, I'm more relaxed. *Keep calm, keep calm.*

Captain Sam Jammal, CO, H&S Company

McCusker was a hyper kind of guy, always doing something. He's a good guy. One day he came up and he wanted to paint everything in desert camouflage. Everybody was rolling their eyes! The guy's all heart. He did a damned good job.

My biggest fear was that I was too lackadaisical about what was happening that day. I was falling asleep as I moved up to the breach. It was kind of boring. It wasn't what I thought it was going to be. I was more excited in Khafji than I was on G-Day.

I was dozing off. Cigarettes and chewing gum. I'd eat just to stay awake. Maybe I was nervous and just didn't realize it. I ate four MREs between the line of departure and the time we went through the minefield.

Captain Joe Fack, FAC

We got across the breach, the minefield was unbelievable. It was just like they tossed them on the road. A lot of mines were big enough that you could see them with the naked eye. When you went around the mines, and the engineers, which were attached to India Company, said that the cardboards [which would keep them from detonating] were still in a lot of the mines. So we got through there at dawn.

Captain Sam Jammal, CO, H&S Company

I remember walking up with Captain McCusker and joking with him. He had a canteen, and I asked him if I could have a swig. He gave it to me. It wasn't water—it was Chivas Regal. It tasted damn good. We didn't drink on Saudi soil. We drank on Kuwaiti soil.

Major Craig Huddleston, Battalion XO

Now it starts to get light, the sun starts to come up, and it's getting close to when Task Force Ripper and Task Force Poppa Bear were to launch the main attack through the minefields. And we started hearing firing, small arms, and then some louder things going off. And then artillery opened up behind us. Friendly artillery, outgoing.

We get a report from Kilo Company that they are in the trenches and they're taking small arms fire and they're starting to clear the trenches. India Company was going to block to the west a little bit. They report thirty-five to forty vehicles on the horizon—enemy vehicles. And we said, "Here we go. This is it."

Captain Joe Fack, FAC

The Dragon guys thought they saw twenty-seven vehicles in a row, because they saw some heat signatures. So all hell broke loose. We called in the Dragons and shot some stuff up. We didn't have TOWs, because they hadn't gotten through the breach. The vehicle lane wasn't open yet.

Lieutenant Ivan Wray, Artillery FO, with India Company

The Dragons attachment said, "Sir, take a look at this." I had no idea what it was I was looking at. It was upwards of twenty-five or thirty colored objects moving away from us.

I thought they were going to be sweeping around, maybe get to our flank, because we were really weak at that point. All we had was straight infantry on the far side of the breach. All the artillery, all our tanks, everything, was behind us. I get a target location for that, I'm not too sure if I want to start firing all this up and let them know we're here, letting them know where we are.

Kilo gets up. We're on the backside of a little uphill slope; Kilo Company, Captain Pappa, gets up there, and then all of a sudden I hear a Dragon go off. I said, "What the hell is going on?" I hear Corporal Daniels calling a fire mission.

I go, "Oh, Christ! Here we go again." What it turns out, Dragons saw a box or some kind of an object there at two thousand meters. The Dragon shoots. One of their own people was calling, "We're taking direct fire." What it actually was, was the engineers behind us blowing up the mine.

So the coordination was lacking in the initial stage of the breach. I hear the boom back there, which is a little bit startling but I understand what's going on. The Dragons were about five or six hundred meters over the slope. I can't see them. I'm going to have to get some artillery out there to ease the pressure from them so they can pull back within the confines of the battalion, get our perimeter a little bit tighter. As it turns out, it was a false alarm.

Everybody gets calmed down. We led out further to the west. Nobody ever figured out what it was they saw.

Captain Leon Pappa, CO, Kilo Company

Just at first light we were already through. I got through around 0510 or 0515. Colonel Garrett called me on the radio—"Are you through?" That's what he kept asking, and I kept saying, "Not yet." The recon guys had already started marking some more lanes. You could hardly hear Colonel Garrett, because the wind was blowing real bad. It was raining. McCusker had to go west, and I'd be the first one to go east, so the colonel kept saying, "Are you through? Are you through?" I couldn't get through until McCusker did.

It was about five-ten, five-fifteen, when we crossed to the other side. We had to be across by five-thirty, we were told.

I went east. We started moving. I must have gone a little too far north, because I had planned to keep my right flank on the tail end of the belt. According to aerial photos, the enemy had some bunker complexes there. By the time I had the company moving, I had two platoons up and one kind of tucked back on the right side.

I remember saying to the platoons, "Okay, we should be starting to see some trenches now if this is accurate." Right about that time—again you're not sure if this is really happening—I saw a flash. I didn't think anything at first, because it was raining and we were getting some lightning. Then I did hear it. It went over our heads.

We started taking fire that hit behind us. I don't think they could see my company at this point. What I thought they saw was Lima. We were heading east. Normally I ran with a pretty sizable wedge. I could get that company spread out probably, in depth, five hundred to a thousand meters, something like this, so I was keeping them a little tighter.

It was First Platoon up on the right and Third Platoon on the left; I was tucked in between, and my other platoon at that point was in trace. The belt was to our right. I couldn't visually see the belt, but they did get some trenches and some bunkers. We were getting fire from somewhere over here. It looked like a thousand meters out. It was high silhouette. I didn't know what kind of vehicle it was. My initial impression was it was a goddamned tank, but I don't think it was.

The more I thought about the rounds, they didn't sound high enough caliber as a tank, so I think it was a Panhard [Iraqi reconnaissance] vehicle, which had a 90-millimeter gun.

Unfortunately, the Saudis had them too. I could just make out the top. It looked too boxy to be a tank. It was maybe a thousand meters away; you could hear its rounds going over.

The initial thing was, *He's fucking firing at us!* I think my two platoons were in pretty good position. Who was really a little out in the open was my headquarters group, and I remember we all kind of laughed because there were some knolls not far away, and I said, "I think that might be a good spot," and we all hightailed it over there.

I wanted to get one of the platoons up higher because I had Dragons. In the meantime, I probably had artillery on the thing in about two minutes. I had a corporal that was an FO—outstanding. They offered me a lieutenant months before that, because I used to have a lieutenant FO who had gone up to be the arty liaison, and I said, "No, I'm happy with Corporal Daniels." I wrote him up for a Navy Achievement Award. A real good kid.

It was a little funny that morning, because we were shooting a preregistered target. We got a good first round. I said, "Tell them to fire for effect." The fire for effect landed way over here. I said, "You're shooting fire mission 418, aren't you?" "No, sir, I thought you said 419." It was like that with the wind blowing. We shot maybe three artillery missions in the space of about five to ten minutes.

In the meantime, I understand the colonel was trying to get the tanks up, because I'll admit initially I said to him (and I took a lot of ribbing over this), "Suspected main gun tank rounds." In retrospect, I think it was something smaller. I think the silhouette wasn't high enough for a BMP, but it could have been. I think it was a Panhard. After the shooting stopped, we moved on another two or three clicks to the phase line—I think it was Silver—where I was supposed to stop. We kicked out patrols and that was basically it.

When we'd started moving, I had heavy guns brought up for me. I did this to stir things up. I had them recon by fire after the last artillery missile hit, and everybody was seeing ghosts. Right at this same time, my First Platoon commander said he had movement in the bunkers. There was this pause. I said, "What are you waiting for me for?" He had an initial apprehension like this isn't the "K ranges" anymore at Camp LeJeune. "What are you waiting for? My blessing? Take him."

I could hear some grenades. Some Dragons were fired. An antitank weapon blew one bunker up. Then, no reports. They said a cat low-crawled out for about three hundred meters. That lieutenant has taken a lot of crap about that—the fight at Cat Hill or something like that.

I think what really made the Marines feel better was our own artillery going over their heads. They could hear it and you could hear them cheering down there. When my radio operator knew we had a mission going out and he heard me say, "Shot out," he would yell "Incoming" over the platoon net. I think it made them feel better that "Hey, we can get some stuff out."

I told Colonel Garrett, "Sir, I was trying to stir stuff up because I didn't know what was up there." Everybody was jumpy. The FAC was yelling at me to use some Harriers he had, and I did.

Captain Mike McCusker, CO, India Company

Iiams is now at the center, holding there, while the engineers are marking these mines, getting ready to blow them. The company is coming through on foot. The vehicles are coming up, and it just starts to get light. We're digging, digging, digging in, because we're on the far side and we don't want to get caught there without holes. The next thing I know, the driver says, "Sir, there are twenty-seven things out there through the night-sight." I thought, *Holy shit, this is all I need!*

So I call back to battalion to see what was up. Nothing was up at the time, so Ivan Wray calls for a fire mission on what's out there. Just as he is whipping them up, Kilo Company had come through and runs into a vehicle, which they shoot. Then he starts calling for air, and he gets priority for air and artillery. We're reporting that back to battalion—he's shooting artillery and air is coming in. These twenty-seven things are out there, but you can't tell what they are except they are a heat source for our night-sight.

Major Craig Huddleston, Battalion XO

I couldn't talk to the colonel. I said, "I've got to get up there." I was tasked with being the traffic director at the breach in the minefield. So I grabbed the tank and the two LAVs and my vehicle, and I said, "We're going forward. Tank, your job is to start shooting if you see targets. You're no longer a mine clearer. You're our armor."

We take off, hell bent for leather, for the minefield. It's only about a kilometer away. We're behind a little rise. I come around the top of the hill, and there I see all of our vehicles lined up to go through this one breach, and off to my right there's all this firing going on, small arms. I see some Dragons going off, Dragon missiles going off, and I see artillery impacting out in front of our men. I said, "Geez, we've got to get going." I turned around to look at the tank and there's nobody behind me. I'm out there with my own vehicle by myself.

Colonel John Garrett, Battalion Commander

We called in artillery. Air showed up. But this firing was going on, and all we had was a foot lane through the minefield, and I had to get my heavy guns and TOWs through there. I thought, *I guess I made the wrong call, because we're not going to be able to defend ourselves.* Plus, there were these brigades of Iraqi armor, and we still didn't know where they were.

Captain Mike McCusker, CO, India Company

I get on the line with the colonel and say, "Hey, sir, we're stuck here, but we're trying to break a lane." He says, "I need a lane through for the vehicles." So I went up to the engineers and said, "We need a lane right here for the vehicles to go through." I sent Iiams and one of the engineers to walk the lane out to where the vehicles are, while I stay with the engineers, and we marked all the mines and blew them and cut the wire. The area has now been prepped, and the colonel is coming through first.

Colonel John Garrett, Battalion Commander

I said, "I've got to get the tank up and get him through." Well, the tank had thrown a track. So he couldn't come up. He was not available. So it appeared that there was no way to get the vehicles through. So Sergeant Iiams, the recon team leader, who is just wonderful, came up and said, "Sir, I think I can get the vehicles through." I said, "What do you mean—you think you can get the vehicles through?" I got in and we just drove through where he thought we could go, and it worked. So we had two tracks, and then we got the heavy guns, the TOWs, and everybody in, and then it was all over because everybody was in position.

Sergeant William Iiams, Recon Team Leader

At that time, we couldn't get the heavy guns through. We couldn't get our TOW vehicles through. I think there were some BTRs, some BMPs coming. The minefield hadn't been blown yet. The antitank mines hadn't been blown. The engineers and myself went over and started putting sticks [of explosive] on all the antitank mines.

We blow all the antitank mines. That gave a way for Colonel Garrett and some heavy guns. I ran back and got them and ran them up and got them through.

Corporal David Bush, S3 Driver

I was with the main command group. After that we started moving out. I was in the back with the position locating system. We were following a trace, so I had to keep having to tell the driver and the captain, "You've got to turn to your left about four degrees, go thirty-five degrees for another two clicks, and that's where they're at," because you couldn't see anything. It was so dark, you couldn't see anything. So that's what I did all night long. It took us all night, and the first troops started having close calls with almost stepping on mines. Nobody got killed. Nobody was injured there—it was easy. It made me feel good, getting through it, not having any losses, not having any kind of fighting going on, no problems.

The thing is the war went smoother than any training operation I've ever been on. Training operations are usually backed up, held up doing something. The war was like a training operation but doing it right.

I drove through the breach about four times going back and forth. They got everybody through and set up outside for a couple of hours on the other side, on the north side of it, got everybody moving through, the logistics train—resupply. They were way back behind us. We made sure everybody knew what was going on. I had it easy during the war because I was in a vehicle. These people, line companies, man, they had sixty-, seventy-pound packs on their backs, and they walked from where the breach was—probably fifteen clicks or so. They walked the whole thing. They walked all day and night long, then went through a breach site. I just drove; I was awake the whole time. There was no problem doing that. I was up for it.

Captain Mark Davis, Battalion Logistics Officer

So we pick up everything up and we walk up to the breach. They laid in. The BAS was portable and they lay in. I've got a radio with a frequency for the battalion, so I know they're going through the breach. They've done their leader recce. It's just now becoming dawn. The companies are goin' through.

I'm pinching myself left and right. I'm talking to the logistic support on the radio. They're asking what I want. They had this code thing set up where the States were chow, birds were ammunition. Water was some type of animal. So if you wanted a day of chow for your battalion, you asked for one "Montana"; if you wanted the ammunition for the battalion, two canaries. He was asking me, "Do you want this Montana?"

We go through the breach. There was concertina wire to the left and right, as far as the eye could see. It just went forever. While this is all going on, before we drive across it, I walked back over to the battalion aid station. The BAS guys are saying, "Sir, this is combat, where's the casualties?" I said, "Let's be thankful there aren't any." They were actually bored, they were falling asleep. They were bored. I thought, *This is the greatest war that could ever be.*

They had erected the BAS; now they tore it down, took it to the other side, laid it out again. It took about two hours to tear it down and two to put it back up again. It didn't take so long to put the tent up, but when you started putting the stretchers up inside, breaking out the equipment, that was what was time-consuming. Making sure the oxygen tanks were fired up, ready to go. Those were the hard things.

During the past months the corpsmen would come back to the BAS for specific training to learn how to do certain things. Each day on the training schedule they'd have it down where they'd be treating a certain type of injury. They'd do things blindfolded. We had a pretty competent medical staff. I was real impressed with them.

Colonel John Garrett, Battalion Commander

Whatever was shooting at us went away. We dug in a defense, and then a few hours later we started taking prisoners as we pushed out, and I think that's pretty much the way it was up and down the line. Once the attack was obvious, then the Iraqis just started collapsing.

Major Craig Huddleston, Battalion XO

It turns out the small arms fire was nervousness on the part of our Marines. The vehicles that India Company saw were pretty much decoys. The Iraqis had made decoys out of water tanks, fuel tanks, and they really looked pretty good, and that's also what our Dragons were shooting at. At sunrise on a rainy, hazy, windy day they looked real, and as we got up there to see what they were, we realized we'd been suckered. The bottom line was the minefields were not attended. Most of the mines were not even armed—they were all surface laid. It was a very minor obstacle for us and we went through it fast. By mid-morning we had three breaches opened up. Most of the 3rd Marines were through, the LAI battalion was through, most of 1/12 was through, and we were continuing to expand outward.

I looked at the minefield; it was so extensive, and it went horizon to horizon, further than we could see, millions of mines. I think the Iraqis got lazy. They got to the point where they were laying so damned many mines, they just tossed them on the ground. Their discipline was poor, and they just said, "The gunny said put the mines out. The mines are out." Had they defended it, it would have been difficult but not impossible. It wasn't the boogey man we thought it was. The minefield was maybe only one hundred meters wide. All the mines were surface laid. The wire obstacles were minor. It was easy to get through the mines with the wire obstacles. Their fighting positions were poorly constructed. They didn't have much cover, they weren't very deep. We would have had a fight if they wanted to, but we'd have beat them up pretty bad there.

Colonel John Garrett, Battalion Commander

We were on the right flank, and Task Force Grizzly was way over on the left flank so that we had the two flanks anchored. We were actually the first ones across—either that or we were tied with Grizzly. I don't know which, but our two units on the flanks were the first to cross the border and the first through the obstacles.

The other reason to get the vehicles through was not only to protect us, but we had to get them out so they could get out quickly and give a credible blocking position against the tanks that we thought might come through.

Captain Joe Fack, FAC

We had artillery shooting over our heads, but it wasn't incoming to us. We were digging in along this road right here, and the platoons identified that we were in a minefield. So everybody said, "Okay, let's get back. Let's get the hell out of here." Kilo Company was on our right flank. They went right through a minefield and identified it. They were within two hundred meters into the minefield when they said, "Oh, by the way, we've got mines all around us." They were kind of worried about that.

We heard an explosion right in the 2/3 area. It was a grenade going off. I guess the grenade fell, the pin came out, and the guy blew up.[3]

Captain Joe Fack, FAC

After everything calmed down, we started doing recons. Captain McCusker and myself reconned the bunkers to make sure nobody was there. The living spaces were plush. They were real nice. The ones that we went into looked like a command bunker. They had like two rooms where people could live, like bedrooms constructed of walls and stuff like that in a lot of the bunkers. They had long trenches that were covered up with sand. It looked like nobody had been there for a while, at least a week or two weeks, and the sand was already getting into the bunkers. There were a lot of Rockeye [bomblets] in the area and stuff like that. You had to watch where you stepped.

Corporal David Bush, S3 Driver

We go up a little workers' camp and we set up there. We were sitting in there, and we find a building, get the communication wires running, getting hooked up so we could talk to everybody. We didn't really dig in too hard.

Sergeant William Iiams, Recon Team Leader

We pulled into an old abandoned town. It was a morale boost since there were so many Iraqis giving up. Plus we ended up in the middle of an onion field. All the troops had fresh onions with their MREs. It's kind of crazy. People were eating onions.

21 / Prisoners

Major Craig Huddleston, Battalion XO

I'm glad the Iraqis didn't defend. In any case, as it became apparent to all the Marine forces that this first offensive was going to be a piece of cake, the mission started changing; we had a boundary change between us and our adjacent unit, which was Task Force Poppa Bear. One of their first objectives they ignored and gave to us, which was very large . . . we called it a worker's camp.

We took off on that same day with India Company, myself, some heavy guns, some TOWs—and away we went to clear this huge built-up area. It had been abandoned, but it turns out it had been an Iraqi division headquarters. What we found in there is of historical significance, and I don't know if it's ever been developed—we found a copy of the order which called for the destruction of the Al Wafrah oil fields. In addition, it had the task organization of the destruction teams and their names. We had a Kuwaiti liaison with us, who translated it for us. We sent it up to the chain of command. It clearly listed the four-man teams that were to destroy each well. And of course, that's what happened. The Al Wafrah oil field was totally wrecked. I hope that the Kuwaitis have the order and that they have sifted through all the POWs and have the people responsible.

We spent a quiet night up there. We got organized in the town. Regimental headquarters moved up behind us, both of the other battalions are to our rear. They're standing down somewhat. The threat is not so great as we thought it was going to be. About nine o'clock the next morning, a passing

Huey reported to us that a tank battalion and an infantry brigade were moving in our direction. It was about ten kilometers away from us. There was no time for the rest of the battalion to join up with us or for us to join up with the rest of the battalion. We decided that if the enemy was attacking, our best bet was to remain in the town and to stay down.

I went forward with a rifle squad, some psyops people, a TOW squad, and a heavy machine gun squad to do reconnaissance and also to see if these folks were maybe trying to surrender, because we had an indication they might be. The helicopter pilot said, "They don't look like they're trying to fight." We came up and hit the second defensive belt, and there they were—a tank battalion and about two thousand infantry moving at us.

By this time we organized four Cobras and four A10s, Air Force aircraft; they were circling overhead. The lead Cobra went up and put a laser spot on the lead tank to get a range. As soon as that laser went out, they all stopped, they all got out of their tanks, and fell into battalion formation, waved white flags, and surrendered, as did about two thousand infantrymen.

They have to come through the minefields to get to us. The first group comes through, a little delegation of five tankers, and they said, "We just want to quit. We want to surrender, how do we do that?" We said, "Come on. We'll take you."

Captain Joe Fack, FAC

The XO, an arty FO, and myself and the TOW vehicles were the whole task force. I had five Cobras, two A10s, a Huey, and all the close air support that I could get. The Cobras were in back of us. There was one Cobra leading us up. We were right below him just in case he had to shoot something.

Corporal David Bush, S3 Driver

They just wanted to surrender. They were throwing their stuff off, running towards us, throwing their weapons down. Then their own troops started shooting at them. So they wanted to surrender. They got sixty or seventy right there. The Iraqis just gave up.

Sergeant Major Bo Pippin, Battalion Sergeant Major

Of course I was surprised to see all of this. I think in the first radio call, they said, "We got sixty-five enemies." Then the guy on the radio came back and said, "Make that one hundred." The third call that came back, he said, "These damn guys are all over the place. There're hundreds of them." I think the total that day, that got somewhere around sixty-five hundred enemy POWs for our regiment; that happened a lot—they gave up without a fight.

We're dealing with all of these prisoners, trying to capture them, and we start taking incoming again. We think its U.S. artillery, so we call around to shut it off. It turns out it wasn't U.S. artillery at all. It was Iraqi artillery and mortars, and they were killing the hell out of their own people. I saw them put a lot of rounds into about 2,000 people in formation. Out of all that group of 2,000, we ended up getting about 120 people. The rest of them either ran back to their fighting holes, were killed, or were captured by the 1st Marines, who happened to come up on the flank closer to them and grabbed them.

Those were our first prisoners. It was kind of a shock. They were well fed. They had new uniforms on. They had a lot of money. They had good equipment. They looked to be in good health, but their morale was shot. I wanted to say that was a result of the air attacks. The Iraqi soldiers said no. Most of this unit, said the Iraqi captain I was talking to, was released from Iranian POW camps in December. "We went home and were immediately sent to Kuwait. We just want to go home." They didn't want to fight. They just wanted to quit.

All the prisoners we captured after that, it was the same story. All we had to do was appear and they asked, "What took you so long? We just want to surrender." They weren't bad off. They weren't starving. They weren't decrepit. They were good-looking soldiers. Most of them had brand-new uniforms, new boots, new clothes, warm clothes, gas masks, helmets, everything they needed to fight with. They just didn't want to fight. They'd recently been paid; they all had brand-new money on them—Kuwaiti money. They just wanted to go home and be done with war.

Captain Joe Fack, FAC

There was also an infantry battalion that was trying to surrender over on the right flank from us. I think that the regimental XO was out there trying to do his part, make sure that nothing happened. Once the infantry guys started surrendering, their own 82 mortars started shooting at the POWs that were surrendering. I tried to get the OV10s to identify where the mortars were coming from, because they had the capability of identifying where it was.

They finally did identify it, but it was two hours later. I don't think the mortars killed anybody. Their shooting was pretty bad. They got pretty close to us, but I was calling up the OV10s, going, "Hey, they're getting kind of close to us. See what you can do for me." There were a couple of areas that came in that they couldn't identify because there was cloud cover and all the smoke and haze that was coming from the burning oil fields.

The next day our mission was getting to Kuwait International Airport—everybody except for two platoons of India Company that stayed back. One platoon went up; Captain McCusker and myself stayed back. While they were up there, we captured forty-five more POWs, plus a PRC 63. Our part in the war was ended right here. We never did get up to Kuwait International.

Major Craig Huddleston, Battalion XO

We passed the next day in relative calm. The war was raging around us; we'd hear a lot of things. We were told we were displacing to Kuwait International Airport. We're going to liberate the city. You could have knocked us over with a feather. We'd only been at it for four days, less than four days. We knew the war was over.

Colonel John Admire, CO, Task Force Taro

Three-three conducted the night infiltration, penetration, and breach of the first Iraqi obstacle barrier. Two-three secured the division's right flank from the Saudi-Kuwaiti border north to the first barrier. On 25 February, 1/3, as Task Force X-ray, conducted the Marine Corps' only helicopter-borne assault of the war by attacking and securing the Burgan oil field.

Major Craig Huddleston, Battalion XO

I was with the Saudi breaching force that made three or four lanes through the barrier. Their engineers went up and made these lanes through the tank ditch in the first berm along the border and to the initial barrier belt, the minefields. When it was time to go, there was a mass of vehicles, three, four, five lanes wide. Miles long, all flying the Saudi flag, just roared into Kuwait. It was an incredible, incredible sight.

All around us things had been happening to indicate the Iraqis were not fighting. When we got up to Kuwait International, there were a lot of Marine forces up there already. There was a lot of battle damage all around us—dead tanks, dead vehicles, dead people. The place was an inferno with all these oil wells burning all around.

Along about dusk, the battalion commander came back with his orders. He said, "We will defend this sector. The war is not over. Don't give up yet. There are still bad things out there. So maintain your dispersion and dig in deep." I don't think many of us paid much attention to him; we knew the war was over.

Captain Joseph Molofsky, Liaison to the Saudi Brigade

They went into Kuwait International. Americans, Task Force Taro, was held outside the city. The Saudis liberated the city. The Force Reconnaissance Platoon leader that was with me, Brian Knolls, drove up there the night before, linked up with some Kuwaiti resistance, drove to the American embassy, and actually raised the first flag at the American embassy. It was unoccupied. He beat out a special operations Delta Force SEAL team operation that was out on a boat with millions of dollars worth of equipment that was going to be used to justify next year's Special Op budget. Young Lieutenant Knolls and five of his filthy, dirty kids preempted Delta Force. That was fun.

I'll never forget riding into the city with the Arabs and the reception we got. It must have been kind of like Paris in World War II. People dancing in the streets. Arabs firing weapons in the air. People crying. Old Arab women running up to you and grabbing you. Unheard of. Children screaming. Intersections blocked. When you'd drive up, these militiamen would run out in the middle of the intersection and move everybody aside and let our vehicle pass. People grabbing you. Old men crying and kissing you. I'll never forget it—never!

Captain Mark Davis, Battalion Logistics Officer

We waited about a day or two. The word comes that we're going to go to Kuwait International Airport. "Holy shit! We're going that far that fast?" "Yes, we are!"

We ordered everybody up and we started driving north. We drove to a breach where one of our task forces had gone through. As we're driving through, I see one American vehicle and it was a tank, one of our tanks that had one of its threads blown off. No other American vehicle was anywhere to be seen. There's numerous tanks, Russian tanks, on either side of the breach, smoked out, burned out. You could see where one of the task forces came through and dropped their mine plows and their rakes and their wheels and kept going.

Now it's starting to get dark at nine or ten o'clock in the morning. We finally get through all this and we're right in the oil fields and the smoke. It's twelve o'clock noon and it's pitch black, black as midnight. We stopped for a piss call. We put on the headlights. It was almost blackout driving conditions. We drove a little bit further. I look and there's fifteen, twenty oil wells just spewing burning oil just as fast as it could come out of the hole and burn. I looked at this and I said, "That son of a bitch. Now he's not just ruining Kuwait. Now we're talking about the world environment."

We got back in the vehicles and drove forward. We drive through this smoke. There must have been over 150 or 200 folks in some sort of quasi-military formation. These guys just walked out of the smoke and gave themselves up.

Just south of Kuwait International Airport, we stop again for another halt. The wind is blowing from the north. In a 180-degree arc, I counted no less than forty-seven oil wells, on fire. It was just as black as pitch.

We go to Kuwait City through the airport. They're trying to figure out where we're supposed to go. I'm thinking that we should just follow the signs, so we did. We stopped along the side of the road. As we drive in, there's some Iraqi APCs with a body or two lying beside them. There are M60 tanks over there. It looks like they had a fight at one time. There were hulks [burned-out vehicles] over here but none from our forces.

We stopped before we got right into Kuwait International Airport proper. People started driving by, waving Kuwait flags. Girls, men, women, children, everybody. They were saying, "Thank you, thank you, thank you," as they drove by. I looked and thought about how this scene had been played before. They freed France. They freed this and that. I am in the midst of history right here, and all I can think about is where I am going to get water for the battalion. I finally started checking on chow, on ammunition.

They gave us a section of the airport, and we bedded down and stayed there for about three days. We were waiting for someone to make a decision on whether they're going to keep us up there or take us back. They told us to not go into the airport buildings, so we didn't. We dug in positions around the airport.

The word finally came out on what we could take back as souvenirs, and I had to turn the rest of the gear in. I went to Colonel Counselman, the division G2, with a truckload of AK47s. He told me that he didn't want to have a thing to do with them, so we ditched them somewhere.

The first thing that everyone wants to know is when we are going home. Nobody knows. It took nearly a month to figure out to do with the MPS equipment that had to be turned in. Finally we got it separated from the stuff we brought from Hawaii and turned it in.

Colonel John Garrett, Battalion Commander

We moved up to Kuwait International Airport. By the time we got there, it was all but secured. We did some clearing operations, didn't hit any resistance really, except that we did take one Scud in the afternoon.

Major Craig Huddleston, Battalion XO

As the company commanders turned to walk away, there was a Scud missile that impacted about a thousand meters from where we were. It got our attention right away, and entrenching tools were flying. We dug in for the night.

The next day Kuwait City was liberated. We got a chance to go around and see a few things. I went off with a few folks and went to Iraqi III Corps forward headquarters in the basement of this building and saw their plan and their orders.

The reason I believe the war was over so quickly was that the preponderance of the Iraqi forces in Kuwait were oriented toward the ocean and were preparing to defend the city. Their orders said the same thing. The division commanders were prevented from launching any but mobile counterattacks and could conduct no major movements except on the orders of Saddam Hussein himself. They had about five divisions in the Kuwait City area on the beach and five Special Forces brigades in the city defending the city from the beach. They had one brigade at the airport. By the time they reoriented and tried to face us, that's when the U.S. Army went into Iraq and the war was over. They had absolutely no options left. We knew after that first day, it was all going our way. Better than we had expected.

Then we moved out, went back to our division support area by motor march, all the way back to Kuwait City within a couple of days. It happened real fast. *Get out of Kuwait. We're going home!* Our spirits were pretty high. We took the coastal road all the way back to our division support area at Niko Bay.

As we traveled down the coastal road and got closer to Saudi Arabia, we saw the effects of the initial days of the war. Iraqi equipment littered everywhere on both sides of the road and on the road itself. The road was so full of bomb craters that we had to dodge them. We saw the rocket launchers that had been harassing us. They were dead and blown to pieces.

Some of the Marines were disappointed. They trained so long and prepared so well, and then it was over before they knew what happened. The results didn't seem to relate to our preparation for the war. It happened so fast and was so massive that their initial reaction was disappointment. They wanted to mix it up a little more.

The first thing Colonel Garrett did when we got back to the division support area was call the battalion together in small groups by company and explain to them that they should not be disappointed and that they had done a tremendous job. "The fact that we didn't take any casualties doesn't mean that you're any less of a Marine than those who have gone before you. All it means is that you should have more respect for the people that preceded you. At the same time, you should take pride in your accomplishments, because no one's ever done anything like you've done. Perhaps next time we won't be so fortunate, so count yourself lucky."

Major Dan Stansbury, Battalion Operations Officer

We went through a lot of Iraqi bunkers. They had a tremendous amount of ammunition left. There were antiaircraft guns with rounds in the chamber and ready to fire. There was a lot of clothing and food. They were really well stocked. A well-disciplined force that really wanted to fight could have caused us some problems. Then again, you've got to take into consideration they were being bombed continuously for thirty days. Command and control, discipline, and supply chains had been destroyed.

If we had been facing a force like the Japanese in World War II, a very committed force, it could have been pretty tough all the way around. Just going through that breach, a couple of guys in a couple of bunkers could have made it tough for us right from the first. I'm very thankful they didn't have the mental toughness of the Vietnamese or the Japanese.

When the fighting ended, just one hundred hours after the ground war began, the Marine part of the invasion force had captured, destroyed, or damaged 1,060 tanks, 608 armored personnel carriers, 432 artillery pieces, and 2 Scud launchers. The Marines in the assault had 5 killed and 40 wounded. The 3rd Battalion, 3rd Marines was unscathed and was to return home with the enviable record of none killed and none wounded by enemy action in Desert Storm.

23 / Yellow Ribbons

In the same manner in which 3/3 deployed to the Middle East, they returned home in increments.

Major Craig Huddleston, Battalion XO

The low point of the whole thing was waiting to get out. We turned our equipment and ammunition in and had absolutely nothing to do except wait to go home.

For me, it took almost three weeks. It was rough. I was as sad as I've been, because the food wasn't very good and there were maybe thirty thousand of us in a place designed for five thousand. We overtaxed the food; we overtaxed the water supply; we overtaxed the phones. There was a little PX there, and it took about three hours to get into it. Lines to phone home lasted all day. It was nice that they had those things, but the aggravation . . . *It's over, let's go home.*

When we finally got out of there, it was pretty good. We were real happy to go. All of the commanders had been struggling to keep the Marines occupied. The last week we were there we had a cookout every afternoon—steaks, chicken, hamburgers—but even that got old. We just wanted to go. For our battalion it had been a thirteen-month deployment. We were ready.

We finally got on the airplane. It was Hawaiian Air and it was great. Everyone said, "Aloha." There we were—filthy, dirty, nasty Marines. At the airfield Senator [John] Glenn, who was a Marine, waved at us. General Boomer came up and said good-bye to us and told us we'd done a good job.

We got on and sat down. This was the nicest environment we'd been in in seven months. As soon as the doors closed and the air conditioning went on it was great. They played a Whitney Houston tape of her singing the national anthem, and there wasn't a dry eye in the house. Again the flight crew was very appreciative. They told us how proud they were and said, "You can't believe what's going to happen when you get home."

Captain Kevin Scott, CO, Lima Company

We took off and, looking out the window, you could see the oil. It was devastating, covering the ocean for miles out to sea. It was washed up on the beaches. These guys really messed up the ecological system.

Major Craig Huddleston, Battalion XO

Anything the flight crews could do for us, they did. We ate good food. It was wonderful. We stopped in Rome and we weren't supposed to get off, but a few of us did. There were some Italian policemen there when I got off with four or five Marines. They didn't speak English, but they rushed up and were shaking our hands and slapping us on the back. I couldn't believe it.

Colonel John Garrett, Battalion CO

In Rome, the ambassador came on board and gave everybody ice cream. In New York, TWA opened up all their offices, and the guys got to call anywhere in the world they wanted, for free. In L.A. they had coffee and cookies set up. When we got back to Honolulu, they had a band and a contingent of Vietnam vets. As a group they have probably been happier about this than anyone else. I am one of them. They could be resentful about this, but they're not. They're unsung heroes.

Major Craig Huddleston, Battalion XO

My plane went from Rome to Shannon, Ireland. We hit Shannon about five minutes after midnight on St. Patrick's Day. The bar was open, and we made the most of it. It was the first alcoholic beverage we had in seven months. Not long after we arrived, a congressional junket came into the bar. There were about forty congressmen and senators and their staffers. We had a helluva party. We stood around and drank beer with them, and the congressmen were telling them what a great job we'd done. We were astute enough to tell them that they'd done a great job too. We had a kind of a mutual admiration society.

We got on the airplane and flew to Bangor, Maine, and got in about 0200. We were told that we had to get off, that there was a welcome home for us. We'd been on the airplane for a long time and were tired. We all took our shaving kits with us. We came around a corner, and here was a VFW honor guard made up of everything from World War I vets through Vietnam vets. They were smiling and slapping us on the back. We didn't know what to think.

About another fifty meters and we went through double doors. I opened the doors and it was like I'd been shot. There were about five hundred people in there with banners and balloons and screaming and yelling and cheering. Two high school bands were playing. It was two o'clock in the morning, and they've got a reception line and you're walking through and they're just pounding us on the back and telling us how wonderful we are. They were kissing us, hugging us, giving us food and beers. I mean there were some people in there . . . Hell's Angels, hippies, grandparents, grandchildren, people our own age. They're just yelling and throwing confetti and streamers. We were absolutely taken aback. They were asking for our autographs, offering some homemade pie. "Here, you'd better have some beer to go with that." This went on for about two hours, with people yelling and dancing on chairs. I talked to one couple that had been there for nineteen hours straight, welcoming flight after flight. It knocked us out.

1st Sergeant Wylie McIntosh, Weapons Company

They treated us great. I flew back on a TWA airplane, and it was like coming home to Mom from scout camp. The flight crew did everything in the world. They autographed our menus and guys' casts. We autographed their white shirts.

We landed in New York. Having come home from Vietnam and kind of having to sneak into town just to keep from getting rocks or spit on, I could not believe it. We got off the plane in New York at one o'clock in the morning. This was not prime time. There were thousands of people there, cheering. It was like a football game, really exciting. I sat down in a bar for my first beer in seven months, was really looking forward to it. A gentleman sitting there plopped down four hundred dollars and said, "Hey, everybody here wearing desert suits, drink this up." I was really impressed.

Captain Kevin Scott, CO, Lima Company

As I walked off the plane in Bangor, I wondered if my mother- and father-in-law could be here. They were down in Brunswick, Maine, and my father-in-law had been in the Army. We came around the corner and started down the ramp, and there they were—my mother- and father-in-law. I spoke to them and the people of Bangor, Maine, who had come to the airport and were treating us fabulously. They were hugging and kissing us and saying, "Thank you." It choked me up to come home to that, even though my mom and wife had been telling me that the nation was behind us. I found it hard to believe that our nation had risen to the occasion and was supporting our servicemen. They were supporting us 100 percent.

Major Craig Huddleston, Battalion XO

Finally they told us we'd have to get back on the plane in Bangor, and the people didn't want to let us go. They were holding us back. We walked back down the corridors and the VFW is still there. They're slapping us on the back again. We passed a flight of inbound men. They were mostly Air Force guys, and they looked like we did a couple of hours ago. They were all bedraggled, had beards and red eyes. We had all these yellow ribbons tied around us, flowers and flags, food and everything. They looked at us, and we told them that they were not going to believe what was going to happen to them. Sure enough, as we were boarding the airplane, we heard it start all over again. It was wonderful!

We got on the airplane and flew into Seattle. There was no one to meet us there, and that was fine because we were really tired. By now we had been on the airplane for twenty-four hours. We were on the last hop to Honolulu. As we taxied down the taxiway at Hickam Air Force Base in Hawaii, the pilot grabbed two of our guys and had them standing up in the escape hatch on top holding the national colors and our guidon. We pulled in and everybody's there, the families. It was really, really wonderful.

As we got off the plane, Hawaiian Air, they stuffed an envelope in every

Marine's pocket. I looked at it later. They had given each of us a free round-trip ticket to go anywhere in the islands.

Captain Kevin Scott, CO, Lima Company

As I walked down the carpet, people were yelling and screaming. Standing at the end of the tarmac was my wife.

Major Craig Huddleston, Battalion XO

I saw my wife and we came back to the base. As we pulled into the battalion CP area, the band was there and they were playing music. There were garbage cans lined up that were full of cold beer and sodas. There were working parties established to grab our baggage off trucks and deliver it to us. The press was there. The armory was full of armorers so the Marines could turn in their weapons. We were all done in half an hour and on the way home. It took me awhile to get over the experience.

Yellow Ribbons
Albuquerque 1991

I wander out of the airport restaurant
Curious Cautious
Stand by a purple pillar
Watch the noisy crowd of people grow
and grow and grow.
Silver foil balloons
Welcome banners
Eagles on T-shirts
Lots of flags
Yellow ribbons
Everywhere.
Passengers scurry through
this happy mob, as if
Embarrassed, a little, to clutter
The Path.
Finally, Returning Warriors
Pierce the circle

are devoured by laughing,
Sobbing, women,
Cheering, Hugging
Men.
Fierce . . . with joy.
I watch all this.
Ashamed of my selfish thoughts.
This is Now.
The Past is gone.
Forever.
Slowly, the Happy Mob moves left
Toward the escalator
To the parties,
parades, vacations,
Lives.
Minds accepting—it's over
No one seems to see
the quiet cowboy standing
by the purple pillar
Holding his hat
In his hand.
—Rod McQueary—Marine, Vietnam veteran, cowboy, and poet

24 / Parting Shots

Captain Leon Pappa, CO, Kilo Company

I thought at first that maybe there was something wrong with me at Kuwait International Airport. I was actually a little disappointed that it was all over. I think this is typical of what the troops think of an officer, that all he wants to see is the fights and the recognition. It wasn't that. For one, I knew I'm glad we're going home, because we've been gone a long, long time, plus the Okinawa thing. But I knew that for Kilo Company it was the beginning of the end for me. It was a selfish motive when I realized I was going to lose the company. I was thinking, "We're never going to be this close-knit again, never have this sense of urgency."

Captain Mark Davis, Battalion Logistics Officer

The war is something I will never forget. The emotional roller coaster you were on. The *Oh, shit, we're doing it, someone is shooting at me*. I'll never forget when we were in Al Mishab and went into Khafji listening on the radio for the guys who came out of Khafji with their turrets turned to the rear. The Saudi guys were just sitting there. They were going to handle it. Then the liaison officer said, "This has turned sour. They're shooting at us." I'll never forget the feeling that these guys were not playing fair. War ain't a game.

Lieutenant Ivan Wray, Artillery FO, with India Company

These kids, these are post–Vietnam generation guys. They grew up disenchanted with a lot of things. They weren't there for the country, in my opinion. They weren't there even for the Marine Corps. What I saw, what really got me in the heart, was that camaraderie, that—for lack of a better word—love.

It really sunk in when the assistant division commander came to talk before the January deadline. He came to talk to us about combat. He had been in Vietnam, and he talked about feelings. He said, "I know you're going to do well." He goes, "What does a man fight for?" The first answer was by Lieutenant Jimenez, who said, "Love." That's incredible. Most of the things I hear are "anger." The Marines were real professionals. You could see it in their eyes. They had to take care of the Marines that affected their immediate world.

The biggest thing was to see these kids I cared so much about and have this self-doubt, thinking, *What will I do if I see these men I care so much about . . . get killed?* I'd get teary-eyed when I'd see these guys; they'd be working and just smiling, laughing, twenty hours a day—literally, at some points. I'd say, "My God, it's not the pay, it's not the food, and it's not the girls back home who broke the hearts of a lot of these guys. It wasn't for the Marine Corps; it was for that man next to you." I said, "Good God! I'm just proud to be here." That was probably some of my best days in the Marine Corps in my career; I've changed in that sense. I do believe in love again. It changed me.

1st Sergeant Wylie R. McIntosh, Weapons Company

The war's over and they stopped short of Baghdad. That's disappointing. Everybody had planned to have lunch or dinner or something in Baghdad city. I was truly disappointed and most of my company was. Really disappointed.

Staff Sergeant Don Gallagher, Platoon Sergeant, Weapons Company

I wish we wouldn't have stopped. Probably Marines, and other servicemen, would have lost their lives, but I think as long as Saddam is over there in power, he's laughing at us. He never lost power. As long as that madman is over there and he's got the capabilities, it might take another ten years, he'll be back into full strength and he won't be stupid next time. He won't wait.

I feel the young Marines did an outstanding job. Once the red flag went up and they realized they were going to do this mission, I never once saw a

Marine who was scared or a coward. They did their job. But there are some damned good Marines who got out because of the war. They had their taste of it and that's it.

Major Craig Huddleston, Battalion XO

We thought for sure Saddam was a goner. But it didn't come to pass. We didn't realize that until we were back here already. I can't speak for everybody, but the general sense I have is we stopped too soon. We could have gone on easily. But then again, everybody's quick to point out, that wasn't the mission; the mission was liberating Kuwait, not to dethrone or destabilize another sovereign nation and be the aggressor. The mission was to liberate Kuwait. Had we decided to go on in and destroy Iraq and destabilize the entire region, we could have done it. If I was the one making the decisions, which I'm not, but had I been in national command authority, I would have said, "Carry on."

Major Dan Stansbury, Battalion Operations Officer

Overall, the American support was the biggest plus. I grew up in the sixties and remembered the Vietnam War, watched the TV, watched all the hard political things that were being done incorrectly. This time, at least, waging the war, I was glad to see that the command structure pulled back and let the war fighters make war. I was very glad to see that. I think that lesson has got to continue to be reinforced so we can't make a mistake like Vietnam ever again.

Captain Mark Davis, Battalion Logistics Officer

I've been a Marine for ten years. After seeing what's happened in Russia now and what's happening in the world, I did not think that Mark Alan Davis would find himself in a Humvee in the middle of the desert going north to fight. I didn't think I'd ever see that. That was a surprise to me. I wanted to savor that. I wanted to burn it into my brain so that I would never, never, never forget. It was the chance of a lifetime. For me, it's like the final test, like a doctor with his internship. For me this was the final test: Do I have what it takes that when the chips are down, the shit is flying? Do I have what it takes to stand there and say, "This is what we need to do?"

Sergeant Major Bo Pippin, Battalion Sergeant Major

We lost a lot in Vietnam. Unfortunately our Vietnam veterans suffered for that. We could have accomplished just as much in Vietnam as we did in the Gulf if given the opportunity. Everyone knows Vietnam was a political situation, therefore the military didn't have control of it. President Bush, God bless his soul, he gave us the authority to go in and fight a military war and be victorious about it.

I am sure this experience changed a lot of young Marines. I know he's got a better opinion of himself; I also think he's seen the value of what our defense of this nation is all about. I think he's got a better understanding of what the Marine Corps is, all the armed forces. I think he's got a better understanding of what we're here for and how proud we are. I think fellas that had no consideration of staying in the Marine Corps are considering it now. We need to hang on to those Marines. We've got to go out there and reemphasize the importance of the value of the Marine Corps.

Sergeant William Iiams, Recon Team Leader

My final assessment of the whole thing was that it's good that these young guys coming out of boot camp are all motivated and think that war is neat; but I'm here to tell you, I think war stinks. I think it's a real terrible thing. I hope I'm never involved in war again. I don't think you really realize, people realize, how easily you can lose your life. When bullets were zinging by me, I thought, *Hey, fuck this. This is not neat. It's not cool.* Seeing dead people. Going through Iraqi stuff, we saw pictures of families. It's a real testament to experience. I think that God really looked over the United States. I thank all the American people for their support and encouragement. They really helped us out.

I felt cheated that Saddam Hussein's still in power. I felt cheated. But going back to my studies, who are you going to put in there? A Kurd leader? Do you put in an Islamic leader? Who do you put in there? Who's going to make things better?

I think the United States as a whole expects the Marine Corps to be a certain thing. I think the United States expects the Marine Corps to be fit and to be sent anywhere. "Send the Marines." That's easy to say, but there's a standard we have to keep. I love the Marine Corps and everything it stands for.

Captain Joseph Molofsky, Liaison to the Saudi Brigade

Nobody can compare their experience with something like Vietnam, but I'll tell you, you've got to give the kids a lot of credit. When they rode out on those artillery raids, they were in the dark in unfamiliar terrain, a couple kilometers south of what they were told was one hell of a capable force that had tremendous ability to wipe out an entire grid square, and they went anyway. Nobody hesitated. Nobody complained. They went up there thinking that there's a good possibility they were all going to get killed, and they went anyway. You've got to give them credit for that.

1st Sergeant Wylie R. McIntosh, Weapons Company

The institution, the society, had created the Marines. A person that joins the Marine Corps today has something inside that's the same thing as it was in 1775. The Marine today has a little more education, and we've got ten thousand times better gear, but there's still something special about a Marine.

Captain Mark Davis, Battalion Logistics Officer

There's something about a man that's going into combat with another guy. There's a bond, the camaraderie like a football team or basketball team, that buddy that you grew up from high school with. It transcends all that. I was closer to these guys here than any of my own brothers.

Lieutenant Ivan Wray, Artillery FO, with India Company

Before we went through the breach, I was talking to Jim Harris, Jim Glenn. We were sitting there, and I popped out some Dostoevsky: "The more I see of mankind in general, the less I believe in mankind in particular, but the more I see of mankind in particular, the more I believe in mankind in general." I think that's great. It just made me believe that passion counts, and life only matters if you care. I cared a lot about those men, and I still do.

Captain Joseph Molofsky, Liaison to the Saudi Brigade

The biggest thing we did wrong is that we let Saddam live. In the Arab mentality, weakness is vanquished. When a man is down, that's when he's finished. Failure to finish him is a sign of weakness.

So for all that we did, in the minds of the uneducated Palestinians and the unwashed masses in the Arab world we actually lost. Because had we won, then Saddam would be dead. And they cannot understand, they will never accept that we truly won if he is still in power. That is the justification to them that he in some way was a victor. I don't know if our leaders understand that completely. He needs to be dead, and we were there and we were poised. All the manpower was there and everybody was pumped up for it. We should have rolled to the Turkish border, and we should have finished his army once and for all. Because we didn't, those tanks that are not destroyed will someday roll into Jerusalem and the American forces will fight them again.

I will deploy again sometime during my career back to the Middle East to finish what could have been finished this time. I feel very strongly about that. We blinked when we should have gone for the jugular. Americans are soft. Had the positions been reversed, he'd have slaughtered us to the man—just to make a point. Absolutely. So that's my big regret. We were there. We could have done it. We didn't finish it.

25 / The Years After

Captain, now Colonel, Molofsky was right—as were others of the 3rd Battalion, 3rd Marines who wished Saddam Hussein had been toppled in 1991 or who predicted that the job would have to be finished at a later date. They had to wait for a dozen years for it to happen.

The first Gulf War showed America and the world that we once more had a first-rate military organization and that we had the will to use it in the name of freedom and democracy. The immediate aftermath of the war, however, weakened that perception. For one thing, although the elder President Bush encouraged Saddam's opponents to rise up against their oppressor, he left Saddam and his Baathist Party with the means to cruelly and effectively suppress any competition to their murderous regime. They took full advantage of this, and there is no evidence that their hold on power was ever seriously challenged.

The United Nations and the United States did place restrictions on Saddam that remained in place for the period between the wars. One restriction was the establishment of no-fly zones in both the northern and southern parts of the country. Another restriction was the agreement with the Saudi government to leave U.S. forces on Saudi soil to provide an area presence and discourage Saddam from further adventures at the expense of his neighbors. This latter arrangement had far-reaching and tragic consequences when the presence of infidels on the sacred soil of Saudi Arabia provided resentment in the Muslim world, particularly with its violent and anti-American agent Osama bin Laden.

But this problem was yet to manifest itself. Less than two years after the stunning U.S. victory in the desert, the American public, whose thoughts were centered on the economy rather than on foreign affairs, rejected the reelection of President George H. W. Bush.

The Clinton administration, with no experience in foreign policy, exacerbated the problem of America's image in the Arab world with its seeming weakness of will. The debacle in Somalia in 1993 signaled to Saddam Hussein that he could play cat-and-mouse with American and U.N. restrictions. His forces sometimes signaled their defiance of the no-fly order by firing on aircraft that were enforcing the policy.

Then there was the question of weapons of mass destruction (WMD). Before the 1991 war, the world had concrete evidence of Iraq's WMD. Iraq had, without question, used them against Iran in their long, mutually disastrous war and against the Iraqi Kurds. Most important of Saddam's defiant actions was his inflexibility regarding the U.N. inspection teams headed up by Dr. Hans Blix. The final ejection of the U.N. inspectors from Iraq rang alarm bells throughout the world. The echoes of these bells reverberated even louder after 9/11, when the United States had good reason to fear that a rogue nation like Iraq might pass WMD along to terrorists for use against the United States.

Less than a year after 9/11, the world's opposition to the Saddam regime was fractious. To much of the Muslim world Saddam was a hero, despite his 1990 invasion of Kuwait. In the eyes of millions of Muslims, he was the defiant leader against the colossus United States, which was, after all, still on sacred Muslim soil and the main supporter of the hated Jewish state. Among the nonaligned countries of the U.N., many were looking to trade opportunities with Saddam and were agitating for the lifting of sanctions.

Of America's traditional western "allies," only Britain, through Tony Blair's efforts, stayed the course. The Germans, whose avoidance of war is a by-product of our post–World War II policies, opted out early. The French, always on the lookout to make a quick franc, abandoned us for trade reasons and for their continuous quest for a French-dominated Europe.

In March 2003 the denouement of the Baathist drama in Iraq began. Coalition forces, consisting mostly of U.S. and British military units, launched simultaneous ground and air attacks. Using maneuver warfare, and technology that had improved dramatically in the years between the wars, coalition forces decimated or routed the Iraqi army in weeks. Over the next few months, Saddam Hussein's murderous sons were located and slain when they refused to surrender, and Saddam himself was found hiding out in a dirt hole and captured.

The victories of both wars were powerful stimuli for patriotism, which had lain dormant since the divisiveness of the Vietnam War. Well trained, well equipped, and, most importantly, well supported by the United States public, America's young men and women were once more restored to the respectful position they have always deserved.

Glossary

.50-cal gun: A U.S. .50-caliber machine gun; also called a heavy machine gun or heavy gun. Often referred to as 50s.

12.7 machine gun: The Soviet-made equivalent of our .50-caliber machine gun.

77: PRC (Portable Radio, Communication) 77; the basic tactical radio used by U.S. ground forces in the First Gulf War.

104: PRC (Portable Radio, Communication) 104; a radio that permits ground forces to talk to aircraft.

120: A Soviet-made 120-millimeter rocket.

1:50,000: A tactical map; used by all sorts of ground, and sometimes air, units.

203: A U.S. 40-millimeter grenade launcher.

360: A 360-degree perimeter.

531: An Iraqi APC.

A6: An attack aircraft used by the U.S. Navy and Marine Corps.

A10: An attack aircraft used by the U.S. Air Force. Nicknamed the Warthog for its ungainly appearance.

Adjust rounds: The Marines firing artillery or mortars may be miles from the target and cannot see it. Moreover, artillery and mortars are an area-fire weapon that are not as precise as, say, rifle fire. Forward observers (FOs) or others trained in the use of artillery act as spotters for the artillery fire and direct it on to the target with adjustment rounds.

Alpha: For the letter "A," often used to designate an assistant; e.g., S3 Alpha is an assistant operations officer.

Ambush: In the context of Desert Storm it is a combined arms raid.

ANGLICO: Air and Naval Gunfire Liaison Company.

APC: Armored Personnel Carrier.

Artillery Liaison Officer: A liaison officer from an artillery unit serving with another type of unit, usually infantry.

Arty: A common abbreviation for artillery.

Astro rocket: A 300-millimeter rocket used by Iraq in the Gulf War. Manufactured in Brazil.

AT4: A portable, disposable antitank weapon used by the United States.

Atropine: An anti–nerve gas agent. Carried in small syringes with a built-in needle for self-injection.

BAS: Battalion Aid Station; staffed by doctors and medical corpsmen, all USMC battalions have a BAS.

BBC: British Broadcasting Company.

BDA: Battle Damage Assessment; an estimate of damage caused by friendly units on an enemy force.

Blood agent: A chemical agent designed to cause death by altering the blood in a person. Difficult to protect against, as it tends to break down the filters on gas masks.

BMP2: An infantry fighting vehicle used by Iraq.

BSSG: Brigade Service Support Group; the logistic support unit for a brigade.

BTR50 and BTR60: Armored personnel carriers used by Iraq.

C-130 transports: Cargo aircraft used by the Marines for hauling personnel and materiel, and for refueling other aircraft.

Cammies: Camouflage; used most often in reference to camouflaged uniforms.

Chem lights: Chemically based lights that put out a dull glow and no heat.

Chopped: Temporarily assigned.

CIT: Counter-Intelligence Team.

Clackers: Detonating devices.

Claymores: Directional antipersonnel mines.

Click: Slang for kilometer.

CO: Commanding Officer.

Cobras: Helicopter gunships used by USMC.

COC: Combat Operations Center; location from where a battle is directed by an organization.

Combat service support: A generic term for those units and facilities that provide logistic support to combat units.

Comm: Communications.

Conex boxes: Large metal containers that offer ease of loading and unloading from ships.

Corpsman: Medical corpsmen; members of the U.S. Navy assigned directly to USMC units.

CP: Command Post or Headquarters.

Danger close: Used to describe friendly fire that is endangering friendly units as well.

Deuce and a half: A two-and-a-half-ton truck.

Deuce gear: Abbreviation for 782 gear; individual field equipment.

DIA: Defense Intelligence Agency.

Doc: A medical corpsman.

DPICM: Dual-Purpose, Improved, Conventional Munition; an artillery round that bursts in the air, scattering the target area with small bomblets. The bomblets in turn bounce from the ground before detonating to cover a wider area.

Dragon: A U.S. portable, wire-guided, shoulder-fired antitank weapon.

DSA: Division Support Area; a logistics base located to the rear of a division area.

EEIs: Essential Elements of Information; the things a troop commander needs to know about the enemy and terrain.

E&E: Escape and Evasion.

E-tool: Entrenching tool; a small folding shovel carried by infantrymen.

F18: Fighter aircraft.

FCT: Firepower Control Team.

Fire for effect: Artillery or mortar fire delivered to a target after the spotter rounds have located it correctly.

Fire-sack: On-call fires for artillery or mortars. An area on which fire from these weapons has been preplotted, and sometimes prefired. This insures rapid, accurate fire on this area when needed.

FO: A forward observer, or spotter, for artillery or mortars.

FPF: Final protective fires; these are preplanned and preregistered fires, used as a last resort when a unit is in danger of being overrun. Whenever possible, they are prefired; that is, they are fired when there is no danger, to ensure that the coverage of the defensive position is complete and accurate.

Frog7: A Soviet-made rocket. Frog is an acronym for Free Rocket Over Ground.

G2: The intelligence officer serving on a general staff.

G-Day: Ground Attack Day; the day the ground war was to start against Iraq.

GPS: Global Positioning System; a navigation system that uses satellites to determine one's position at any point on the earth's surface, within a few feet, in all weather.

Gray Navy: Unmarked aircraft used for clandestine purposes.

Guidon: A small unit flag used by Marine rifle companies and aircraft squadrons.

Gunny: Marine slang for gunnery sergeant. Gunnery sergeant is both a rank, pay grade E-7, and a title for the operations sergeant of a Marine rifle company.

H&S: Headquarters and Service; the company in a Marine battalion with the responsibility for most administrative and logistics matters.

HARM: High-speed Antiradar Missile.

Harrier: The USMC attack aircraft that has the capability of taking off and landing vertically, much like a helicopter.

HAWK: An antiaircraft missile. Hawk is an acronym for Homing All the Way Killer.

Headquarters Commandant: An additional title carried by the H&S company commander when the battalion is in the field; responsible for camp layout, sanitation, messing facilities, and the like.

Heavy guns: .50-caliber machine guns. In the Gulf War, they were normally mounted on a vehicle.

HF: High Frequency; a type of radio.

HMMWV: The modern-day replacement for the jeep. Pronounced Humvee. Also referred to as a Hummer.

Huey: Generic term for the HU1E and later model helicopters of the same type.

ID: Identification.

Intel: Intelligence.

Joint Operation Graphic Air Map: A map used by combat aviators.

K-Ranges: Training ranges.

LAAW: Light Antitank Assault Weapon; a shoulder-fired weapon that entered the U.S. inventory in the 1960s. At the time of Desert Storm it was being phased out in favor of the more powerful AT4.

LAI: Light Armored Infantry. There is now a battalion of these in each Marine division.

Lat and Long: Latitude and longitude.

LAV: Light Armored Vehicle.

Leader recce: Leader's reconnaisance.

Leatherman: The brand name of a multipurpose tool that has pliers, wire cutters, knife blades, screwdriver blades, etc. It reminds one of a large Swiss Army knife.

LVTP: Landing Vehicle Tracked, Personnel; an obsolete term for a machine now called the Amphibian Assault Vehicle.

M-16: The service rifle for U.S. forces.

M49: A liquid cargo tanker.

M-60: The standard machine gun for U.S. forces.

MACS: Marine Air Control Squadron; the air traffic controllers for Marine aircraft.

MAG: Marine Aircraft Group; generally made of three or more aircraft squadrons.

MEB: Marine Expeditionary Brigade; a force that normally consists of at least a Marine regiment and a Marine aircraft group. Usually commanded by a major general or brigadier general.

Mech ops: Mechanized operations.

MEF: Marine Expeditionary Force; a force that normally consists of at least a Marine division and a Marine aircraft wing. Normally commanded by a lieutenant general.

Minus: Used by the military to denote that not a full unit is engaged in the activity described. For example, a Marine infantry company, minus, would be a company that had perhaps only two of its three platoons deployed on an operation.

MOPP: Mission-Oriented Protective Posture; clothing and equipment worn to protect against chemical or biological agents.

MOUT: Mechanized Operations in Urban Terrain.

MP: Military Police.

MPF: Maritime Prepositioning Force; a maritime organization that has warfighting material positioned on ships at strategic locations around the world.

MPS: Maritime Prepositioning Ships.

MRE: Meal Ready-to-Eat; today's field ration.

MRL: Multiple Rocket Launchers.

MSR: Main Supply Route.

NBC: Nuclear, Biological, and Chemical.

NCO: Noncommissioned Officer.

Nerve agent: A chemical agent that attacks the body's central nervous system.

NVG: Night-Vision Goggles.

OD: Officer of the Day.

OP: Observation Post.

OV10: A type of aircraft.

Overwatch: Watchful guard; a security or guard force to prevent someone from coming on their flank or their rear.

P7: LVTP-7 amphibian tractors; also called amtracks, tracks, or amphibian assault vehicles.

Pam II Chloride: An anti–nerve gas agent.

Panhard: An Iraqi reconnaissance vehicle.

Piss-cutter: Slang for garrison cap. Also known as a fore and aft cap.

Position Location System: An early type of GPS.

POW: Prisoner of War.

PRC63: Peoples Republic of China 63; an armored personnel carrier of Chinese manufacture. Widely used by Iraq.

Psyops: Psychological Operations.

PT: Physical Training.

PX: Post Exchange.

Rack: Bunk.

Recon: Reconnaissance.

Resections: A method of finding one's position using a compass and map.

Rockeye: Bomblets.

RPG: Rocket-Propelled Grenade. An antiarmor weapon of Soviet manufacture.

RPV: Remotely Piloted Vehicle. A large model airplane with a video camera attached. Used for unmanned reconnaissance over hazardous areas.

RTO: Radio Telephone Operator.

Rucksack: Pack.

S1 or G1: Personnel and Administrative Officer.

S2 or G2: Intelligence Officer.

S3 or G3: Operations Officer.

S4 or G4: Logistics Officer.

Sagger: A Soviet-manufactured antiarmor missile.

Sand table: A miniature mockup of the battle area that commanders use for planning purposes.

Satcom radio: Satellite communications radio.

SAW: Squad Assault Weapon. A light machine gun.

Scud: Medium-range missile used by the Iraqis.

SIMCAS: Simulated Close Air Support.

Six-by: A 2 1/2-ton or 5-ton truck with six drive wheels.

SRI: Surveillance, Reconnaissance, and Intelligence.

Stars & Stripes: Newspaper of the U.S. military.

T55: A Soviet-made tank.

T62: A Soviet-made tank.

T72: The latest Soviet-made tank.

TACP: Tactical Air Control Party; a team made up of a pilot and his radio operator, whose mission is to control tactical aircraft on the ground for the ground forces.

TAOR: Tactical Area of Responsibility.

TOW: Tube-launched, Optically Tracked, Wire-Guided missile; the most powerful antitank weapon in the U.S. inventory. TOWs can be used by ground vehicles and by some types of aircraft.

TRAP: Tactical Recovery of Aircraft and Personnel.

Tribals: Native clothing.

Twenty-nine Palms: A huge U.S. Marine Corps base in the California desert.

Utilities: The Marines' field uniform.

V150: An American-made mechanized infantry vehicle used by Saudi forces.

VHF: Very High Frequency. A type of radio.

Weapons Company: The company in a Marine infantry battalion that has .50-caliber machine guns, TOWs, and 81-millimeter mortars.

WMD: Weapons of Mass Destruction.

XO: Executive Officer. The second in command of a unit.

Notes

Introduction

1. Vincent C. Thomas Jr., "The Restructuring of the Marine Corps: A Look at Yesterday and Tomorrow," *Sea Power* (September 1992).

Chapter 1. The Alert

1. Charles J. Quilter Jr., *U.S. Marines in the Persian Gulf, 1990–1991: With the I Marine Expeditionary Force in Desert Shield and Desert Storm*, History and Museums Division (Washington, DC: US Marine Corps, 1993), 3n. Hereafter referred to as Quilter, *I MEF*.

2. Ibid., 7.

3. The Platoon Leaders Class program was one of several sources for commissioned officers in the Marine Corps.

Chapter 2. India Company Leads the Way

1. Quilter, *I MEF*, 8.

2. A FAC, or forward air controller, is a Marine aviator assigned to a ground unit. His mission is to call in air strikes, medevacs, and the like for his ground brethren. The Marines learned several wars ago that the best air support for their infantry units was through communications between an aviator on the ground and one in the sky.

Chapter 4. Cement Ridge

1. Lat and long is military shorthand for latitude and longitude, a precise measurement of one's location on the earth's surface.

2. A grid square is a square kilometer.

3. ANGLICO stands for Air and Naval Gunfire Liaison Company. It is a Marine Corps unit whose mission is to provide expertise in calling in Marine air and naval gunfire to allied and U.S. Army units. In this case they were attached to the Saudi brigade.

Chapter 6. Holidays

1. November 10th, the birthday anniversary of the founding of the Marine Corps, is always celebrated, no matter what the conditions.

Chapter 14. The Battle for Khafji

1. The vast majority of the information about this battle came from participants. However, I consulted two other sources. They are: Charles H. Cureton, Lieutenant Colonel, USMCR, *U.S. Marines in the Persian Gulf, 1990–1991: With the 1st Marine Division in Desert Shield and Desert Storm* (Washington, DC: History and Museums Division, Headquarters, U.S. Marine Corps, 1993), 26–42; and Michael R. Gordon and Bernard E. Trainor (General, USMC, Retired), *The Generals' War: The Inside Story of the Conflict in the Gulf* (New York: Little Brown, 1995), 267–81.

Chapter 15. With the Recon Teams in the City

1. DPICM is a type of artillery round that explodes in the air, discharging many bomblets. The bomblets fall to the ground, bounce and then explode, thereby increasing the kill radius.

Chapter 17. Khafji Retaken

1. Although the call signs and cryptographic keys the team had were expired, the team managed to maintain fairly secure radio operation anyway though a brevity code devised by Corporal Richard Fitzpatrick, a fellow recon Marine.

2. Doc Callahan had ten years experience with Marine recon. He was widely liked and respected by all the Marines with whom he served.

3. Colonel Admire and Captain Molofsky had a view of the significance of the battle of Khafji that was shared by General Myatt but somehow escaped the planners in CentCom Headquarters in Riyadh. In their book, *The Generals' War*, Michael Gordon and General Bernard Trainor argue that General Schwarzkopf's failure to understand this resulted in adherence to a plan that permitted Saddam Hussein's Republican Guard forces to escape when they could have been destroyed instead. General Myatt agrees.

Chapter 18. Movement West to Attack Position

1. Marine convoys were often a colorful sight. Marine Corps doctrine calls for its forces to be deployed no more than 50–80 kilometers from a beachhead port. The

distances of Saudi Arabia quickly ate up most of their assets. Some help came from the U.S. Army, which helped by supplying tankers. However, the most ingenious solution was devised by Marine Lieutenant Colonel Timothy "Trucks" Taylor. Colonel Taylor received permission to lease civilian vehicles, and he pressed a wide variety of transports into service. These ranged from tractor-trailer combinations, to interurban buses belonging to the Saudi Public Transportation Corporation, to colorfully painted ten-ton trucks that the Marines called "circus trucks." This collection of vehicles, which eventually reached fifteen hundred in number, were referred to as "Arab Motors." Volunteer drivers were also called into duty and used. Quilter, *I MEF*, 28–29.

2. The Miracle Mile and other support wonders were created by the Direct Support Command under the leadership of Brigadier General, later General and Commandant of the Marine Corps, Charles C. Krulak. In seven days, two Marine engineer battalions constructed a huge supply depot thirty-five kilometers southwest of the "elbow." This depot included the largest ammunition supply point ever created by the Corps, a five-million-gallon fuel farm, and a complete naval hospital with fourteen operating rooms. It also had two airstrips that could accommodate C-130 transports. Krulak dubbed it "Al Khanjar," which is Arabic for a type of short sword. Ibid., 55–60.

3. This was a man-portable line charge. First it would fire an explosive line into a minefield, and then the line would be detonated. The idea was to explode the mines before troops or vehicles could come into contact with them.

Chapter 20. The Breach

1. Atropine is a poisonous, but not fatal, alkaloid made from the belladonna plant. It is used as an antidote for some nerve agents.

2. H. Norman Schwarzkopf, CentCom News Briefing, 27 February 1991. As reported in: *U.S. Marines in the Persian Gulf, 1990–1991: Anthology and Annotated Bibliography*, Charles Melson, Compiler (Washington, DC: History and Museums Division, Headquarters, U.S. Marine Corps, 1992), 53.

3. PFC Adam Hoage of 2/3 was dismounting from a truck when the pin on one of his grenades caught on the truck and came out. Hoage knew the situation was hopeless and quickly stepped away from his comrades. The explosion killed him and wounded another Marine. Cureton, *U.S. Marines in the Persian Gulf: 1st Marine Division*, 61.

Index